THE ECONOMICS
AND POLITICS
OF SPORTS FACILITIES

THE ECONOMICS AND POLITICS OF SPORTS FACILITIES

Edited by Wilbur C. Rich

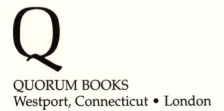

QUORUM BOOKS
Westport, Connecticut • London

Library of Congress Cataloging-in-Publication Data

The economics and politics of sports facilities / edited by Wilbur C. Rich.
  p. cm.
  Includes bibliographical references and index.
  ISBN 1–56720–317–5 (alk. paper)
  1. Sports facilities—Economic aspects—United States. 2. Sports facilities—Political
aspects—United States. I. Rich, Wilbur C.
  GV429.E36   2000
  338.4′7796′06873–dc21   99–056365

British Library Cataloguing in Publication Data is available.

Library of Congress Catalog Card Number: 99–056365
ISBN: 1–56720–317–5

First published in 2000

Quorum Books, 88 Post Road West, Westport, CT 06881
An imprint of Greenwood Publishing Group, Inc.
www.quorumbooks.com

Printed in the United States of America

∞™

The paper used in this book complies with the
Permanent Paper Standard issued by the National
Information Standards Organization (Z39.48–1984).

10 9 8 7 6 5 4 3 2 1

To Isadore A. Rich, my brother
A mentor and counselor for student athletes

Contents

Preface

Although this is a relatively short book, it discusses many of the major problems confronting professional sports, sports franchise owners and their host cities. *The Economics and Politics of Sports Facilities* is designed to provide a readable introduction to sports politics in America. This book grew out of a roundtable discussion on sports stadiums I organized for the New England Political Science Association. Although sports is not a major topic among nonurban political scientists, many follow the progress of their local sports teams. Others do not take professional sports seriously. They study political power, leadership, violence, intrigue and conflict among governments. If they read this book, they will discover that professional sports contain all of these elements.

This book is about *games* that generate millions of dollars and engage the energy and time of leading local politicians. Sports teams have become cultural icons and the *game* is more than a game. Ergo, stadiums and arenas are more than predictable architecture. In many ways they are part of the cultural definition of a city. Sports is definitely a subject that deserves serious attention by social scientists. Some of the contributors to this volume are among the leading social scientists who watch and study the sports industry.

This book is an appeal to those who would take the *game* over the edge, stripping away its fantasy content and transforming the *game* into a bottom-line business enterprise. This book also takes a sober look at what the sports industry is doing to our economically distressed cities.

I would like to thank Professor Stuart Nagel for his invaluable support from the inception of this symposium to its initial publication in

Policy Studies Review. Professor K. Tom Liou did a masterly job of edit-
ing and producing the Spring 1998 volume in which the symposium
appeared. I am grateful to Elinor J. Kim, my student research assistant, for her work on the manuscript during summer 1999. I would
also like to thank Eric Valentine of Quorum Books for his encouraging
and helpful assistance in transforming a successful symposium into a
book. Finally, I would like to acknowledge that several original contributors revised their essays and also to welcome the new contributors to this expanded volume.

Introduction: Professional Sports, Economic Development, and Public Policy

The United States has become the undisputed center of a multi-billion-dollar professional sports business. The transmutation of sports into a billion-dollar business is one of the true epics of American capitalism. Professional athletes can now make millions of dollars playing a game they learned as a child. They are performing in stadiums that would be the envy of the ancient Greeks and Romans. To call these new facilities athletic stadiums or arenas would not do them justice. Some of these structures resemble mini-malls, offering a variety of things to do in addition to watching the game. Others exemplify the social stratification of society, with their fancy luxury boxes for the rich while others offer plenty of plain seats for the nonrich. Stadiums have become a signature of their host city. Even as these stadiums are getting bigger and fancier, no one associated with professional sports seems to be satisfied. Cities are now competing with each other to build elaborate and more expensive stadiums and arenas. These structures are monuments to the centrality of sports in American culture and to how wealth is expressed through sports. The question is, who's wealth are these structures representing? The city? The owner? The taxpayer? Of the thirty National Football League (NFL) teams, twenty-seven play in publicly owned stadiums. This paradox of a privately owned enterprise that is subsidized by taxpayers will most likely continue.

Beginning in the 1990s there has been a building boom in professional sports stadiums. Between 1960 and 1990 a total of sixty new facilities were constructed for professional sport franchises. The cost of these new facilities is escalating. Past estimates indicate that building a stadium cost $500 million in 1960, $1.5 billion in 1970, and $1.5 billion in 1980. This figure can hit the $5 billion mark in the 1990s (see Lathrope 1997, 1148). Yet even with all of this experience of stadium construction, planners often underestimated the final cost. For example, the estimated cost of the Louisiana Superdome was 367-percent higher that its projected cost. The actual cost of the stadium construction was about 73 percent above its projected cost (see Baim 1994).

The purpose of this volume is to inform citizens, especially those who love professional sports, about the rising cost of building and maintaining sports arenas and stadiums. More important, the purpose is to examine the economic consequences for cities investing in stadiums. These are issues that affect not only the fans but all citizens. It is not just the city residents who are required to share the cost of building a stadium; increasingly it is the entire state that is mobilized to the save a sports franchise.

At the outset it should be emphasized that this book does not take an antistadium stand, nor does it argue that stadiums should be completely privately funded, although some may draw that conclusion. The authors in this volume are involved with the debate about the direction of professional sports, the cost of sport facilities, the role of local and state governments, and the impact on sports fans. None of the authors should be considered anti-professional sports. Instead, they are more concerned about the tactics of owners, the complicity of elected officials, and the lack of public accountability of owners. The authors believe professional sports franchise owners have serious credibility problems that concern the financial future of their teams. Advocating the public accountability of franchise owners is not a new idea. The bedrock of a democratic society is accountability. Although owners are not public officials, they are the trustees of the city's image. If they decide to act irresponsibly, many people will be hurt. For a variety of reasons, some owners are teetering on the brink of instability that may require more government regulation of their sports.

As we move toward the millennium, there are a number of reasons to rethink the relationship of cities and their state governments to professional sports.

VOODOO ECONOMICS RUN AMOK

First, the economics of the sports industry are increasingly uncertain. In the 1980 presidential election, candidate George Bush accused candidate Ronald Reagan of using voodoo economics because his ideas were based on faith rather than economic rationality. Voodoo is a variant of primitive religion that requires its believers to rely on magic and spirits to make things right. The religion makes outlandish claims and predictions. The cost of building stadiums and paying players is also out of control, salary caps notwithstanding. One of the themes running through this volume is the unrealistic financial calculations that seem to affect everyone connected with sports. Stadium proponents treat million-dollar and sometimes billion-dollar proposals as if they are just a matter of putting together the right package. According to this view, the fans will believe anything, the bankers will fund anything, and the politicians can sell anything.

Because television is providing most of the revenue, it is now in a position to influence the owners' policies about expansion plans and game rules. The network contracts make it possible for the owners to pay players million-dollar salaries. There is so much money involved that local television affiliates are being asked to share the cost of paying for the National Football League contract. There is also continuing competition between the networks and cable outlets. With the proliferation of media outlets, these companies need programming. Some believe that sports will become so profitable that they will only be seen on pay per view. Others doubt those days are near, because the advertisers are mostly focused on a mass audience.

Another reason for focusing on sports stadiums is that financing is not well understood. Economists have found that "part of the stadium financing game seems to be keep the details of the financing package a bit vague and imprecise" (Zimmerman 1997, 207). Others would argue that those costs are but a fraction of the costs of presenting the game. Taxpayers have to share in the cost of building stadiums. A billionaire like Paul Allen asked the city of Seattle to share the cost of building a new stadium for his Seahawks. Robert Kraft first asked for a new facility for his New England Patriots, but finally settled for $70 million to pay for the infrastructure for a privately funded stadium that was built on the same site as the old stadium.

An equally vexing problem in discerning the total cost of stadiums is calculating the hidden costs. Teams will release data about the initial agreed-upon construction-cost sharing but little is revealed about the continuing cost of the stadiums to cities. Although the NFL has commissioned some studies of stadium cost, those data are not readily available to the public. Researchers suspect that there are all types of private deals that affect the cost of producing the game. We have no idea what sports equipment companies are paying teams. We do not know what owners make off concessions and parking. We do know that one of the reasons that the owners seek new stadiums is to provide more luxury boxes. We know that corporations entertain clients at games and write it off as a business expense. We know that some owners are seriously considering the so-called Carolina Plan, in which fans purchase the rights to particular seats and have the option to sell those rights. This mini-investor scheme is used to pay for the cost of a stadium.

Ferreting out the hidden costs of stadiums should be the job of the local media. Is the media doing an effective job covering sports and stadium building? In Chapter 10, Robyne S. Turner and Jose F. Marichal discuss the role of newspapers in the sports business. They examine who gives what statements in support or in opposition to a stadium. Wilbur C. Rich, in Chapter 11, also examines how the media gets caught up in the "theater" of owners and politicians and loses its objectivity. In chronicling the story of the Boston Megaplex proposal and the quixotic attempt by the city of Hartford, Connecticut, to lure away the New England Patriots, he demonstrates how owners and politicians used theater tactics to gain public support. Both chapters stress the importance of the politics behind the headlines. The careers of politicians and the reputations of owners can become entangled in the twist and turns of the story. Consequently, they spend an incredible amount of time, and sometimes money, to come across as the good guy in this drama. A subplot in the theater of stadium politics is how owners make and remake their reputations.

STADIUMS AND LOCAL POLITICS

The third reason for this volume is the need to examine how cities reply on sports franchises and stadiums as tools for revitalization and place selling. Many old cities are in the process of rebuilding their central business districts to lure the convention and tourist trade. The entire downtown area is now being transformed into a tourist center. Some city boosters believe this is necessary to sell the city to outsiders. Many city leaders believe if they do not sell the city, it will not survive. The steel mills and manufacturing plant are not returning to Rust-Belt cities. They must find new reasons to exist and to create an exciting location for new residents and businesses. This is also where the nexus of local politics and economics of stadiums meet. There are a variety of theories about the motives of the coalitions behind stadium building.

The debate over the theories of city politics and economic development is of intense interest among political scientists. Not since the late 1950s and early 1960s have so many scholars been attracted to the question of who rules cities. In the 1960s there was a classic debate between Floyd Hunter and Robert Dahl on whether there was a single elite or several elites that dominated city politics. Today that debate has evolved into a discussion over who makes economic development decisions. Stephen Elkin's *City and Regime in the American Republic* (1987) compares the works of Paul Peterson and Ira Katznelson and concludes that their work represents the rediscovery of the normative conception of city politics. In *Urban Trenches*, Katznelson argues that urban politics is a contest for power between classes and races. In *City Limits* (1981), Peterson argues that a city's interest is more than the sum of competing interests within its borders. He asserts that the city has a unitary interest which responds to a competitive economic environment. Cities act like businesses. They seek to maximize economic returns on the resources they control. As such, they maintain an exchange relation with mobile wealth. City policies attract or repel different types of mobile wealth.

The "who makes economic decisions" debate was joined by Clarence Stone in the late 1980s. Stone and Sanders's *The Politics of Urban Development* (1987) disagrees with the conclusions of market theory. Using case studies of cities, Stone and his colleagues sought to present examples of nonmarket forces that drive politics. Following Elkin's lead, Stone's work focuses on the composition of governing regimes in cities and the process of decision making. A fuller elaboration of regime theory is presented in Stone's *Regime Politics: Governing Atlanta, 1946–1988* (1989). Stone locates the mechanism for decision making. Stone concluded that social production rather than social control explains the informal decision-making style of Atlanta elites. More specifically, the black elected officials and the white economic leaders in Atlanta worked cooperatively to advance the interests of their city. They understood that they needed each other to make economic decisions work. The contrast between regime theory and market theory revolves around whether politics or economics is paramount in the decision matrix. Regime theory argues that politics matters and economic decisions flow from political accommodations. Market theory argues that that economic markets determine the politics. Thus politics is limited by the city's economic resources and by the need to attract investors. This debate continues and informs us about stadium politics.

Following Stone's lead, other political scientists have identified three types of regimes which govern city sports (see Pelissero, Henschen, and Sidlow 1991). The first type is a corporate-dominating governing regime. Such a regime promotes the corporate agenda, which now seems to be directed toward downtown development. This is the classic pro-growth machine elite (see Molotch 1976). According to Pelissero, Henschen, and Sidlow, corporate regimes have traditionally supported new and renovated stadiums as a tool for economic development. They believe that "first-class" cities need the proper amenities to attract and keep businesses. They are more likely to define their cities in competitive terms. This type of regime is in a better position to lobby for a sports franchise, rally support for a new stadium, and defend itself against possible franchise raiders. Owners who work with this type of regime and in this type of environment are the envy of their respective leagues.

The second type of regime is called a progressive regime. This type of regime promotes a more comprehensive and inclusive agenda, and is more inclined to consider neighborhood group interests in making economic decisions. These regimes are less likely to support "growth machine" projects or downtown stadiums if they do not coincide with city and community interests. They can challenge the growth machine. This is not to say that such cities will not support sports stadiums, but rather that the political leadership usually makes sure it does not alienate members of the community. The politics of such cities are very delicate. Elected officials, particularly the mayor, govern with the support of several coalitions, and are not in the position to make arbitrary decisions about stadiums. Owners find the progressive environment more conflictual. Getting a stadium built in this environment requires a considerable amount of political skills. It also helps if the team in question is competitive or a winner.

The final type of regime is called a caretaker one. A caretaker governing regime is merely serving its time, not asserting any agenda. Caretaker regimes are beset with problems, because they have little or no mandates. They are not elected to do anything specifically and do not have a close relationship with economic leaders. If such a city gets a franchise, it is usually the result of the efforts of a high-profile entrepreneur acting without open assistance from elected officials.

THE STRUGGLE FOR ACCOUNTABILITY

The final reason for examining sports stadiums is the continuing search for accountability from franchise owners. Again, this theme runs throughout this book. Management theory holds that "any group or individual who can affect or is affected by the achievement of an organization's purpose is a stakeholder" (Mason and Slack 1997). Ergo, fans have a stake in what a sports franchise produces. The product is entertainment. If the fans boycott a team or refuse to watch them on television, then it affects the value of the team. A team without a supportive fan base cannot survive. If a team loses the socioemotional ties with its fans, and the team loses incessantly, players and coaches may be fired, ownership can change, and, ultimately, teams can relocate.

This is why any discussion of stadiums has to take into consideration the relationship of a team with its host community. After receiving a financial subsidy from the taxpayer, do owners have any moral obligation to consider the interests of the host community? In theory, owners are granted the privilege of using the city's name, public airways, taxpayer money, and public infrastructure to make a profit. Owners have made a social contract. Implicit in that contract are social obligations. As the value of the franchise increases, the sense of obligation to the city also increases. If Al Davis asks the city of Oakland to pay for the return of the football Raiders to the Bay area, does he have an obligation to stay in the city? Mr. Davis has made it clear that the Raiders are his team and that he will do what he wants with it. It is not just Davis, but several owners who have used the threat of moving to force their host cities to give them more of whatever they think they need stadiumwise to be competitive.

Accountability is made even more problematic with corporate takeover of local franchises. These megacorporations span the entire nation and even the world. The giants of the corporate world have staked claims on the world of sports. The venerated Disney Corporation owns a professional hockey team, the Mighty Ducks of Anaheim. The corporation also owns 25 percent of the Anaheim Angels. The corporate giant General Electric owns Madison Square Garden, the New York Knicks, and 15 percent of the New York Rangers. The Tribune Company owns the Chicago Cubs. Comcast owns SportNews sports channel and the Philadelphia 76ers. Communication moguls Rupert Murdoch and Ted Turner each own major league baseball teams. When Ted Turner's company merged with Time Warner Company, the deal included the Atlanta Braves, the Atlanta Hawks, and the Atlanta Thrashers hockey franchise. Murdoch paid $350 million for the Los Angeles Dodgers baseball team. Alfred Lerner paid a record $530 million for a new Cleveland Browns football team.

In 1998 it was estimated that fifty-two public companies own parts of 130-odd major sports teams in America. Why do communication companies buy professional teams? With the proliferation of media outlets, these companies need programming. We live in a twenty-four-hour sports television world. ESPN and ESPN2 provide incessant sports fare and commentaries. If one is addicted to sports, the overlapping of sports seasons prevents sensory deprivation.

This corporate takeover translates into great political and economic power. This is in addition to the great personal power it bestows on corporate leaders. It allows owners to associate with some of the most famous people into the world. Aside from providing instant celebrity status and membership into the highly visible national glitterati, owners play Daddy Warbucks to athletes, many of whom come from disadvantaged backgrounds. Indeed, the sports business is amenable to Horatio Alger stories, since athletes are selected based on performance and individually crafted skills. Supposedly talent offsets the racial and social disadvantages of players. Minority players are marketed as sport heroes to all Americans, regardless of race, color, religion, or creed. Although sports marketing is beyond this book, its impact on sport is enormous and is one the driving wheels behind the escalating cost of sports.

To shed some light on the issue of cost, relocation, and stadium building, this book is divided into four parts. Part I deals with the history of sports and sports stadiums. The lead chapter provides a historical perspective regarding the evolving relationship between cities and sports. Steven A. Riess, a longtime student of the history of sports, looks at the changing role of sports in cities. The author finds that interest groups, politicians, and owners play a critical role in the promotion of sports and its relationship to cities.

In Part II, the economics of sports stadiums is examined. Economists Andrew Zimbalist and Robert Baade have become town criers, warning cities about the dangers of investing in sport franchises with virtually no guarantees. They have found little supporting data for the development claims of owners and their advocates. The authors examine the economic rationale for sport stadiums as a technique for economic development. They focus on claims and actual benefits the cities derived from investing in sport franchises.

In Part III, several case studies are presented of cities attempting to use sports franchises as tools for economic redevelopment. To bring the discussion closer to the economic dilemma facing cities, we have included some case studies of individual cities and how they have coped with hosting their franchises. Included in those case studies are Chicago, New Orleans, Detroit, Phoenix, and Boston. In Chapter 4, Richard Temple Middleton discusses the politics of stadiums and the governing regime in Phoenix. Phoenix is an example of the rise of Sun-Belt cities and their supposed leap into the big time. In Chapter 5, Robert K. Whelan and Alma H. Young illustrate how the Zephyrs and the New Orleans Arena played a role in regional development competition. Lynn W. Bachelor examines stadiums in Chapter 6 as part of what she calls "solution sets." Politicians often use "tried and true" solutions for new problems, regardless of whether there is a good fit. This phenomenon has been observed in many city-revitalization programs, and it applies to stadium building.

Cities with recently built stadiums are at a slight advantage over those with old facilities, but they cannot be complacent. A new stadium ages as soon as it is completed. The next city will build a domed stadium, one with more luxury seats, one with a sports mall, one with more parking, or one connected to a shopping mall. As the cities of Atlanta and Chicago have proven, a new stadium can sometimes be constructed next door to an old one. In Chapter 8, Edward I. Sidlow and Beth M. Henschen chronicle the building of Comiskey Park II, Oriole Park at Camden Yard, Jacobs Field in Cleveland, and Comerica Park in Detroit. Neil J. Sullivan provides cities with a strategy for playing the baseball stadium game in Chapter 9. As these case studies prove, it is a game where even smart players can lose. The long arm of franchise costs even reaches down to the minors. Chapter 7, by Arthur T. Johnson, details the risks of minor league baseball. Drawing upon data from particular cities, he is able to compare city responses to the pressures of sports investment.

Finally, Part IV deals with how the media covers sports and how owners can use the media to create a mood in their host cities. The media is critical to the presentation of stadiums to the taxpayers. Jose F. Marichal and Robyne S. Turner, and Wilbur C. Rich, discuss what the public knows and how they know it.

As for the future, no one can predict it. We live in a strange period in the history of sports. We hope this book provides some thoughts and insights that can guide city leaders in their approach to sports franchise owners. We also hope that the public will be able to ask better questions after reading this book.

REFERENCES

Baim, Dean V. 1994. The Sports Stadium As a Municipal Investment. Westport, Conn.: Greenwood Press.

Brinkeroff, Joel. 1997. Stadium Politics. *California Journal* 28, no. 1: 40–44.

Elkin, Steven. 1987. *City and Regime in the American Republic.* Chicago: University of Chicago Press.

Katznelson, Ira. 1981. *Urban Trenches.* New York: Pantheon Books.

Lathrope, Daniel J. 1997. Federal Tax Policy, Tax Subsidies, and the Financing of Professional Sports Facilities. *South Texas Law Review* 38: 1147–1165.

Mason, Daniel, and Trevor Slack. 1997. Appropriate Opportunism or Bad Business Practice? Stakeholder Theory, Ethics and the Franchise Relocation Issue. *Marquette Sports Law Journal* 7: 399.

Molotch, Harvey. 1976. The City as a Growth Machine. *American Journal of Sociology* 82: 309–331.

Pelissero, John, Beth Henschen, and Edward Sidlow. 1991. Urban Regimes, Sport Stadiums, and the Politics of Economic Development Agendas in Chicago. *Policy Studies Review* 10: 117–129.

Peterson, Paul. 1981. *City Limits.* Chicago: University of Chicago Press.

Rosentraub, Mark. 1997. The Myth and Reality of the Economic Development from Sports. *Real Estate Issues* 22: 24–29.

Safir, Adam. 1997. If You Build It, They Will Come: The Politics of Financing Sports Stadium Construction. *Journal of Law and Politics* 13: 937–963.

Stone, Clarence. 1989. *Regime Politics: Governing Atlanta, 1946–1988.* Lawrence: University of Kansas Press.

Stone, Clarence, and H. Sanders. 1987. *The Politics of Urban Development*. Lawrence: University of Kansas Press.

Zimmerman, Dennis. 1997. "Who Benefits From and Who Pays for Stadiums? Evidence From Some Recent Deals." National Tax Association Proceedings (December 8), pp. 204–211.

HISTORY OF STADIUM POLITICS

When fans reflect upon history they usually recall the sports icons, the Babe Ruths, the Johnny Unitas, the Bobby Orrs, and the Bill Russells instead of the facilities the great players played in. Few think of the old stadiums that play a big part in the history of sports, such as Ebbets Field, Connie Mack Stadium, RFK Stadium, and Wrigley Field. Wrigley Field is the only stadium that remains an active ballpark and will remain so for a long time. If one reads sports history, it shows that these sports monuments were built as tributes to the game. These stadiums have lasted for years. Now they are considered dinosaurs. Their demise will be more than a loss of historical structure, but parts of sports history. We live in a time when historic stadiums are unequivocally being replaced with new ones. The new ones will not have the shelf life of their predecessors. Will Baltimore's Camden Yards, Cleveland's Jacobs Field, or Seattle's Safeco Field remain valuable parts of sport history? These facilities cost more and have more luxurious seats, but they will not be the same. To understand why, a brief history of sports is necessary.

Steven A. Riess, a historian, provides us with a brief chronology of the relationship of cities to sports. The relationship started as a oppositional one rather than a supportive one. Before we got the mega-million-dollar stadium and arena deals, cities sought to ban sports because of its linkage to gambling. But as the moral inhibition against gambling declined, a close relationship between city politicians and the entrepreneurs developed. Today gambling is a major part of sports business. Not only are the odds given on the radio, but they can also be found in the leading newspapers. Although only one state legally sanctions gambling on sports, it is done throughout the nation.

1

Historical Perspectives on Sports and Public Policy

Steven A. Riess

American cities from their inception have been called upon to make policy decisions regarding their residents' sporting pastimes. Even in the colonial era, local governments were responsible for protecting public thoroughfares, community norms, and the social order. Thus, as early as 1631, Boston began regulating taverns, which were important sites of gambling sports, and in 1647 banned bowling and shuffleboard because of the gambling nexus. The town permitted useful sports on the Common, but prohibited blood sports, and, as in most colonial communities, Dutch New Amsterdam proscribed Sunday sports because they detracted from God's Day. In 1657 Boston banned football because players in the streets disrupted traffic and trade with their games and even made it dangerous to walk or just stand in the city's narrow streets. Another problem was caused by hunts, when bystanders were occasionally shot, and consequently, in 1710, the General Court forbade shooting at pigeons or targets in Boston (Struna 1979, 3, 9). In the nineteenth century, municipalities built large suburban parks that became important sites for sport, beginning with New York's Central Park, completed in 1858. Cities barred blood sports, including boxing and animal baiting, both of which continued surreptitiously. Prize fighting was only legalized in Louisiana and New York in the 1890s. The gambling sports of the male bachelor subculture, including billiards and bowling, were often forbidden because of the wagering, and horse-race gambling was only permitted at racetracks. Cities also regulated legal private sporting venues, ranging from baseball fields to bowling alleys with license fees. In the first half of the twentieth century, municipal involvement with sports continued in much the same way, seeking to protect public morals and public space. Cities began to build small neighborhood parks, but also started to build stadiums, primarily for amateur athletics and other public uses. States established regulatory commissions, modeled after the New York Racing Commission (1895) and the New York Boxing Commission (1920), to supervise these commercialized gambling sports (Riess 1989, 17–21, 41–46, 132–141, 173–177, 184).

Since the 1950s, and especially the mid-1960s, cities have gone into the business of subsidizing professional sports, especially major league baseball and professional football, by building stadiums to house local franchises. Hardly a year goes by when local governments do not build a baseball field, a football stadium, or a hockey arena whose primary tenant is a private business enterprise. Between 1999 and 2003, local governments are helping to build nine new major league baseball parks, seven professional football fields, and nine arenas for pro basketball or hockey. This policy issue first received important attention in a Brookings Institution study edited by Roger Noll (1974), and in the 1990s became a cottage industry among economists. As Baade (1995, 278) points out, part of the reason has been the concern about "the ongoing American urban fiscal crisis and the extraordinary financial privilege enjoyed by professional sports owners and players."

Despite the voluminous literature on sport stadiums by political scientists, urban planners, and especially by economists, there has been little awareness of the historic background of government interaction with sports businesses. The purpose of this chapter is to examine the historic backdrop to this important contemporary policy issue. Before we can intelligently analyze current public-policy issues that beset municipalities and professional sports, it would be valuable to know the historic relationship between professional sports and local government.

Historian George Lipsitz (1984, 1) has pointed out that the popularity of sports and the close relationship between civic development in cities, the manner of financing, and the method of locating stadiums reflected local historical patterns. Consequently, public debates about stadium building involved larger questions about the nature of a particular metropolis, including clues about how local governments will deal with related developmental issues (Euchner 1993, 20). How far should a city government go to prevent the loss of a team? What were the benefits of keeping the team? What would be lost if the franchise left town? How far should a city government go to attract a team if it had none? What was to be gained? Public-policy analysis would benefit from a long-term historical perspective on the issues involved in public support of private sport facilities. This chapter will examine aspects of the historic relationship between professional sports and urban government, emphasizing the origins of public financing of major league baseball stadiums.

EARLY PUBLIC-POLICY ISSUES IN
MAJOR LEAGUE BASEBALL

Urban politicians were directly involved with professional sports for well over one hundred years. They were invariably ardent sports fans, and more importantly, were among the earliest sports entrepreneurs. In the late nineteenth century, when prize fighting became a successful commercial enterprise, the first boxing managers and promoters were commonly big-city politicians who had the connections to arrange bouts and the political clout to stage the fight at a time when the sport was widely banned. Operators of major racetracks were invariably politicians or men allied to machine politicians who had the influence to protect a business that was constantly under attack by moral reformers (Riess 1988, 99–121; 1989, 171–194).

Even professional baseball team owners were commonly professional politicians. They did not employ their influence to get the municipality to build them ballparks, but they did use their clout to get cities to subsidize their investment in more modest way (Riess 1989, 194–202; Vincent 1981, 45–53). Political connections helped teams get protection against interlopers, secure inside information about ballpark sites and transportation developments, keep down licenses and other fees, and secure police protection. In Chicago this included the assigning of city police to provide security inside (Riess 1980, 58–61, 75).

A number of public-policy issues that involved professional baseball at the turn of the century included the suppression of ticket scalping, especially at the World Series, and gambling. How ardently should the police clamp down on these crimes? Sports gambling, especially off track on horse racing, was a huge illegal business. There was a lot of wagering on boxing and even on baseball, the one major professional sport whose appeal was not based on gambling, and which alone had a reputation for honesty. However, betting on baseball was a popular pastime, inside and outside ballparks. People bet on which team would win, but also total number of runs, and even if a pitch would be a ball or a strike (Riess 1980, 75, 61–63). Another important policy issue was Sunday baseball, which was widely banned in the Northeast and South for violating the American Sabbath. Midwestern and Western cities were generally more liberal on this question, and most of their cities had professional Sunday ball by the 1890s. The legalization of Sunday sport became an important ethnocultural issue in the early twentieth century. It was backed by pietistic small-town WASPS who wanted to affirm their status and cultural heritage, and hoped to exercise social control over the working-class urban immigrants. New York City did not get Sunday baseball until 1919, while Boston waited until 1929 and Philadelphia and Pittsburgh until 1933 (Riess 1980, 121–149; Lucas 1971, 163–175). However, the city fathers kept a tight rein on Philadelphia baseball, since the Phillies and Athletics had a difficult time getting a beer permit after the end of Prohibition, which cut off an important revenue source. They encountered a strong coalition of temperance advocates and neighborhood bar owners who kept the parks dry until 1961, when the sale of beer in cups, for the safety of players and umpires, was permitted. By then the Athletics were long gone. The intent was to use the license fees to help pay for a new ballpark for the remaining team. Sunday beer sales were not legalized until 1972, when the Phillies were playing in the year-old Veterans Stadium (Kuklick 1991, 72–73).

There are only a handful of cases where a city provided land for a baseball team. In 1870 a group of prominent Chicago boosters organized the White Stockings to promote their city. One year later, the club played in the new National Association of Professional Baseball Players, the first professional baseball league at a lakefront site located on municipally owned land. The land had been donated to the city by the federal government with stipulations that it not be used for profit-making ventures. The field burned down in October in the Great Chicago Fire. In 1878 the White Stockings, now in the three-year-old National League (NL), returned to their original site. Five years later the team built a state-of-the-art facility there, but in 1884 was compelled to move by the federal government because the terms of the lease had been broken when the city allowed a private business to use the field (Riess 1980, 86).

While teams built and owned their ballparks, the public had a vested interest in their location because of the anticipated impact on the repose of the community, the influence on land uses, and the impact on property values. In a few instances community opposition to the construction of a ballpark became a public issue, such as in March 1903, when the American League (AL) announced that it had obtained a site for a future ballpark at an underdeveloped section of Manhattan around 155th Street. Local real estate owners fought the plan, fearing for their future property values, the introduction of deleterious new businesses, and the general demoralization of the neighborhood. Their resistance was almost surely orchestrated by Andrew Freedman, a major power in Tammany Hall and himself a prominent realtor, who had just recently sold his majority share in the New York Giants and had promised to help keep out the interloping American League. The matter went to the Washington Heights Board of Improvements, which by a three-to-two vote rejected a bid to have a street opened through the proposed site (later the site of Columbia Presbyterian Hospital). The Highlanders (later known as the Yankees) had their own political clout through Frank Farrell, one of the gambling czars in the city, and Bill Devery, the former police chief. Their political clout helped protect their investment against continued community opposition before the Board of Estimate (Riess 1980, 91).

Fan safety was a significant matter of public policy. Baseball parks in the late nineteenth century were extremely dangerous buildings, often firetraps that had been flimsily constructed. There were plenty of episodes of fields catching on fire. In 1894 alone, four major league ballparks burned down. Usually fires occurred when the stands were empty, but in Chicago, on August 6, with 6,000 in the park, the West Side grandstand became enflamed. Hundreds were injured, mainly from a panicked crowd that pushed spectators into the barbed wire in front of the stands The Polo Grounds in New York was the scene of serious problems. In 1897 the platform connecting the bleachers to the grandstands collapsed under fans rushing to get out of the rain. Six years later the cheap stands in Philadelphia gave way, killing twelve and injuring hundreds (Riess 1980, 95).

In the Progressive Era municipalities responded to such hazardous construction by enacting new building codes. The codes dealt with matters like requiring inspections by fire marshals, tightening regulations about building materials, establishing fire limits, and regulating roofstands. These were seating areas constructed on buildings that overlooked the ballpark. Cities like Chicago, Detroit, and Philadelphia all had roofstands outside the field. In 1929, when the World Series was played in Philadelphia, the rooftop stands produced a lot of money for the property owners and raised property values. After the 1934 season, team owner Jack Shibe put up a "spite fence" in right field to destroy the competition (Kuklick 1991, 73–76). In 1909, when Chicago revised its building codes, it specifically addressed ballpark safety. The codes banned roofstands and the construction of wooden ballparks that seated over 5,000 (which meant its major league fields). This decision did not effect the building of Comiskey Park in 1910 (one year after Shibe Park in Philadelphia and Forbes Field in Pittsburgh), which had always been planned as a modern fire-resistant grounds. However, the new law had an important impact four years later when the Federal League claimed major league status. The Chicago Whales' new North Side Park, named Weeghman Park (today's Wrigley Field) had to be built with expensive fireproof materials (Riess 1980, 94–97).

THE CONSTRUCTION OF THE FIRST
PUBLIC SPORTS STADIUMS

By the late nineteenth century, cities were developing athletic sites like baseball diamonds, tennis courts, and even golf courses to promote participatory sports (Riess 1989, 62, 132). Then, in the 1920s, state colleges began building large football fields where spectators could root for their state's team. These trends encouraged municipalities, beginning in 1914, to construct public sports stadiums that were intended to encourage amateur athletics and promote the reputation of the cities. San Diego led the way in 1914 with a $150,000 concrete oval facility, paid for by a bond issue funded by revenues from taxes and admission fees. The 30,000-seat structure was operated by the Board of Park Commissioners and used for baseball, football, and chariot racing. In the 1920s several local governments constructed huge outdoor sports facilities to encourage athletics and promote the reputation of their cities. The first was Pasadena's 52,000-seat Rose Bowl, built in 1922 as a joint project with the Tournament of Roses Association for $325,000. The Rose Bowl was soon followed by the Los Angeles Coliseum in 1923; the first section of Chicago's Soldier Field (Riess 1989, 144; Bale and Moen 1926, 198) and Baltimore's $500,000, 80,000-seat Memorial Stadium, both in 1924; and Philadelphia's Municipal Stadium in 1926.

The Los Angeles Coliseum was the most famous of these municipal stadiums, serving as home field for the University of Southern California football team, the site of the 1932 Olympic Games, and, after World War II, the home of the Rams of the National Football League. Los Angeles's city government was traditionally weak, but it did have a powerful political elite of wealthy WASP bankers, realtors, and publishers operating behind the scenes. They composed the local political regime that included downtown corporations, developers, financial institutions, urban planners, and clients of the development (Pelissero, Henschen, and Sidlow 1991, 117–118).

Los Angeles's chief power broker was Harry Chandler, the immensely wealthy publisher of the *Times*, whose goal was to promote Southern California. He and his fellow boosters decided after World War I to respond to the recession and the accompanying sharp decline in tourism by actively promoting their city. Mayor Meredith Snyder appointed a committee of 100 boosters to the California Fiesta Association, reorganized a year later as the twenty-two-member Community Development Association (CDA). The chairman of the eight-man executive board that set its agenda was William M. Garland, a prominent realtor, and president of the Chamber of Commerce (Riess 1981, 51–55).

The CDA's primary goal was to put Los Angeles on the map by securing the Olympic Games for Los Angeles. Prior host cities for the Olympics included Athens, Paris, St. Louis, London, Stockholm, and Berlin (the scheduled site of the canceled 1916 Games), with Antwerp scheduled for 1920. All but St. Louis were world-class cities. This would enhance their city's prestige, supply a lot of free publicity, and promote future development. The CDA knew that to achieve its goal Los Angeles first needed a stadium big enough to house the event and also be used for athletic meets, football games, conventions, and festivals (Riess 1981, 53).

In 1919 the boosters first proposed building a 75,000-seat publicly financed facility. They wanted the city to float a bond issue to pay for it or lease the CDA a parcel of Exposition Park, located ten minutes from downtown by car near the USC campus, where it would then build a multipurpose facility. The Coliseum would be rented to the city and county for ten years for $475,000 apiece, and afterward would be turned over to the local governments. The city and county approved a plan to finance the stadium, but voters turned it down in a referendum, a typical Los Angeles response to bond issues. The CDA then took it upon itself to build the grounds, regardless of the public vote. The CDA got the city to give it seventeen acres in Exposition Park for a new stadium and agreed to pay the building costs through rental fees. The CDA set up a syndicate to underwrite an $800,000 below-prime-rate loan secured by the good name of the city and county. The arrangement's legality was questioned, but was affirmed by several jurists who argued that the CDA was simply representing the city and county in constructing and maintaining the Coliseum, and that whatever the elected officials did was by definition in the public interest. Thereafter there was little public opposition to the project except from the reform Municipal League that complained about the costs of construction, the subsidization of middle-class entertainment, and the impropriety of private control of a publicly funded building. The league found it presumptuous for self-designated power brokers to assume they knew what was best for the city, especially when the electorate had opposed the bond issue (Riess 1981, 54–58).

The regime's actions in the Coliseum project reflected its substantial power. These movers and shakers had never been elected or appointed by anyone but themselves. They were self-selected, accomplished men who took for granted that they knew what was in the best interests of their community, and so acted. In this case the public interest coincided with their own particular interests. In hindsight, the CDA acted with considerable foresight, which enabled Los Angeles to become the first major metropolis to open a municipal stadium. Yet the project also reflected their arrogance and lack of confidence in the public and elected officials (Riess 1981, 62–63).

The CDA's project was a great success. In 1923 the International Olympic Committee selected Los Angeles to host the 1932 Games, pending completion of a 75,000 arena. The CDA built its facility efficiently and relatively untainted by obvious political cronyism. The cost of the Coliseum when completed in the late 1920s was $1.9 million. One-half of the construction costs were born by the $499,225 the city and county each paid in rent. In return they gained joint control of the Coliseum after the Olympics. The region got a huge new sports complex that seated over 100,000 by 1932, and provided a great home for West-Coast athletic competition, especially USC and UCLA football (Riess 1981, 55, 63).

The Coliseum was completed much more cheaply than Chicago's Soldier Field, constructed by the South Park Board at the approximate site where Daniel Burnham's Chicago Plan of 1909 had proposed a facility for sport and other great events. Originally known as Grant Park Stadium, it was soon renamed Soldier Field in honor of deceased World War I servicemen. Architects Holabird and Roche won a competition to design a 100,000-seat u-shaped amphitheater which they modeled after the Parthenon, conforming to the adjacent Field Museum's neoclassical style. In 1920 voters approved a $2.5-million bond issue, but the project was scaled back to half the projected seating capacity when no construction bid came in under $4.33 million. The original plans were subsequently completed after voters approved additional $3-million bond issues in 1924 and in 1928 for a total cost of $8.5 million. The overruns were attributed to the difficulties of construction on reclaimed land, the elegant classical accouterments, and kickbacks to Park Board President Edward J. Kelly. The field was used for many great events, beginning in 1926 with the International Eucharistic Congress, which attracted over 200,000, and the Army–Notre Dame football game that drew 100,000, and the 1927 Dempsey–Tunney "long-count" heavyweight championship rematch, attended by 104,000 who paid a record gate of $2.6 million. The largest sporting crowd was 115,000 for the 1937 Austin–Leo high school football championship game. The field is still operational, and has been the home of the Bears since 1971 (Duis and Holt 1978, 170–173).

The municipally publicly financed stadiums of the 1920s provided models for Cleveland, Miami, Dallas, New Orleans, and El Paso, which all built public stadiums during the Depression, the latter four for postseason football bowl games to promote tourism (Riess 1989, 145; Bale and Moen 1926, 198). The man most responsible for the park was William R. Hopkins, who was the Republican city manager. His goal was to complete the Mall, a park by Lake Erie surrounded by major government buildings including City Hall and the public library. Hopkins sought to complete the Mall with a multipurpose stadium. The Indians president Ernest Barnard wanted to expand the Indians ballpark that had less than 30,000 seats, but it was in a crowed neighborhood of working-class homes that left no space to expand and provide necessary parking. The owners wanted to sell the team, and a new park would enhance the franchise's value. Barnard believed a new park would draw at least 750,000 fans, and thought that a contending team could draw another 500,000 spectators. The City Council voted 23–1 to put a $2.5-million bond issue on the ballot. The local business elite got behind the project and published a report that predicted the stadium would be used for business meetings, orchestral performances, boxing, soccer, and track and field. The voters approved the project and construction began in 1930. It opened on July 2, 1931, with a musical concert, followed the next day by Max Schmeling's successful heavyweight title defense against Willie Stribling. In 1931 the *Plain Dealer* described the stadium as "a monument to the progressive spirit of the city's people." The first baseball game was on July 31, 1932, against the Athletics, seen by 80,184, then the largest crowd in professional baseball history. However, the Depression severely hindered attendance, which only reached 387,936 that season. The Indians used Municipal Stadium throughout the 1933 season, the first full-time use of a city-owned field by a major league team. However, attendance remained poor. Crowds were still hurt by the Depression, and also the poor quality of the Indians and the cold climate at a site adjacent to Lake Erie. The cavernous field was not designed with baseball in mind, and always looked empty and uninviting. In 1934 the Indians only played there on Sundays and holidays, playing the rest of the year at the old Lake Park. Twelve years later Bill Veeck bought the Indians, improved the quality of the team, and moved them back to the stadium. Attendance rose from 558,182 in 1945 to 1.5 million in 1947. One year later, when the Indians won the World Series, they set the major league attendance record of 2.6 million (Torry 1995, 206–207, 209, 212–213).

THE HISTORIC IMPACT OF BASEBALL TEAMS ON NEIGHBORHOOD DEVELOPMENT

The public has always had a vested interest in the location of ballparks because of the potential impact on the community's tranquillity (i.e., noisy crowds, disorderly conduct, increased street traffic), their influence on land uses (especially businesses that catered to a sporting clientele like saloons and restaurants), and their impact upon property values (popularization of undeveloped areas and decline of established residential communities). Research into the impact of ballparks upon land uses and property values in Atlanta, Chicago, and New York from 1900 to 1930 found they had relatively little impact on property values and land uses in established locales other than in the blocks nearest the entrance way. For instance, when Comiskey Park opened in 1910 some small shops were opened by the front gate to take advantage of the traffic, including McCuddy's Bar, whose owner had been told of the construction in advance. This was the only area around the park whose property values appreciated differently than the rest of the neighborhood, tripling in five years. Furthermore, ballparks had relatively little impact on underdeveloped localities, other than to publicize them and promote confidence in their future growth. On the other hand, the property values at the Cubs' West Side Grounds tripled shortly after the Cubs abandoned the field and sold it to the state for the Illinois State Hospital and Medical School. These facilities had a much greater impact on land use than the old ballpark (Riess 1980, 94, 97–100, 102–104, 108–111).

The Polo Grounds had a limited impact on its Washington Heights neighborhood because it was separated by natural boundaries like the Harlem River and Coogan's Bluff. Brooklyn's Ebbets Field area underwent a great boom, reflecting its presence in the thriving Flatbush neighborhood. The ballpark contributed to the boom by publicizing the area, but the main factor was the improved public transportation that made Flatbush a desirable bedroom neighborhood in the 1920s. The Yankees moved in 1923 from the Polo Grounds, where they had been renters for a decade, to Yankee Stadium in the Bronx. This was expected to greatly enhance the future of the borough. Boosters predicted the area would boom and the field would encourage the rise of small restaurants, bars, and garages catering to baseball fans. The stadium added to the boom in its immediate vicinity by creating an anticipated source of revenue for local merchants, advertising for the locale, and psychological backing for investors. However, it was a minor contributor to its West Bronx neighborhood, much less the entire borough's progress. Far more important were the new county court house and the construction of apartments on the Grand Concourse caused by the construction of the Jerome Avenue line of the IRT subway. The subway enabled thousands of New Yorkers to live in the new apartment buildings because it provided cheap and easy access to their jobs in Manhattan (Riess 1980, 108–110).

Historian Bruce Kuklick (1991), who has carefully studied the relationship of Shibe Park to North Philadelphia, presents a somewhat contrary view. He argues that when Shibe Park was first built in 1909, "Baseball led the way in the real estate move north of the Pennsylvania tracks after the hospital (and other noxious industries) disappeared" (p. 41). Kuklick argues that the ball club had a modest but positive impact on the community that included row houses, empty lots, and industry: "The blocks immediately around Shibe Park were a peculiar walking industrial zone. The park solidified economic stability through various kinds of employment and often directly contributed to the quality of the housing stock. Baseball made for ancillary employment that gave neighbors an overriding interest in their land. The stadium generated parking lots, residential rooming, the rooftop seats, eating establishments, and bars, all stimulating residents to look after their property." Community residents worked the low-paying seasonal jobs in Shibe Park as vendors, ushers, ticket takers, ticket sellers, groundkeepers, and cleaners (pp. 100, 165).

URBAN POLITICAL REGIMES AND
THE SUBSIDIZATION OF SPORTS STADIUMS

Today the relationship between urban politics and sports is different than in the early twentieth century. Politicians, except for Governor George Bush Jr., a minority partner in the Texas Rangers, do not own sports franchises, yet their relationship to the municipality is still very important. Beginning in the 1950s politicians, especially in cities without professional sports teams, made special efforts to attract or keep major league franchises that included subsidizing ballfields and indoor arenas. Politicians went after a sports franchise just like they would industry and businesses that would improve the community's tax base and quality of life (Riess 1989, 244). Keeping a franchise or bringing in a new team enhanced a mayor's personal image, demonstrated his community spirit, and made points for him with urban boosters, contractors, the construction trades, and the tourist industry. On the other hand, a politician who opposed expensive new parks and arenas ran the risk of being labeled an unprogressive killjoy who let a beloved team leave town or failed to bring in a much-desired sports franchise. These politicians were invariably backed by powerful local elites who were vigorous advocates of such big-ticket items as stadiums and convention centers that benefit banks, real estate development, and tourism (Euchner 1993, 59–60). Local regimes were also under a lot of pressure from franchise owners, many of whom have a great deal of political clout even if not directly involved in politics, like the owners of companies like the Chicago Tribune, Anheuser-Busch, and Disney, and individuals like Ted Turner and Wayne Huizinga. On the other hand, there has been little negative fallout for officials if a team was lost on their watch (Danielson 1997, 114). Furthermore, even if politicians had to raise taxes to pay for ballparks or arenas, repercussions were usually not too loud, especially since those levies fell disproportionately on tourists. Groups that criticized the concept of sports as an agent of economic development or believed such funds could be better used for social-welfare programs had little input in policy decisions.

Political scientist Charles Euchner (1993) argues that "building stadiums and courting sport franchises have become major parts of city agendas as the emphasis of urban leaders has shifted from redistribution to development." Mayors in the 1960s and 1970s focused on social programs, but with the problems of fiscal crisis and economic stagnation, mayors like Edward Koch of New York, William Hudnut of Indianapolis, and Frederico Pena of Denver centered on economic development. Euchner points out that once cities began to stress sports franchises as vehicles for economic development, "cutthroat competition among cities for teams was inevitable" (p. 6), since there were few teams and lots of cities to go around.

Local regimes hoped that by drawing a major league team to their town they would be adding a valuable new asset, enhancing the town's prestige, and demonstrating community spirit. Boosters believed that the presence of sports teams could help build feelings of community among disparate people. In the late 1960s journalists frequently claimed that exciting pennant races in St. Louis in 1967 and Detroit in 1968 curbed summer riots (Rader 1983, 293), and attributed Mayor John Lindsay's reelection in 1969 to the Miracle Mets. The sports franchise would create a positive attitude for tourism and commerce, promote economic development, raise revenue, and entertain local residents (Riess 1989, 244).

The principal anticipated benefit was the stimulation of economic activity. A 1987 study of Milwaukee claimed the Brewers brought in $212 million in direct and indirect revenues. A study in Philadelphia one year later estimated its four major league teams would produced $343 in economic benefits for the city and an additional $233 for the rest of the metropolitan area. Advocates emphasized the dramatic economic impact of such events as the Superbowl, which by 1986 was reputedly worth $226 million to New Orleans and $119 million six years later to Minneapolis (Danielson 1997, 105–106).

PUBLIC SUBSIDIES AND THE MIGRATION
OF FRANCHISES

In 1953 the Boston Braves, the "second" team in that city, moved to Milwaukee, a city that had been without major league baseball for fifty-two years, lured by a publicly financed ballpark. This was the first major league franchise shift since 1903. Milwaukee's quest was led by boosters like the Chamber of Commerce, the Milwaukee *Journal*, and especially brewer Frederick Miller. Political leaders made available County Stadium, which had originally been built for a minor league club, and expanded it to meet the needs of a major league team. The politicians saw a team as a means to gain prestige for Milwaukee and promote economic development. The Braves were a big success at the box office, and for a few years were the most profitable team in baseball. Furthermore, in their first season, the Braves reportedly attracted $5 million in new business to the city. They brought "an electric vitality" that seemed to affect all local business and bolster the city's second-rate self-image. The Braves won pennants in 1957 and 1958 and the World Series in 1957. Thereafter, attendance declined, particularly after 1961, once the team slipped out of the first division, popular players were traded, and few efforts were made at promotion (Gendzel 1995, 537, 539). In 1962 the Braves were purchased by Chicagoans with no loyalty to Milwaukee, and even though Milwaukee had the second-best major league attendance between 1953 and 1965, they soon decided to move to Atlanta for better media opportunities (Zimbalist 1992, 128). This move foreshadowed a growing problem in major sports, with owners increasingly from out of town, often major corporations with little if any connections to the home town.

Prior to the announcement of the move, Milwaukee had already responded to the outside owners by offering to renegotiate the stadium lease. Then, once the owners made their plans public, Wisconsin Attorney General Bronson La Follette hit the team with an antitrust suit. The state claimed that the National League had conspired to restrain trade and harm Wisconsin's economy by approving the transfer without offering another team. This was the first time a state had sued a major league team for violating an antitrust law in state court. Local courts ruled that the team had to stay or be replaced. However, the case was lost on appeal in Superior Court because of baseball's exemption from the antitrust laws (Gendzel 1995, 550).

The Braves were replaced by the Brewers in 1970, formerly the Seattle Pilots. To keep them from moving, Wisconsin is subsidizing a new field to replace County Stadium. In the spring of 1994 a statewide referendum to create a special sports lottery for constructing a park was opposed by 64 percent of the voters. Only the Milwaukee metropolitan counties supported it. Nonetheless, in 1995 Governor Tommy Thompson, best known for leading the national fight to cut welfare, secured an increase in the sales taxes in Milwaukee and the collar counties of 0.1 percent to fund a $250-million project. As Gendzel (1995, 564, 532) points out, while municipal leaders might have been indifferent to the problems of jobs leaving town, they went ballistic to protect a major league franchise.

Atlanta went after the Braves like Milwaukee itself had gone after the Braves. The point man was Mayor Ivan Allen Jr., an unabashed booster, who got the city to build the $42.4-million Atlanta–Fulton County Stadium in 1964 in anticipation of getting a team. Local political leaders welcomed the team with open arms, perceiving it as a way to go "big league" and promote the city's reputation. The city had made the decision while, as historian David Goldfield (1982) noted, "The city's abundant poor required special appeals to secure what was left over" (p. 196). Terms were extremely favorable; the city even picked up the legal costs of the antitrust case. The team's radio–TV package rose from $400,000 in Milwaukee to $2.5 million in Atlanta. Historian Glen Gendzel (1995) interpreted the transfer of the Braves from Milwaukee to Atlanta as the product of "competitive boosterism," in which local elites promoted economic development by encouraging new enterprises to migrate to their city (p. 351). Did the city earn any direct benefits? Economist Dean Baim (1990, 20) found that the stadium lost nearly $20 million in its first twenty-five years.

The next major league migrants were the St. Louis Browns, who moved to Baltimore in 1954, where they played at the publicly owned Memorial Stadium, and the Philadelphia Athletics, who moved to Kansas City in 1955. In 1947 Baltimore started construction on Memorial Stadium to replace the old Municipal Stadium. Built on the exact same site as its predecessor, the new stadium was an immediate success, and by 1950 had earned the city $329,659 through rent and concessions. The city's goal was to attract big-league sports teams, and residents in three elections approved a total of $7.5 million in new bonds to improve the facility and bring it up to standard. Among the improvements was an upper deck that brought the capacity to 50,000 seats. In 1953 the Colts moved in, followed by the Orioles one year later (Miller 1992, 188–189; Hamilton and Kahn 1997, 247).

Philadelphia politicians in the early 1950s, including Mayor Joseph Clark, did not give much attention to the possibility a team might leave, or that the municipality should subsidize a team to stay put. Baseball was not a high priority for Clark or his constituents, who were unhappy with the poor quality of the Athletics, the ambiance at old Shibe Park (renamed Mack Stadium in 1953), the price of concessions, and the undesirability of the location in what had become an increasingly dangerous neighborhood. In the early 1950s, when the local government was collecting land and promoting construction projects to revitalize the Central Business District (CBD) and the industrial base, baseball was not seen as promoting these goals. But while towns with major league franchises remained passive, cities without big-league teams, including Kansas City, Minneapolis, and San Francisco, were all interested in stealing the Athletics and were proposing bond issues for new parks (Kuklick 1991, 121, 123–124; Riess 1989, 235). The Athletics ended up in Kansas City, playing at Municipal Stadium, where the city had spent $3 million to refurbish the minor league park previously owned by the new team owner, Arnold Johnson, to fit major league requirements. In 1955, after the A's had left, Richardson Dilworth was elected mayor of Philadelphia. He was not as interested in the city's economic base and high culture compared to other Democratic patricians, but believed that professional sports added "an irreplaceable zest to the city" (Kuklick 1991, 136). The city commissioned the "Municipal Sports Stadium Study," which concluded Mack Park was too old, had poor parking, and had a poor location in a dangerous neighborhood. The report recommended public funding for a new park. Dilworth supported a public multipurpose stadium that promised the best cost–benefit return, but his advisors warned him that the public would not support a bond issue (p. 137). It would be several years before Philadelphia would build a new ballpark.

The most important migration of the 1950s was that of the Dodgers and Giants to the West Coast, which dramatically altered the geography of major league baseball and shattered the hearts of Brooklynites. Furthermore, as Neil Sullivan (1987), an expert in public administration at New York's Baruch College noted, "The Dodgers were more than a business. They represented a cultural totem, a tangible symbol of the community and its values" (p. 18). Most scholars blame Walter O'Malley for deserting Brooklyn and taking the second-most-profitable team in the National League to greener pastures, thereby grievously harming the borough. Sullivan argues that O'Malley wanted to stay in Brooklyn, buy land, and build his own multipurpose stadium to replace undersized (albeit highly profitable) Ebbets Field, whose neighborhood was becoming unsafe and less accessible to Long Island automobile commuters. O'Malley was concerned about the team's future, because after World War II Brooklyn had undergone significant demographic changes tied to middle-class white flight (suburbanization) and an increasingly lower-class population of people of color, conditions that would eventually hurt attendance. His preferred site was in downtown Brooklyn (Atlantic and Flatbush Avenues), but city leaders felt that this site was too valuable for a ballpark and should be saved for other uses with greater developmental potential (pp. 38–40). O'Malley sought help from the city to get the land through eminent domain, but O'Malley had to first convince master builder Robert Moses. Moses supported helping out the Dodgers, but not in downtown Brooklyn, and not as a Title I urban-renewal project, though he never had any compunction about using urban-renewal laws for projects he favored. Moses preferred a site at Flushing Meadows, in Queens, where the World's Fair was held in 1964. O'Malley also encountered roadblocks from other local government leaders, ranging from the borough level up to the mayor, state officials, and members

of regional planing authorities, as well as the local business community. The city's multilayered decision-making process, growing public
suspicions about the value of public works, and conflicting political
pressures slowed down its response to O'Malley. Furthermore, no one
remotely believed that O'Malley would leave Brooklyn for parts un-
known. Robert Moses and Mayor Robert Wagner were the only individuals who could break through the red tape, but they had no desire
to do so. Along with other city fathers they misread the seriousness of
the situation, which was understandable given the historic stability of
major league baseball in the first half of the century (Sullivan 1987, 44,
47–57, 120–133; Euchner 1993, 16–17).

On the other hand, Los Angeles Mayor Norris Poulson, his regime,
and the powerful county board wanted major league baseball to cer-
tify Los Angeles's status as a first-class city. They started trying to get
a baseball franchise in the early 1940s, but their first success was getting the Cleveland Rams to move there in 1946 in competition with
the Dons of the new All-American Football Conference. O'Malley's
preferred site was at Chavez Ravine, the last vacant sector in the general vicinity of downtown Los Angeles, previously reserved for public housing that many residents felt was "creeping socialism" aimed
at benefiting Mexicans and Mexican Americans. In 1952 voters rejected
plans for the city housing authority to build public housing at Chavez
Ravine (Hines 1982, 124, 13–39; Sullivan 1987, 84–86).

O'Malley offered to trade for the site, putting up Wrigley Field, a
minor league ballpark in Los Angeles that he had just acquired from
the Wrigley family. Despite this step, O'Malley still had a lot of bridges
to cross, having to deal with the state, county, and city, the courts, a
voter referendum, and neighborhood activists prior to final approval
of the land deal that required a two-thirds majority of the city council.
A hard-fought referendum was in doubt until the very last moment,
when a telethon featuring Hollywood stars including Debbie Reynolds
and Ronald Reagan helped gain the voters' approval. It passed by
24,293 votes out of 666,577. The county subsidized O'Malley's move
by providing him with 300 acres of free land worth up to $6 million, a
ninety-nine-year lease on parking, $4.7 million in new roads, and other
concessions. This was an outstanding business decision for O'Malley
and a great coup for L.A., which got a major league team and a tax-
generating property, but a devastating blow to Brooklyn, which never
recovered (Sullivan 1987, 160; Lowenfish 1978, 79–80; Henderson 1980,
267–286; Lipsitz 1984, 8–9). Sullivan gives the impression that O'Malley
was eager to build his own field in California as he had promised in
New York. However, the Dodgers president had originally wanted
Los Angeles to build the field for him. As Poulson (1966) remembered,

we promised "O'Malley the moon . . . and Walter asked for more. . . . He would expect us to build him a ballpark" (pp. 200–201).

As Euchner (1993) points out, the move west by the Dodgers into Los Angeles and the Giants into San Francisco involved the same kinds of issues that dominate contemporary stadium politics. They included public versus private development, eminent domain, competing economic-development strategies, neighborhood resistance, and fragmented local political processes: "Most important, the long, drawn-out series of threats and negotiations—in which the owner of a franchise ratchets up demands by entertaining the competing bids of two or more cities—still drives stadium politics" (p. 19).

The attitudes of government officials regarding the subsidizing of baseball franchises changed in the 1960s with the rapid deterioration of Rust-Belt cities, and planners looked to baseball as a panacea. Since the 1960s city leaders have been prepared to go to any length to keep a franchise. As economist Andrew Zimbalist (1992) noted, while "a city reaps unquantifiable benefits from having a team, cities that have teams and lose them are likely to encounter an image problem" (p. 138). Between 1966 and 1970 several cities built sports stadiums and arenas in the downtown area, including St. Louis (Busch Stadium), Philadelphia (Veterans Stadium), Pittsburgh (Three Rivers Stadium), and Cincinnati (Riverfront Stadium). These were all Rust-Belt cities that were losing population or economically declining cities that built municipal stadiums in downtown areas to keep their sports franchises and to promote urban development. This was a big change from the historic locations of major league ballparks on the suburban fringes in middle-class residential areas or undeveloped sites, although sports arenas had long been sited in entertainment zones in or near the CBD. Private downtown ballparks had previously avoided the downtown because of exorbitant property costs, but municipal subsidizing of land purchases (often obtained through eminent domain) and construction costs changed that. Urban planners advocated downtown sites to promote civic development, save Central Business Districts, build confidence in cities' futures, and, if domed, to serve as convention centers. These new edifices were usually located close to downtown hotels and near major highway interchanges, with ample parking to facilitate suburban fans.

The new stadiums built after the mid-1960s were very expensive facilities. Atlanta's multipurpose Fulton County Stadium, built in 1964 in, admittedly, a region of cheaper construction costs, cost $314 a seat or $19 million, compared to fields built in St. Louis, Anaheim, and San Diego in 1966 and 1967 that averaged $25 million. By 1970 parks cost from $750 to $850 a seat, or around $45 million for Riverfront in Cincinnati and $50 million for Pittsburgh's Three Rivers Stadium and Philadelphia's Veterans Stadium. Projects planned at relatively reasonable rates (which had helped convince the public to support them), like the renovation of Yankee Stadium, often ended up with huge overruns. In 1971, when New York took over the field, it announced that refurbishment would cost $24 million; the final bill was $106 million; plus, the Giants left for New Jersey in 1976. The cheapest field in this era was Buffalo's 70,000-seat Rich Stadium, completed in 1973 as a football-only edifice to keep the Bills in town, which cost $23.5 million (Quirk and Fort 1992, 162; Riess 1989, 241–242).

O'Malley's Dodgers Stadium, completed in 1962, was the last privately built baseball park. The Florida Marlins now share Pro-Player Stadium, privately built in 1987 with the Miami Dolphins). By 1970–1971, 69.7 percent of all facilities used by major league sports teams were publicly owned and 23.7 percent were privately owned (6.6 percent were affiliated with universities). Only hockey still mainly used private facilities (66.7 percent), typically in older multipurpose arenas. On the other hand, a small share of baseball stadiums (30.4 percent), football fields (22.6 percent), and basketball courts (16.3 percent) were privately owned. By 1988 the proportion of privately controlled baseball parks had declined to 20.8 percent and 7.1 percent for football (Okner 1974, 325–326; Riess 1989, 239). Three years later 70 percent of all indoor arenas in the United States and Canada were publicly owned.

Public subsidization of private franchises was not limited to construction of ballparks and arenas, but extended to more modest assistance, such as underpricing of rents and various fees. Direct subsidies included purchasing broadcast rights, and indirect subsidies included constructing highways and exit ramps and giving up future revenues because the edifice was tax exempt. Benjamin Okner (1974, 335–343) estimated that in the late 1960s sports facilities received an average direct government subsidy of $400,000, and $8.8 million in indirect assistance. He found that revenues were enough to cover operating costs, but not enough to also cover amortization and interest charges (also see Noll 1974, 29–32). In 1970, when the Seattle Pilots moved to Milwaukee, the county charged just $1 in taxes for the first million tickets sold, and then just 5 percent thereafter. Seven years later, when the Brewers drew 1.1 million spectators, the county got just $21,149 in taxes. In New York, when George Steinbrenner bought the Yankees from CBS in 1973 he had the city rewrite the lease so that he could deduct maintenance costs from rent. Thus, in 1976, when the Yankees grossed $11.9 million, the city ended up owing the Yankees $10,000 instead of the $854,504 it would have made under the old contract. In 1978, *Sports Illustrated* estimated local government support at $25 million a year (Kennedy and Williamson 1978, 71–72). Recent audits found that in 1989 the Yankees paid no rent at all, and often the maintenance deduction resulted in rental payments of under $200,000 (Zimbalist 1992, 138).

Domed stadiums, modeled after the Houston Astrodome, which cost about $41 million, were particularly expensive. Overly optimistic urban planners built domed facilities as civic monuments that were expected to become centers for public entertainment and attractions for conventions and other businesses expectations that were rarely achieved. Lipsitz (1984, 10–13) found that in Houston the project provided few public benefits while offering private investors a great opportunity to make a lot of money with little public control. The Astrodome was built in 1965 by a former mayor, Judge Roy Hofheinz, owner of the Astros, and his partner, oilman Bob Smith, who owned the prospective site that previously had little value because it tended to flood. The city came up with $3.7 million and $31.6 million in revenue bonds approved by a referendum, while Hofheinz and Smith raised their $6 million for the park by selling luxury boxes. Houston's reward was major league baseball and a famous building that from the start was unprofitable. Houston was traditionally a private city that offered minimal public services, and building the Astrodome did not help reverse that trend (Riess 1989, 242). Even more irresponsible was the New Orleans Superdome, originally planned as a $35-million, self-supporting edifice. Louisiana legislators gave the Louisiana Stadium and Exposition District a virtual blank check, and ended up with a $168-million 97,000-seat enclosed field (Burck 1973, 105–106). The true cost was actually about double because of the high-cost bonds purchased to finance the structure. New Orleans never did get a major league baseball team.

Political scientist John P. Pelissero (Pelissero, Henschen, and Sidlow 1991, 118) of Loyola University has pointed out that progressive regimes promoted politics that would purportedly promote development through sports. For instance, he points to Mayor Moon Landrieu of New Orleans in the 1970s pushing the construction of the Superdome to help redevelop downtown. The core of his regime was the local African American community rather than business and civic leaders. The project provided service contracts that rewarded Landrieu's supporters, although the scheme was a huge financial drain and did not turn around downtown.

In New York, for instance, politicians argued for a takeover and rehabilitation of Yankee Stadium to attract tourists, fill up hotels and restaurants, and revitalize its surrounding neighborhood. Borough president Robert Abrams claimed that a new stadium would generate the kind of excitement and energy that New York needed, "not only in real dollars, but in spirit. We're in a psychological crisis. Decisions are being made every day to come to New York, to leave New York, to invest in New York." Abrams argued that fixing up the ballpark would be interpreted as a message to local businessmen that the city was on the way back from its fiscal crisis (Lipsyte 1976, 43). Similarly, in the rapidly growing city of San Antonio the mayor in 1977 justified a $3.7-million improvement of the Convention Center for the Spurs: "We have a great opportunity through the gaining of national stature on the sports scene. This will help attract industry and assist our economy" (Kennedy and Williamson 1978, 71–72).

There is little evidence that downtowns were much improved by sports facilities. Pittsburgh promised that the area around Three Rivers Stadium would get road improvements, a new park, a marina, a hotel, and restaurants, which did not happen. In New York the primary rationale for rebuilding Yankee Stadium was community improvement. However, the residents and merchants in the environs did not get any tangible benefits. Journalist Robert Lipsyte (1976, 41) was told by a local a storekeeper, "That's an isolated place over there. People just drive in and out." New highway access ramps were built, but not, as promised, a park behind the stadium. Lipsyte concluded that the project did not provide the foundation for the reclamation of the Bronx, and failed to restore public confidence and halt white flight.

Busch Stadium, built in 1966 in St. Louis, appeared to positively benefit its neighbors in the old Skid Row section. The Cardinals owner, August A. Busch Jr., was a leader of Civic Progress, an organization that promoted slum clearance, urban redevelopment, and government spending for downtown. Civic Progress got the land near the park declared a blighted area, which meant tax abatements, and formed a redevelopment corporation to acquire land through powers of condemnation and eminent domain. The field was intended to be the center of the city's downtown urban renewal to modernize an old decaying industrial city. Busch and his pals used the downtown park as an entering "wedge to secure tax breaks for adjacent businesses," while the lost revenue was made up by local homeowners and by curtailing city services (Lipsitz 1984, 5). Busch Stadium seemed to have had a big influence in renovating downtown, removing "ramshackle tenements and marginal business establishments" for parking, restaurants, and new stores (Rooney 1975, 112). However, it was just one part of the city's major effort at rejuvenating the downtown, symbolized by the Gateway Arch. In the meanwhile, old Sportsman's Park rusted away along with its industrial neighborhood.

The economic impact of such subsidies fell well short of misguided estimates by paid consultants who typically overestimated the numbers of fans coming from out of town with "new" money, underestimated the alternate use of discretionary money by local folk, and abused the concept of the multiplier. Those reports were less an effort to make an accurate estimate than to convince voters to support ballparks. As Tom Ferguson, ex-president of the Beacon Council that promoted economic development in Dade County, Florida, said, "It's all to sell the local community on making an expenditure" (Whitford 1993, 31). Many of the so-called new benefits really were just local money being shifted around differently since the proportion of out-of-towners attending sporting events was usually exaggerated. Cities and other public authorities were left with inflated bills, financial losses, underused facilities, and few if any long-term improvements.

Beginning with the 1974 Brookings Institution report on the economics of sports (Okner 1974), academic economists have consistently, if not unanimously, took to task the projections made by supporters of municipally financed sports structures (Baim 1994; Baade 1995; Rosentraub 1997). Any consultant who dared provide an unfavorable report would probably be fired or unable to get new contracts in the future. These consultants overestimated the numbers of out-of-town fans attending games with their new money, and underestimated alternate uses of discretionary money by local folk. In New York and Chicago, for instance, few football tickets were sold to out-of-towners. Fans attending ball games at Yankee Stadium in the Bronx did not tarry in the neighborhood and spend money, but jumped right back into their cars or the subway and headed straight home.

Economists have similarly taken to task the false expectations generated by spectacular events like the World Series, the Superbowl, or the Final Four in college basketball, which are often one-shot deals. The justification was similar to boosters who had supported postseason bowl games, beginning in Pasadena in 1902, to promote tourism. This was especially important during the Depression, when stadiums were built for bowl games in Miami, Dallas, New Orleans, and El Paso. Superbowls are largely rotated among milder-climate cities that already are tourist havens, while in the case of the World Series, getting the event depends on having excellent teams, not the newest park (although quality teams have performed better in new parks).

Economists recognize that certain groups do benefit from government subsidies. Dean Baim argues that the subsidies are extremely regressive, mainly benefiting rich franchise owners and newly wealthy athletes, and (I would add) the upper-middle-class fans who can afford the high price of tickets (Baim 1994, 163; Rosentraub 1997, 3–30). There are direct economic benefits that include rent, concession shares, parking revenues, jobs, and taxes. But these revenues are relatively small, especially at open-air stadiums that are vacant much of the year, making it nearly impossible for governments to make up their subsidies.

ECONOMIC DEVELOPMENT AND SUBURBIA

Another major development was the move to the suburbs, especially by indoor arenas, long a mainstay of urban entertainment. These include the Forum in Inglewood, California; the Brendan Byrne Arena in East Rutherford, New Jersey; and the Nassau County Coliseum in Uniondale, New York. These facilities were situated where they would be accessible to well-off suburbanite fans, who comprise a major portion of the audiences for high-priced spectator sports. Furthermore, by 1970 one-fifth of the new baseball and football stadiums were also being built in suburbs like Bloomington, Minnesota, and Arlington, Texas, and the trend continued with facilities like Giants Stadium in the Meadowlands. By 1987, one-fifth of National Basketball Association (NBA) and National Hockey League (NHL) teams were located in the suburbs, but just 12.5 percent of American League teams (Riess 1989, 307, n. 22). These facilities were all expected to be centerpieces in promoting suburban development.

Economists Mark S. Rosentraub and Samuel R. Nunn (1978, 412–413) analyzed the high cost of subsidizing professional sports in their study of the Dallas suburbs of Arlington and Irving. In 1972 Arlington convinced the Washington Senators to move there by building them a $20-million stadium and establishing a corporation to buy media rights to the ball games for $7.5 million. Irving got the Cowboys to move from nearby Dallas by raising a bond issue to pay for a new $35-million stadium. Suburban leaders hoped to gain prestige and enhance their community's tax base. However, the entire stadium profits from Texas Stadium (Arlington) between 1972 and 1975 were completely eaten up by operating expenses. Enough money was made in 1976 to retire stadium bonds for the first time, but there was still no revenue for the city. Neither town made much from sales taxes, despite all the traffic passing through, nor did any financial benefits spill over into adjacent cities. Paying for the baseball field left Arlington with the lowest bond rating of any comparable Texas city (Rosentraub 1997, 433). In 1988 Arlington sold the park to the Rangers for the bargain price of $17.8 million, following the prior privatization of St. Louis's Busch Stadium in 1980. Arlington subsequently spent $35 million to finance a new stadium (the Ballpark in Arlington) that was completed in 1994. It was paid for by a sales tax, mostly paid by nonresidents, and the city will probably pay off the bonds five years ahead of schedule (Rosentraub 1997, 436). Rosentraub found that "as the new suburban franchise locations matured during the 1980s . . . new entertainment and business complexes may have resulted in comparatively better fiscal performances in the two suburban cities" (p. 440).

The most ambitious suburban sports development was the Meadowlands Complex, just five miles from New York City, which included the 76,500-seat Giants Stadium, the 35,000-seat Meadowlands Racetrack (built in 1976 at a cost of $302 million), and the $75-million 20,000-seat Brendan Byrne Arena. The Meadowlands, a former dump, had enormous potential because 20 million people lived within an hour's drive. The 1971 master plan of the Hackensack Meadowlands Development Commission mapped out, in addition to the sport complex, office buildings, factories, hotels, and housing, much of which was completed on schedule soon after Giants Stadium (Riess 1989, 245). The commission did not claim that development required the sports complex (which it did not), but that its presence and the accompanying publicity expedited investment (*Chicago Tribune*, November 10, 1985). The Meadowlands was the closest open space to New York City, and would have undoubtedly boomed with or without a sports stadium and the New Jersey Sports and Exposition Authority.

The Meadowlands was one of the most successful publicly owned stadiums. In 1989 it had a $5-million profit in net operating income, charging the highest rent to any NFL football team. Yet Quirk and Fort (1992) also found that it was one of the most heavily subsidized, to the amount of $8 million. By subsidy, the authors meant net operating income less depression, capital return, and property taxes foregone. In other words, "the amount by which revenues fall short of covering all the costs that would have been incurred if the facility were operated by a private owner" (p. 171). It was surpassed by Riverfront, the Kingdome, the Astrodome, the Silverdome, and Byrne Arena, with $10-million subsidies, which in turn are dwarfed by the $43-million Superdome subsidy. In addition, the Superdome has the highest annual negative income ($8 million). Quirk and Fort estimated that in 1989 the total public subsidy to major sports tenants was about $500 million (pp. 166, 171).

PUBLIC SUBSIDIES OF SPORTS STADIUMS
IN THE 1980s AND 1990s

Despite the available economic data, cities continue to subsidize sports franchises, either to keep them in town or to attract them to their towns. The regimes continue to rely on unsubstantiated forecasts by well-paid consultants to support sports as an economic-development tool. On occasion, civic leaders might recognize that subsidizing a team is something done for psychic returns that residents seem prepared to pay, especially if the costs don't come directly from their own pockets. In the remaining section, we will consider several cases of recent municipal subsidization of baseball teams.

BALTIMORE

Scholars have particularly examined how sports teams manipulated Baltimore, which in the 1970s lost 13 percent of its population and in the 1980s was fifth among fifty-eight cities as measured by urban distress (Miller 1992, 104). By the mid-1960s Memorial Stadium's negatives, including poor accessibility, distance from the interstate, and limited parking, made it a losing financial proposition for the city (Quirk and Fort 1992, 250). Furthermore, the local franchise owners, Jerry Hoffberger of the Orioles and especially Carroll Rosenbloom of the Colts, began to put pressure on the city. In 1965 Rosenbloom warned the city that it might lose the teams without a new stadium. The Colts owner was ignored then, but repeated his demands two years later. The city responded it could not afford a new stadium and was having a hard time maintaining the old stadium. Douglas Tawney, director of the Department of Parks and Recreation, recommended a $10-million overall that would include 15,000 parking spaces and luxury boxes, which mollified Hoffberger but not Rosenbloom, who felt the Orioles had a better stadium contract (they controlled stadium concessions) and were favored by the city (Miller 1992, 202).

Rosenbloom announced in February 1971 that he would move out of the city when his lease expired one year later. There was not much response by the city or neighboring counties, but Governor Marvin Mandel did get the message, and soon supported a new stadium. In 1972 his administration created the Maryland Sports Complex Authority to establish, without state funding, a sports complex for metropolitan Baltimore. Its members were mainly drawn from the city's pro-growth leadership, who saw a stadium as a means to help redevelop the city center (Miller 1992, 203–204). By then Rosenbloom had already left Baltimore, having traded his team for the Los Angeles Rams.

Discussions soon developed about acquiring Camden Yards as the site. Camden Yards was located in the Inner Harbor, a former blighted area of abandoned warehouses, redeveloped in the late 1970s into an upscale zone of offices, hotels, restaurants, and tourist attractions. The location was very accessible, adjacent to the interstate highway, and had a lot of parking in the evening (Quirk and Fort 1992, 253; Miller 1992, 300). A feasibility study reported that the neighborhood was becoming poorer, older, and racially mixed, and endorsed a new domed 70,000-seat stadium at Camden Yards that would cost $114.1 million and help revitalize the area. Mandel and the Sports Authority tried to promote popular support for a plan to sell bonds to finance construction, but in early 1975 voters approved a referendum barring the use of public funds for a stadium (Miller 1992, 205–206).

In 1976 Indianapolis began to court the Colts, whose owner Robert Irsay had alienated fans by his inept management, causing a drop in attendance. Three years latter Irsay was openly talking about relocating unless there was a $25-million renovation of Memorial Stadium or a new stadium. The local power elite thought this was idle chatter, since Irsay already had extremely favorable terms in his lease, and especially since NFL rules required league approval for such a move and that was considered unlikely. Nonetheless, Irsay's actions and the sale of the Orioles to Edward B. Williams heightened fears about the teams. In 1980 Governor Harry Hughes tried to encourage the teams to stay put by approving a $22-million appropriation to expand the field with more seating and luxury boxes and create 2,000 more parking spaces if the teams would sign fifteen-year leases, but neither franchise agreed to the terms. The Orioles instead called for a baseball-only field in the CBD that the local elite opposed, especially because of high prevailing interest rates and the need for state and federal funding. Furthermore, a study by the Baltimore *Sun* had reported that the Orioles had directly generated only about $2 million for the city's income, and the parks director reported that the city was making no money from professional sports at Memorial Stadium (Miller 1992, 294–298).

Mayor William Schaefer wanted to avoid building a new stadium and the accompanying huge debt service it would have brought, especially since the city had more pressing problems. He preferred giving teams more-favorable leases (Euchner 1993, 105), which left the teams and the city at an impasse. By 1983 Schaefer was concentrating on the Orioles because it seemed the Colts were determined to leave, which they did, moving to Indianapolis in the middle of the night on March 29, 1984. This shocking event seemed to demonstrate "Baltimore's worst fear about itself. It was a second-rate town again" (Richmond 1993, 65). The city considered suing the Colts and the NFL as a monopoly. Baltimore had experience in the courts, having originally won the rights to the Colts franchise as a result of a lawsuit against the NFL in 1952 (Euchner 1993, 110). Instead, Schaefer decided to work together with the NFL to gain a new franchise (which it got when Art Modell moved the Browns from Cleveland in 1995). The city did try to use eminent domain to contest the Colts' action, but the courts ruled that the Colts were now out of the state's jurisdiction. Euchner has suggested that a better tactic would have been to claim the Colts had not bargained in good faith, and thus, under NFL by-laws and the limited antitrust exception of football, the Colts "might have owed Baltimore the right of first refusal" (p. 111).

The departure of the Colts and the Orioles' continued complaints and rumblings convinced Schaefer to support a new municipal stadium. Schaefer inaccurately believed the Colts had been worth $25–30 million in economic activity in terms of jobs, entertainment, and taxes, "All the things that keep a city alive" (Miller 1992, 299). Schaefer wanted to use professional sports to help revitalize his city, which under his leadership was gaining a reputation for pragmatism and vigor. New sports stadiums would restore the city's public image, offer large construction contracts, and promote economic development (Euchner 1993, 119). Up to then Schaefer had been focusing on rehabilitating rowhouses, revitalizing the oceanfront at the Inner Harbor, and promoting a sense of community in the neighborhoods (Miller 1992, 299).

Schaefer was moving far ahead of public opinion on the stadium issue because he did not want to lose another franchise on his watch (Euchner 1993, 119). The mayor organized a task force that recommended a controversial new downtown facility that became a big issue in the 1986 democratic gubernatorial nomination. His opponent, Attorney General Stephen Sachs, and suburban Washington assemblymen preferred a park nearer Washington that would make the Orioles more of a regional club. Schaefer was also opposed by legislators from the stadium neighborhood, who wanted the field fixed up or replaced at the same site. A state commission investigating four potential sites recommended Lansdowne, a Washington suburb, for the site, with the expensive Camden site third (Miller 1992, 299–300).

Historian James Miller (1992, 302–303) claims that Schaefer's victories in the primary and the general election set the stage for decisive action. Immediately after his victory in the general election, Schaefer called for action, and one month later the Maryland Professional Sports Authority presented a plan to build the downtown stadium Schaefer wanted at the Inner Harbor, along with a second field for football. In late March 1987 he submitted legislation for a $200-million ballpark to be funded by tax-exempt bond issues and a lottery, which was approved one month later. The quasipublic Maryland Stadium Authority was established to select the site, condemn property, raise funds, pay for the eviction of residents, and coordinate construction (Euchner 1993, 120).

Camden Yards, an intimate park designed in the style of the early-twentieth-century fields, had been a great success, drawing several million fans annually. Average attendance rose from 29,458 for the last four years of Memorial Stadium to 45,034 in the first five years at Camden. It is especially popular with out-of-towners, who comprise 30 percent of the spectators, or triple their share at Memorial Stadium. About 70 percent of first-time attendees were from elsewhere. The success of Camden Yards has encouraged other cities to build retro ballparks. Yet Hamilton and Kahn (1997, 245–246, 253) argue that even at Camden Yards the cost to the public has outweighed the financial benefits. The stadium has generated enough new revenue to more than cover capital and maintenance costs; however, all surpluses have gone to the Orioles and not the city. The state and city lose about $9 million a year on the park, and another $12 million from the national economy.

CLEVELAND

Another city that badly needed a new stadium was Cleveland, where residents and jobs were taking flight and the franchise was the laughing stock of the American League. The stadium had always been a poor ballpark, with thousands of empty seats located far from the playing field (Rosentraub 1997, 245–249; Torry 1995, 206, 216–217). By 1983 Governor Richard F. Celeste knew the Indians might move without a new stadium. Nonetheless, one year later he opposed a countywide ballot to finance a $150-million 72,000-seat domed stadium for the Browns because he believed that raising property taxes was a bad way to finance a stadium. Future mayor Mike White denounced the stadium as a "sport palace for the Republican privileged" (Torry 1995, 220). Local businessmen gave a nonbinding offer to pay half of the costs, but the county defeated the proposal by 100,000 votes. Republican county commissioner Vincent Campanella and Republican Mayor George Voinovich encouraged county officials, prominent businessmen, and representatives from the Browns and Indians to form the Greater Cleveland Domed Stadium Corporation. They wanted to secure a downtown site, preferably in the Central Market area, a decrepit part of the CBD. It was difficult to form a consensus about securing public money, especially since many local Democrats were not on speaking terms and the Jacobs brothers, the new owners of the Indians, were not known as compromisers. On the other hand, they had a big stake in local real estate, and most observers felt they were not looking to move (pp. 203–204, 206, 215–216, 218–220, 222).

By 1990 prospects for a new baseball park had improved. Mayor White and other leading Democrats was willing to support a new stadium for economic development of the CBD, as a symbol of the city's rebirth, and as a source of community pride (Rosentraub 1997, 255–258; Torry 1995, 222). The proposed park also became part of a package deal to bring the NBA Cavaliers back from the Richfield Coliseum. The movers and shakers got the Cavaliers to agree to a 20,000-seat arena and the Indians to a 45,000-seat ballpark that each would manage by itself. The $344-million proposal was very vague (and underestimated), and the architect's plans were uncertain. About half of the cost, $174 million, would be privately paid from luxury boxes and club seats, plus the Indians would provide $20 million as seed money and nearly $3 million annually toward construction. The city's share

would come from a sin tax on cigarettes and alcohol. Supporters decided to put the bill on the May primary ballot, even though they knew
that such elections tended to draw older citizens who traditionally
voted against tax increases more than younger balloters. They figured
an early election would take advantage of popular enthusiasm that
might wane and the need to sell bonds by the end of the year to take
advantage of certain expiring federal laws. Virtually every officeholder
supported the well-organized and well-financed plan. Advocates sold
the proposal as a developmental project for the downtown that would
cost them each just a few dollars while it would bring in 11,600 construction jobs and 17,000 permanent jobs. Still, the boosters were uncertain of victory, and recruited the help of Major League Baseball
(MLB) Commissioner Fay Vincent, who warned the city council that
the Indians were likely to move without a new park. Voters approved
the plan with 51.9 percent of the vote. The suburban vote carried the
measure, with a 55-percent approval, although 56 percent of
Cleveland's ballots were against it. By the time the project was completed in 1994, the cost of Jacobs Field alone was at least $176 million
(Rosentraub 1997, 258–283; Austrian and Rosentraub 1997, 361–363;
Torry 1995, 222, 224–227).

SAN FRANCISCO

The Giants originally moved to San Francisco in 1957 and played at
the minor league Seals Stadium. Three years later the team moved
into the city-built, $11-million 40,000-seat Candlestick Park, right on
the bay, just fifteen minutes from downtown. Rent was a minimum of
$125,000, or 5 percent of profits, compared to other publicly built parks
that charged 7 percent. The city expected to make $500,000 a year from
the deal (Agostini, Quigley, and Smolensky 1997, 388). However, fans
quickly found the cold winds and foggy weather intolerable; the park
was popularly known as the "Wind Tunnel," or the "Cave of the
Winds." The nation discovered the foul character of the park at the
1961 All-Star Game when pitcher Stu Miller was knocked off the mound
by "the Hawk," as the strong winds were locally known (Andelman
1993, 256–257). Mayor George Christopher had a wind study made
that recommended doming Candlestick. As early as 1967 there was
talk of either dumping Candlestick Park or expanding it, and one year
later the San Francisco Planning and Urban Research Association recommended moving to a more convenient downtown site. Instead, the
city expanded the field for pro football to 58,000 seats. But the Giants
had a hard time attracting fans, and had the lowest attendance in the
majors in 1974 (519,000) and 1975 (522,000) (Agostini, Quigley, and
Smolensky 1997, 389; Andelman 1993, 258–259).

In 1981 the Giants issued a report that declared the park unfit for baseball and urged a domed stadium. Mayor Dianne Feinstein established a task force to consider the park question. One year later the experts recommended a new site at the China Basin, jointly owned by the state and the Port Commission, that would be combined with the Mission Bay development project. This was a very expensive proposal, since the land alone would have cost at least $32.8 million, might be better used for housing, and would take the land off the property-tax rolls. To fund the park, the task force recommended the sale or lease of private luxury boxes, corporation sponsorships, advertising revenue from scoreboard and media, and the sale of the old field. Former Mayor Christopher estimated the project would cost $165 million, and instead suggested doming Candlestick Park (Agostini, Quigley, and Smolensky 1997, 389–390).

Between 1987 and 1990 there were three ballots in the city and three in the region to keep the team in the Bay area, in which voters showed they wanted a privately owned and financed downtown stadium (Fort 1997, 174–175). The first vote was on Proposition W, advocated by Giants owner Bob Lurie, which called for a publicly built park near the Oakland Bay Bridge that would cost the city nothing but valuable land (p. 164). The $80-million funding was to come from bond sales guaranteed by the city and the sale of luxury boxes. Mayor Feinstein did not expect the initiative to pass, but supported it, along with organized labor, most supervisors, and the Chamber of Commerce. Mayoral candidate Art Agnos opposed the plan, as did neighborhood groups and environmentalists like the Sierra Club. Foes were dubious of the no-cost claims, and argued that the project would divert existing taxes to the project, wind up with a financial bailout, and hurt the quality of life. Proposition W went down to defeat, 96,445 to 85,005. Yet at the same time voters approved a $99-million bond issue to pay for parks, streets, and police stations which they felt were more important than a new ballpark. Following the election, Giants' owner Bob Lurie made it clear that if the city did not provide a new stadium he was primed to move elsewhere, even though his heart was in San Francisco (Fort 1997, 164–165, Agostini, Quigley, and Smolensky 1997, 390–391).

Mayor Agnos and his new administration worked to find a way out of the bind and keep the Giants in town to demonstrate the city's vitality and to promote economic development. In 1988 Agnos sought bids for a downtown park as well as a 20,000-seat entertainment and sports arena, and on July 27, 1989, Lurie and the mayor announced plans for a 45,000-seat stadium at China Basin. Lurie saw this as a last shot and was told by the mayor that he could break his lease at Candlestick if the proposal was defeated. Proposition P proposed a joint stadium venture between the city and the experienced Spectator Management

Group, covering development, financing, ownership, and revenue sharing. Voters were impressed by the proposed mix of public and private financing, and narrowly rejected Proposition P by a vote of 87,850 to 85,796. A second ballpark initiative on the ballot, Proposition V, sought to get the Board of Supervisors to consider improving Candlestick Park at private expense. This measure failed 98,875 to 93,599, probably influenced by the earthquake a few weeks earlier at the start of the World Series. The need to rebuild the city's infrastructure put baseball on the back burner (Agostini, Quigley, and Smolensky 1997, 394; Fort 1997, 165–166; Andelman 1993, 260).

Nearby towns also considered the possibility of hosting the Giants. In 1990 San Jose, fifty miles from San Francisco, voted on Proposition H to build a publicly financed $160-million park financed by taxes on entertainment, real estate, and utilities. It was defeated by a vote of 89,269 to 85,313. A companion bill, Proposition G, in nearby Santa Clara County, for a 1-percent utility tax and parking tax to build a $153-million stadium, was defeated by just 2,000 out of 257,000 votes. San Jose's newly elected mayor, Susan Hammer, was a big stadium booster, and three months after taking office formed a commission to determine how to finance a new baseball park. The local press, eager to improve the city's image, vigorously supported plans that called for a joint private–public venture. On June 2, 1992, San Jose voters went to the polls to decide if they wanted to support a $265-million stadium with redevelopment funds and by raising utility taxes by 2 percent ($35 per household). Over $1 million was spent by pro-stadium folk to sign up new voters and educate the public (one-fourth of which was put up by the Giants), compared to about $15,000 for the opposition. However, the bill was soundly defeated, 94,465 to 78,809 (Fort 1997, 166–167; Andelman 1993, 261–264).

Lurie had enough, and in 1992 made a deal to sell the team for $11 million to a Tampa syndicate that intended to move the Giants to their city. Major League Baseball blocked the move, and instead Lurie sold the franchise for $15 million less than its fair market value to a syndicate of San Franciscans organized by Mayor Frank Jordan. The city fathers drew up a new proposal for the China Basin site that would give developers an exemption from zoning regulations (Agostini, Quigley, and Smolensky 1997, 394–395). The proposition was not a detailed financial understanding, but just asked voters to approve a policy statement that called for a privately financed project. The campaign had support from a broad coalition of political and social leaders, organized labor, the gay community, and environmentalists, and was chaired by future Mayor Willie Brown's campaign manager, who had previously opposed municipal support for a new ballpark. The cost was estimated at $255 million, but with no new taxes, no use of general funds, and no taxpayer liability. Of the total, $140 million would come from a private bond issue and $90 million from the sale of the stadium's name, personal seat licenses for 15,000 seats, advertising and concession rights, and luxury boxes. Direct public money would be limited to tax-increment financing from the Redevelopment Agency, while the Port of San Francisco would buy a portion of the site owned by the Department of Transportation and negotiate lease terms with the team. Proposition B was approved by the voters on March 26, 1996, by an overwhelming 101,343 to 51,222 vote. As Fort (1997, 167) points out, voters were willing to provide a valuable public site for the new ball field, but they did not want to pay for it (see also Agostini, Quigley, and Smolensky 1997, 394).

ST. PETERSBURG

Virtually all ballparks were built with the assurance that a baseball or football team would stay there or was about to move in. This was not the case for St. Petersburg's Tropicana Field, whose construction was approved on speculation in 1988. Only ten years later did the facility get its major league tenant, the Devil Rays. Best known as a retirement community, the city had a long history of competition with its more aggressive neighbor Tampa, home of Busch Gardens, the University of South Florida, and the regional airport. The origin of Tropicana Field goes back to 1977, when the state legislature established the Pinellas (County) Sports Authority (PSA), St. Petersburg's answer to the Tampa Sports Authority, which had brought an NFL franchise to the area. As early as 1980 the authority announced plans for a $59-million baseball-only stadium on a twenty-one-acre site owned by the city that fronted on the interstate. The board soon decided that an open-air stadium was not the best solution, and after visiting Seattle's Kingdome, then the only multipurpose stadium making money, the PSA decided to build a downtown multipurpose stadium. Funding was expected to come from special grants, tax-increment financing, or a combination of several sources, including an admission tax or a surcharge at the stadium. Baseball advocates convinced themselves that if a stadium were built, they would get a major league team, presumably one dissatisfied with location, since there were no strong prospects for expansion then (Andelman 1993, 55, 60, 65).

The city's drive for a stadium did not get far beyond the talking stage until, on October 18, 1982, the Tampa Sports Authority announced plans to build their own ballpark next to Tampa Stadium. This pushed St. Petersburg to make a firm commitment to baseball. Within days, the city council granted the PSA a $1 a year, forty-year lease on the sixty-six-acre downtown Gas Plant redevelopment area, plus $7 million to prepare the site for construction. An unofficial steering committee, known as "the Vault," took charge. It included the city manager and his assistant, a county commissioner, two councilmen, and the *Petersburg Times* publisher. There was considerable opposition to the proposed new stadium, especially since taxpayers opposed building before any team committed itself to the city. Calls for a countywide referendum went unanswered because civic leaders knew it would fail. They took their cue from Seattle, where two referendums on the Kingdom had failed and the third had only passed because it had been slipped into a vote on a measure calling for better drainage and improved streets (Andelman 1993, 67–68, 90–91). Furthermore, supporters wanted local government leaders to make the hard decisions on their own initiative, which was what they had been elected to do, as in Tampa, whose stadium had been constructed based on the action of "a group of strong-willed legislators" (Andelman 1993, 92).

On July 24, 1986, the county and city committed to a new $83-million domed stadium, even though baseball commissioner Peter Ueberroth warned them that there was no guarantee the city would get a major league franchise. Nearly half of the costs were to come from taxes on the tourist industry, which avoided putting a heavy tax burden on local residents. Planners expected that tourists would also comprise most of the spectators. The city's main target then was Jerry Reinsdorf of the White Sox, who was promised an annual $10-million media deal and free land for his real estate business to sweeten the pot. The city lobbied intensely in Tallahassee, seeking $30 million to enhance the planed ballpark and build parking lots. Their thirty-one-page report, "Baseball and Florida," projected that the Sox would annually bring in $54.5 million in new business, and $101 million in sales taxes over a thirty-year period. But Reinsdorf chose at the last minute to stay in Chicago when the state government met his terms. Nonetheless, St. Petersburg went ahead with its plans for a dome, with a projected cost was at least $110 million plus $40 million in improvements once a team was secured. The eventual cost of the grounds (including interest) has been estimated by the *Tampa Tribune* to surpass $300 million (Andelman 1993, 9, 14, 18, 20, 263).

These examples offer a valuable model for analyzing the merits of deciding policy issues through the voting process. Citizens in metropolitan areas, rather than elected officials, had to make the hard decisions about whether to finance sports facilities. Fort (1997) found that across the country voters' preferences regarding stadium subsidization "are not being met," and thus direct democracy does not serve the public in deciding policy issues. Scholars have found that stadium issues are ripe for special interest politics, since there is a big payoff for a few and relatively little cost for the many. They prefer the logrolling prevalent in direct democracy because then there can be tradeoffs in benefits and costs. In referendums, the supporters of public financing have typically arranged all the details (financing for the highest amount they think the public will tolerate, leases, and infrastructure payments) and decide when it is most advantageous to hold the vote. When an initiative is an option pushed by someone seriously upset with the status quo, legislators may prefer to let the citizens vote rather than having to make an unpopular decision. Public officials want to have their cake and eat it too. They will usually support publicly financed stadiums rather than lose a team, which they are certain is bad for their careers, but prefer to have the voters approve the means to pay for the subsidization. Yet the referenda have mostly been defeated, usually by narrow margins. The public wants sports stadiums, but not publicly financed stadiums, especially if the funding comes directly out of their pockets. Fort found that from 1982 through 1996 only twelve of twenty-nine referenda on stadia passed (41 percent) (pp. 150–151, 158–159, 161). By contrast, when it comes to representative democracy, virtually no city officials have stood up and said no. One who did was New York's Mayor Edward Koch, who did not support an effort to rebuild Madison Square Garden, and currently Mayor Richard M. Daley, who has reined in the Chicago Bears' quest for a publicly financed facility.

CHICAGO

Considerable attention has recently been given to the relationship between commercialized sport and municipal government in Chicago. In the 1990s the city constructed a baseball park, subsidized the construction of the privately owned United Center, and has debated support of a new football facility to replace Soldier Field. Chicago park advocates justified public support for a ballpark on the grounds of urban development and the strong possibility of losing the franchise. In 1981 Jerry Reinsdorf and his syndicate purchased the Sox from Bill Veeck. Their ballpark, the oldest in the majors, was located in a declining white ethnic neighborhood, separated from the city's largest black ghetto by the massive Dan Ryan Expressway. The presence of a large African American neighborhood so close was hurting attendance. One year later, in return for a promise not to move from this problematic location, the city council approved a $5-million tax-exempt industrial revenue bond to finance twenty-seven luxury suites. The Sox then had much less visibility than their crosstown rivals, the Cubs, who had a showplace at Wrigley Field and were televised virtually daily on WGN-

TV, a superstation. The Sox hired a consultant who advised them to develop a suburban base where there were more potential fans who could afford to attend ball games (Euchner 1993, 135).

Euchner argues that this report dramatically altered the Sox's future planning toward the suburbs. In 1985 they began exploring the option of moving to the western suburbs to be closer to the main group of their fans. The Sox planned to move to west suburban Addison, but lost a referendum there in 1986 despite the support of Governor James Thompson and DuPage County Republican leaders. Then the regimes in Chicago and Springfield got together and established the Illinois Sports Facilities Authority (ISFA) to build a park in Chicago across the street from the old field. Despite coming up with a plan late in 1986, squabbling between Mayor Harold Washington and Thompson over control of the ISFA, community demands for just compensation for displaced residents, and complaints by the Sox over the terms seriously imperiled the project. The Sox were just minutes from leaving for St. Petersburg when a final agreement was reached. The new 44,321-seat Comiskey Park was completed in 1991. It has not been a success. Architecturally, it lacks the flair and excitement of intimate parks like Camden Yards or Wrigley Field, and it has had little economic impact on the neighborhood. Architect Philip Bess lobbied unsuccessfully for an alternate model that would have promoted a wide mix of land uses, employing the blocks facing the field for commercial and residential development of an interactive community where there would be a mixture of residential, business, and cultural activities. This would have encouraged a lot of traffic, which would in turn have promoted a sense of security and galvanized even more business activity (Euchner 1993, 139–159; also see Chapter 8).

THE SAGA OF THE OAKLAND/LOS ANGELES/ OAKLAND RAIDERS

The city that first propelled the franchise-shift mania, Los Angeles, became a major player again in the 1980s. In 1978 the Los Angeles Memorial Coliseum Commission (LAMCC) began to seek a new tenant to replace the Rams, who were moving to Anaheim Stadium in Orange County, a much safer location for spectators than South Central Los Angeles. The 92,000-seat Coliseum was out of date, and half of its seats offered poor viewing for football. Sellouts were rare, making network blackouts possible, and there were no luxury suites. On the other hand, Anaheim promised Rosenbloom and the Rams that it would increase its stadium capacity from 43,250 to 70,000 seats, build new executive offices, give the Rams 100 luxury boxes, and allow Rosenbloom to share in developing a ninety-five-acre parcel adjacent to the field. The

LAMCC, comprised of representatives from the state, city, and county, was a very aggressive agency because it had no independent taxing powers and needed rent to cover expenses that could not be passed on to other government agencies. Discussions were initiated with other teams to replace the Rams, including the Vikings, which helped convince Minnesota legislators to build a new stadium. The LAMCC then turned to the Raiders, whose unfavorable lease at Oakland–Alameda County Coliseum was soon expiring (Euchner 1983, 82–85).

As of 1980 no NFL team had moved out of its metropolitan area since 1962. It had much more success preventing teams relocating than Major League Baseball, which was exempt from antitrust laws. The Raiders correctly anticipated that the league would not permit them to move from Oakland, and so in January the Raiders and the LAMCC sued the league for violating the antitrust laws. The plaintiffs won a huge settlement of $18 million in damages and $10 million for legal fees (Danielson 1997, 149). Oakland then initiated an eminent-domain suit to prevent the Raiders from leaving. The city claimed that it had built the Oakland Coliseum primarily for the Raiders in 1966, and that the presence of the team promoted economic and recreational activity, both important public uses (Euchner 1993, 94). Oakland city officials claimed the Raider migration cost the city $30 million in direct revenue and an additional $100 million in "indirect benefits" (Quirk and Fort 1992, 173). In June 1982, after preliminary rulings, the state Supreme Court ruled that the city had the authority to condemn private property, including the Raiders' franchise. However, the courts ruled on appeal that seizure of the team to preserve "the vague sense of community engendered by the team did not fit the usual understanding of eminent domain" (Euchner 1993, 93). The franchise was not important enough to the city to justify the novel application of the law. Euchner argues that the "fragmented nature of the California political system and culture channeled important issues to the courts in the first place. Once the cases were in the courts, the legal system's rules of admissibility of contestants, issues, and evidence narrowed the range of politics" (p. 80).

In 1982 Al Davis moved the Raiders from Oakland to Los Angeles. The Coliseum package, never more than vaguely outlined, included a $6.75-million loan to construct ninety-nine luxury suites (worth $20 million a year) and most of the revenue from tickets, concessions, and parking. The loan would be forgiven if the Raiders moved out. Davis did not begin construction on the suites until 1987, and then stopped, claiming other structural changes promised by the LAMCC had not been made. Davis claimed that he had the right to abrogate his contract and leave the Coliseum. Davis was then given $10 million by the village of Irwindale, population 1,000, in eastern Los Angeles County, to consider moving there. The wily Davis pocketed the money while he considered other proposals. In 1990 Davis chose to move back to Oakland, which had offered a $32-million franchise fee and renovations of its coliseum. The terms were so generous that they contributed to Mayor Lionel Wilson's defeat in 1991 (Euchner 1993, 87, 96–97, 100).

RECENT JUDGMENTS ON STADIUMS AND
ECONOMIC DEVELOPMENT

Recent scholarship on the impact of sports teams on economic development is consistent with earlier conclusions. Experts agree that teams are small to medium enterprises that "are not economic engines; they have too few employees and involve too few direct dollars to be a driving force in any city or county's economy" (Rosentraub 1997, 176) In no city do they provide as many as 1 percent of the private-sector jobs. In Cook County, for instance, sports accounted for merely 0.24 percent of personal income in 1982 (Baade and Dye 1988, 266).

Economist Robert Baade and virtually every other academic economist remain very critical of municipal subsidization of professional sport. They chastise cost–benefit analyses that have consistently understated direct costs (that usually end up in a net loss) and overemphasized indirect results, usually tied to multiplier benefits (consultants have used multipliers ranging from 1.2 in Pittsburgh to 3.2 in Chicago), not to mention exaggerating the unquantifiable benefits of image and civic pride. Baade and Dye (1988, 8–13) used regression analysis to examine the economic impact of professional sports on nine cities and found a negative impact. Jobs created were mainly low wage and part time. They also studied the image impact in eight cities and found that when corporations make business decisions, they do not give much attention to the presence of a big-league sports franchise. More recently, Baade (1995, 286–289) examined forty-eight cities in the period from 1959 to 1987, including all thirty-five cities that had a major league team in baseball, basketball, football, or hockey, as well as thirteen other large cities. He found that professional sports were statistically insignificant in determining real personal income per capita. In not a single case did having a stadium lead to a positive effect on real income. He further found that in 63 percent of the cases, the stadium had a negative impact, resulting in economic growth below national urban trends.

Baade does point out that there has been increased taxpayer resistance to subsidization. They have seen the high costs of stadium subsidization and resent the benefits going to rich, arrogant franchise owners, who are reaping huge profits and running roughshod over communities, frequently moving to a new field before the costs of the old building have been amortized. The result has been far more scrutiny on public capital budgeting decisions. Since the 1980s, public officials have been trying to get teams to pay a share of costs. Baade and Dye (1988, 267, 273) urge that stadiums be employed together with other potential economic anchors and that governments demand that teams use their own money to build stadiums because that makes them more committed to staying. They found that from 1970 to 1985 only two shifting franchises out of twenty-two were from privately built stadiums. They recommend that the structures be used more frequently and that greater attention be paid to safety by surrounding the stadiums with organic commercial corridors rather than concrete parking lots.

One city that seemed to be a model for sport supported economic development has been Indianapolis. Rosentraub has recently examined the impact of sports on Indianapolis where the city explicitly tried to use sport to promote itself. Downtown Indianapolis was dying in the 1970s like the CBD in other midwestern cities as the white middle-class and job opportunities fled to the suburbs, leaving behind a growing African-American underclass. The regime sought to establish a progressive national image with sports as the foundation "on which to build an amenity infrastructure" and thereby promote the quality of life. The outcome would be positive national attention, the promotion of investment, and the creation of new jobs" (Schimmel 1995, 114, 124).

In 1984 the 60,300-seat inflated-roof Hoosier Dome opened with the Colts as its main resident. The city paid for slightly more than half of the building's $78-million cost, with the rest from philanthropic sources. Indianapolis also established a tennis stadium (the Sports Center) and a velodrome, thereby attracting several national athletic organizations to the city. In the downtown area, $2.76 billion was invested in capital development, over half of which was from the private sector. The city itself only put up 15.8 percent, less than the expenditures of the state or of Indiana University. Rosentraub found that the city was very successful in leveraging funds for its sports strategy, which generated excitement and enhanced its image but had little direct role in economic development. The sports facilities created jobs, but they amount to a mere 0.29 percent of the city's workforce (Rosentraub 1997, 214–216, 218, 221, 236, 239; Schimmel 1995, 140).

CONCLUSION

Urban politicians and associated regimes have had a long relationship with professional sports that goes back well over 100 years to when franchise owners were professional politicians who utilized their clout to help support and protect their sporting investments. In the Golden Age of Sports in the 1920s, municipalities constructed large

outdoor arenas to encourage amateur sport and to boost the reputation of their cities, which they anticipated, would enhance the local
economy. Since the 1950s, cities, especially in the South and West, have
tried to attract professional sports franchises by building them stadiums and arenas, as have suburbs since the 1970s.

In both cases the goals were to demonstrate the improved status of
the community and to promote economic development. Older, established cities have been forced to respond in kind to keep their teams.
They have also justified their expenditures as measures to promote the
city and the surrounding neighborhoods. The subsidies of new ballparks
have not been good financial investments, although they may still be jus-
tifiable expenditures if the public understands and accepts the returns,
which are more psychic than financial. There is a big difference between municipal backing of art museums, zoos, and other nonprofit
urban cultural institutions and the subsidization of a private business
that generates few jobs or little long-term economic development.

REFERENCES

Agostini, Stephan J., John M. Quigley, and Eugene Smolensky. 1997. Stickball
    in San Francisco. In *Sports, Jobs, and Taxes: The Economic Impact of Sports
    Teams and Stadiums*, edited by Roger Noll and Andrew Zimbalist. Wash-
    ington, D.C.: The Brookings Institution, 385–426.

Andelman, Bob. 1993. *Stadium for Rent: Tampa Bay's Quest for Major League
    Baseball*. Jefferson, N.C.: McFarland.

Austrian, Ziona, and Mark S. Rosentraub. 1997. Cleveland's Gateway to the
    Future. In *Sports, Jobs, and Taxes: The Economic Impact of Sports Teams and
    Stadiums*, edited by Roger Noll and Andrew Zimbalist. Washington,
    D.C.: The Brookings Institution, 355–384.

Baade, Robert A. 1995. Stadiums, Professional Sports, and City Economies:
    An Analysis of the United State Experience. In *The Stadium and the City*,
    edited by John Bale and Olaf Moen. Keele, England: Keele University
    Press, 277–294.

Baade, Robert A., and Richard F. Dye. 1990. The Impact of Stadiums and Pro-
    fessional Spots on Metropolitan Area Development. *Growth and Change*
    21: 1–14.

Baade, Robert A., and Richard F. Dye. 1988. Sports Stadiums and Area Devel-
    opment: A Critical Review. *Economic Development Quarterly* 2: 265–275.

Baim, Dean V. 1994. *The Sports Stadium as a Municipal Investment*. Westport,
    Conn.: Greenwood Press.

Baim, Dean V. 1990. Sports Stadiums as Wise Investments: An Evaluation.
    Heartland Policy Study 32 (26 November): 1–20.

Bale, John, and Olaf Moen, eds. 1926. Stadiums. *Playground* (July): 198.

Chicago Tribune. 1995. 28 September.

Burck, Charles G. 1973. It's Promoters vs. Taxpayers in the Superstadium Game.
    Fortune 87: 105–106, 180–182.

Danielson, Michael N. 1997. *Home Team: Professional Sports and the American Metropolis*. Princeton: Princeton University Press.

Duis, Perry, and Glen Holt. 1978. The Classic Problem of Soldier Field. *Chicago Magazine* 27: 170–173.

Euchner, Charles C. 1993. *Playing the Field: Why Sports Teams Move and Cities Fight to Keep Them*. Baltimore: Johns Hopkins University Press.

Fort, Rodney. 1997. Direct Democracy and the Stadium Mess. In *Sports, Jobs, and Taxes: The Economic Impact of Sports Teams and Stadiums*, edited by Roger Noll and Andrew Zimbalist. Washington, D.C.: The Brookings Institution.

Gendzel, Glen. 1995. Competitive Boosterism: How Milwaukee Lost the Braves. *Business History Review* 69: 530–566.

Goldfield, David R. 1982. *Cotton Fields and Skyscrapers: Southern City and Region, 1607–1980*. Baton Rouge: Louisiana State University Press.

Hamilton, Bruce, and Peter Kahn. 1997. Baltimore's Camden Yards Ballpark. In *Sports, Jobs, and Taxes: The Economic Impact of Sports Teams and Stadiums*, edited by Roger Noll and Andrew Zimbalist. Washington, D.C.: The Brookings Institution.

Henderson, Cary. 1980. Los Angeles and the Dodger War, 1957–1962. *Southern California Quarterly* 62 (Fall): 261–289.

Hines, Thomas. 1982. Housing, Baseball and Creeping Socialism: The Battle of Chavez Ravine, Los Angeles, 1949–1959. *Journal of Urban History* 8: 123–143.

Kennedy, Ray, and Nancy Williamson. 1978. Money in Sports, Part I. *Sports Illustrated* 49: 28–36, 71–72.

Kuklick, Bruce. 1991. *To Every Thing a Season: Shibe Park and Urban Philadelphia 1909–1976*. Princeton: Princeton University Press.

Lipsitz, George. 1984. Sports Stadia and Urban Development: A Tale of Three Cities. *Journal of Sport and Social Issues* 8: 1–18.

Lipsyte, Robert. 1976. A Diamond in the Ashes. *Sports Illustrated* 44: 38–43.

Lowenfish, Lee E. 1978. A Tale of Many Cities. *Journal of the West* 17: 71–82.

Lucas, John A. 1971. The Unholy Experiment—Professional Baseball's Struggles Against Pennsylvania Sunday Blue Laws, 1926–1934. *Pennsylvania History* 38: 163–175.

Miller, James Edward. 1992. The Dowager of Thirty-Third Street: Memorial Stadium and the Politics of Big-Time Sports in Maryland, 1954–1991. *Maryland Historian* 87: 187–200.

Miller, James Edward. 1990. *The Baseball Business: Pursuing Pennants and Profits in Baltimore*. Baltimore: Johns Hopkins University Press.

Noll, Roger G. 1974. The U.S. Team Sports Industry: An Introduction. In *Government and the Sports Business*, edited by Roger G. Noll. Washington, D.C.: The Brookings Institution, 3–32.

Noll, Roger, and Andrew Zimbalist, eds. 1997. *Sports, Jobs, and Taxes: The Economic Impact of Sports Teams and Stadiums*. Washington, D.C.: The Brookings Institution.

Okner, Benjamin A. 1974. Subsidies of Stadiums and Arenas. In *Government and the Sports Business*, edited by Roger G. Noll. Washington, D.C.: The Brookings Institution, 325–348.

Pelissero, John P., Beth M. Henschen, and Edward I. Sidlow. 1991. Urban Regimes, Sports Stadiums, and the Politics of Economic Development Agendas in Chicago. *Policy Studies Review* 10: 117–129.

Poulson, Norris. 1966. *Memoirs*. Los Angeles: Department of Oral History, University of California Los Angeles.

Quirk, James, and Rodney D. Fort. 1992. *Pay Dirt: The Business of Professional Team Sports*. Princeton: Princeton University Press.

Rader, Benjamin G. 1983. *American Sports: From the Age of Folk Games to the Age of Spectators*. Englewood Cliffs, N.J.: Prentice Hall.

Richmond, Peter. 1993. *Ballpark: Camden Yards and the Building of an American Dream*. New York: Simon and Schuster.

Riess, Steven A. 1989. *City Games: The Evolution of American Urban Society and the Rise of Sports*. Urbana: University of Illinois Press.

Riess, Steven A. 1988. Sports and Machine Politics in New York City, 1890–1920. In *The Making of Urban America*, edited by Raymond A. Mohl. Wilmington, Del.: Scholarly Resources, 99–121.

Riess, Steven A. 1981. Power without Authority: Los Angeles' Elites and the Construction of the Coliseum. *Journal of Sport History* 8: 50–65.

Riess, Steven A. 1980. *Touching Base: Professional Baseball and American Culture in the Progressive Era*. Westport, Conn.: Greenwood Press.

Rooney, John F. 1975. Sports from a Geographica Perspective. In *Sport and Social Order: Contributions to the Sociology of Sport*, edited by Donald W. Ball and John W. Loy. Reading, Mass.: Addison-Wesley.

Rosentraub, Mark S. 1997. *Major League Losers: The Real Cost of Sports and Who's Paying for It*. New York: Basic Books.

Rosentraub, Mark S., David Swindell, Michael Przybylski, and Daniel R. Mulling. 1994. Sport and Downtown Development Strategy: If You Build It, Will Jobs Come? *Journal of Urban Affairs* 16: 221–239.

Rosentraub, Mark S., and Samuel R. Nunn. 1978. Suburban City Investment in Professional Sports: Estimating the Fiscal Returns of the Dallas Cowboys and Texas Rangers to Investor Communities. *American Behavioral Scientist* 21: 393–414.

Schimmel, Kimberley S. 1995. Growth Politics, Urban Development and Sports Stadium Construction in the United States: A Case Study. In *The Stadium and the City*, edited by John Bales. Keele, England: Keele University Press, 111–155.

Struna, Nancy. 1979. The Cultural Significance of Sport in the Colonial Chesapeake and Massachusetts. Ph.D. diss., University of Massachusetts.

Sullivan, Neil J. 1987. *The Dodgers Move West*. New York: Oxford University Press.

Torry, Jack. 1995. *Endless Summers: The Fall and Rise of the Cleveland Indians*. South Bend, Ind.: Diamond Communications.

Vincent, Ted. 1981. *Mudville's Revenge: The Rise and Fall of American Sport*. New York: Seaview.

Whitford, David. 1993. *Playing Hardball: The High-Stakes Battle for Baseball's New Franchises*. New York: Doubleday.

Zimbalist, Andrew. 1992. *Baseball and Billions: A Probing Look Inside the Big Business of Our National Pastime*. New York: Basic Books.

II ━━━━━━━━━━━━━━━━

SPORTS AND ECONOMICS

As the professional sports business becomes a multi-billion-dollar enterprise, more and more demands are placed on public resources. Proponents of new sports stadiums always pitch them as the great economic multiplier or job facilitator. In fact, exaggerated claims have become the norm in the economics of stadium building. In order to understand the real economics of stadiums, we must separate the "hype" from the reality and the espoused from the actual benefits. The owners' demands for modern facilities has led to excessive demands for tax breaks, loan guarantees, and other financial concessions. City leaders believe that they have no choice but to invest millions of dollars in stadiums. This is done to enhance the city's reputation as a major league city, an image supposedly important for attracting new businesses and investments. Sports scholars and journalists have tried to warn cities that such investments are risky. Yet, some cities seem addicted to what Joel Brinkerhoff (1997) calls "municipal cocaine." In an article in Reader's Digest, Tim Keown (1997) quotes Mark Rosentraub, a leading sports authority, as calling funding for stadiums "a perverse form of welfare." Keown himself calls it a "shell game."

If stadiums and sports franchises are so costly and wrongheaded for cities, why do cities make so many concessions to owners? Why do they fight so hard to keep the home team from relocating? These extremely complicated questions are trying to answer because they raise even more enigmatic public-policy issues that surround sports: Are taxpayers' interests being served in the symbiotic relationship between professional franchise owners and city leaders? Do cities need these amenities to attract residents, businesses, and jobs? Are these franchises reliable vehicles for economic development? What types of jobs do sports franchises provide? What role does politics play in nurturing the sports-industry complex? Who are the major players in sports politics? What is the role of the media? Finally, what does the record show about the impact *of sports franchises on cities? Mark Rosentraub (1997) has called it a myth that sports franchises stimulate economic development. Many economists have also documented the fallacy of sports teams as economic-development tools (Noll and Zimbalist 1997). Yet the chase continues, and the leagues remain ready to add new teams when the money and facilities are right.*

Some cities even build stadiums before they have a team. In St. Louis, politicians convinced the taxpayers that the Trans-World Dome would attract an NFL franchise. The state was willing to service 50 percent of the debt, the city and the county 25 percent each. Adam Safir (1997) reviewed this case, along with the funding in Baltimore, Phoenix, and Seattle, and called for a law to protect cities from this type of debt. Currently, no law mandates that sports-franchise owners must be accountable to the communities in which they are located. When a franchise decides to relocate, there is little a city can do to stop it. Thus, city leaders strive to make their city a deserving location. Accordingly, keeping a franchise has emerged as one of the priorities for elected officials. Is this a good policy for economically struggling cities? If one examines the financing of some of the stadiums, it is not clear that this is the case.

What about the changing economics of sports ownership? As athletes demand higher and higher salaries, professional teams raise ticket prices and demand more luxury boxes in stadiums. Fans continue to complain about ticket prices and the cost of food at concession stands. Despite salary caps and labor agreements, the cost of owning a professional team continues to rise. Are there discernible limits to the cost of professional sports? Can expansion and season extensions solve all the economic problems of professional sports? Besides the fact that millions of dollars of public money are spent on these facilities, the mobilization necessary to attract and retain a professional team represents an important case study of how the economic and political elite work together. Whereas members of the economic elite will compete to secure a sporting franchise, they often exhibit less enthusiasm about solving the other needs of a city. Nevertheless, sports stadiums and successful professional teams are not what investors would call "a sure thing." This part will explore some of the politics and risks associated with professional teams and sports facilities.

Does the financing of sports stadiums and arenas conform to any standards for economic investment? Is state financing of stadiums a form of voodoo economics? Should Congress protect state and local officials from competing against themselves? Why are the taxpayers so willing to be taken for a ride? Could a stadium have negative consequences for local retailers? What type of jobs are being created by a new stadium? Who will get those jobs? Are concessions vendors, security guards, and parking attendants career opportunities? What about the multiplier effect? Andrew Zimbalist and Robert A. Baade, two leading sports economists, look at these questions in the following two chapters.

REFERENCES

Brinkeroff, Joel. 1997. Stadium Politics. *California Journal* 28, no. 1: 40–44.

Keown, Tim. 1997. The Stadium Shell Game. *The Reader's Digest*, November, 153.

Noll, Roger, and Andrew Zimbalist. 1997. *Sports, Jobs, and Taxes: The Economic Impact of Sports Teams and Stadiums*. Washington D.C.: The Brookings Institution.

Rosentraub, Mark S. 1997. The Myth and Reality of the Economic Development from Sports. *Real Estate Issues* 22: 24–29.

Safir, Adam. 1997. If You Build It, They Will Come: The Politics of Financing Sports Stadium Construction. *Journal of Law and Politics* 13: 937–963.

2

The Economics of Stadiums, Teams, and Cities

Andrew Zimbalist

> I am not about to rape the City as others in my league and others
> have done. You will never hear me say, "If I don't get this I'm
> moving." You can go to the press on that one. I couldn't live with
> myself if I did that.
>
> Art Modell, owner of the Baltimore Ravens,
formerly the Cleveland Browns, 1994[1]

U.S. team-sports leagues are monopolies. As such, they maximize their
profits by reducing the supply of franchises below the demand for
franchises from economically viable cities. The result is that cities are
thrust into competition with each other to procure or retain teams.

The tendency of sports teams to seek more hospitable venues has
been exaggerated in recent years by the advent of new stadium technology. This technology replaces the cookie-cutter stadiums of the 1960s
and 1970s with single-sport constructions that maximize opportunities for revenue generation from luxury suites, club boxes, concessions,
catering, signage, parking, advertising, and theme activities. Depending on the sport and the circumstance, a new stadium or arena can
add anywhere from $10 to $40 million in revenues to a team's coffers.
In fact, the economics of new stadiums can be so alluring that demo-
graphically lesser cities (e.g., Memphis, Charlotte, Jacksonville, Nashville) with new stadiums can begin to compete with larger cities with
older stadiums. Thus, the new stadium technology creates new eco-

nomically viable cities, and thereby exacerbates the imbalance between supply of and demand for sports franchises.

This imbalance, in turn, leads cities to imprudently offer the kitchen sink in their efforts to retain existing teams or attract new ones. The cities build new stadiums costing in excess of $200 million, plus infrastructural expenditures and debt-service obligations that often double the cost of the project.[2] Furthermore, when the state government is involved in financially supporting the effort, it generally requires the approval of parallel pork projects elsewhere in the state to secure the necessary votes in the legislature. Frequently, the stadium lease is on such concessionary terms that the city cannot even cover its incremental debt service with rent and other stadium revenues. The public ends up paying for the stadium, only to generate millions of dollars of extra revenue that inevitably is divided between higher player salaries and ownership profits.

While this line of reasoning applies to all the professional team-sports leagues, it applies most forcefully today to the NFL, for two reasons. First, the NFL relies less on regular ticket sales for revenue than the other sports because each team only plays between eight and ten home games each year. Smaller cities can fill a stadium of 60,000 eight times a year with relative ease. Further, in contrast to basketball, baseball, and hockey, where less than 25 percent of total revenues are shared among the teams, in football this proportion rises above 75 percent. Thus, there are more potentially viable cities in professional football. Second, because NFL teams must share 100 percent of their television, licensing, and marketing revenues as well as 40 percent of their gate, NFL teams have a powerful incentive to maximize stadium revenues, which are not shared at all. Although it might trouble Jerry Jones and some other owners, the NFL would be well served by sharing 40 percent of all stadium revenues.

DIMINUTIVE IMPACT

It is a common perception that sports teams have an economic impact on a city that is tantamount to their cultural impact. This is wrong. In most circumstances, sports teams have a small positive economic effect, similar perhaps to the influence of a new department store. First, individual sports teams are not big business. The average NFL team in 1994 grossed $65 million. Compare that to the 1993 Effective Buying Income (EBI) for the metropolitan limits of St. Louis of $21.1 billion. The gross of an average NFL team, then, would account for 0.3 percent of St. Louis's EBI, 0.6 percent of Jacksonville, Florida's EBI, and just 0.05 percent of the EBI of the metropolitan limits of New York City. Before the 1994–1995 work stoppage, the average Major League

Baseball franchise also had gross revenues of around $65 million, while the average revenues in the NBA were approximately $50 million and those in the NHL were closer to $35 million. In terms of permanent local employees, sports teams employ between 50 and 120 full-time workers, along with several hundred low-skill and low-wage, part-time and temporary stadium or arena personnel.[3]

Second, economic studies have shown that most public stadiums and arenas do not cover their own fixed and operating costs. Indeed, using available data for twenty-five publicly owned stadiums and arenas for 1989, Quirk and Fort (1992, 170–171) estimated an average public stadium subsidy (net fiscal cost) of $6.8 million and conservatively projected in excess of $500 million in government subsidies to all professional sports teams in the same year. Operating and debt-service deficits mean that city or state governments have to levy additional taxes. Higher taxes, in turn, discourage business in the area and reduce consumer expenditures, setting off a negative multiplier effect.

Third, virtually all independent economic research has confirmed a diminutive or negligible economic effect from the relocation of a sports team in a city. For instance, Baade and Dye (1990) looked at nine cities over the period from 1965 to 1983 and found no significant relationship between adding a sports team or a new stadium and the city's economic growth. In fact, they found that in seven of the nine cities the city's share of regional income declined after the addition of a sports team or the construction of a new stadium.

Baade (1994) recently updated and expanded this study to include thirty-six metropolitan areas over a thirty-year period (1958–1987) and found that in no case did a new stadium have a statistically significant, positive economic impact on the city's growth, and in three cases it had a negative impact. In one case the presence of a new team had a statistically significant impact on the city's real per-capita growth (Indianapolis). Mark Rosentraub (1997) studied Indianapolis, which put forth an integrated sports-development strategy in conjunction with a downtown redevelopment initiative. The city was fortunate to be able to leverage only $436.1 million of its own funds to attract a total of $2.8 billion in private and public monies. That is, the city paid less than one-sixth of the total bill. Rosentraub's study found that while the number of sports-related jobs increased, sports was too small a component of the local economy to have an appreciable impact. Indeed, most of the employment growth was in low-wage services, and Indianapolis's share in the total county payroll actually declined from 1977 to 1989. Arthur Johnson (1993) studied fifteen cities that host minor league baseball teams and concluded, "The economic impact of a minor league team is not sufficient to justify the relatively large public expenditure necessary for a minor league team" (p. 245; see also Crompton 1995).

PROMOTIONAL STUDIES

Dozens of studies have been performed by consulting firms under contract with affected cities or teams. Predictably, most of these studies have concluded that there would be a substantial, positive impact from adding a sports team. There are several methodological difficulties with these studies.

First, they do not sufficiently account for the difference between new and diverted (or gross and net) spending. People have only so much income that they will spend on leisure and entertainment activities. If they go to a ball game, it generally means that they are not spending the same dollars locally to go to the theater, to movies, to a concert, to dinner, to rent a video, and so on. That is, the dollar spent at a sports event usually replaces the dollar spent elsewhere in the local economy. The spending impact is therefore practically nil.[4]

The main source of net spending is out-of-town visitors to a ball game. With exceptions, such as Baltimore or Denver, this number is usually small for professional sports teams.[5] It consists primarily of the visiting teams and out-of-town media, and most of this will be offset by road trips by the local team and media.[6] Some promotional studies have surveyed fans at a stadium to ascertain whether they are from out of town, and then assumed that the entire estimated expenditures by these visitors during their stay is attributable to the sports team. Yet the presence of out-of-town visitors may be attributable to something other than the ball game (e.g., business, cultural activities, relatives, etc.). In this case only their spending at the ballpark should be counted in the team's economic impact. Indeed, in many cases the ballpark spending should excluded, because these visitors would have spent their money at other venues within the city if no sports team existed. Crompton (1995, 27–29) reviews several cases where visitors attending local sporting event were surveyed and reports that half or more of the visitors were in the city for another reason.

Second, the promotional studies tend to make favorable assumptions about the size of the area being impacted. The smaller the circle around the stadium that is chosen as the impacted area, the greater percentage of attendees at the sports event that will be classified as from out of town and, hence, by assumption the greater will be the net spending.[7] There is, however, little reason for public-policy makers to endorse such a parochial view of economic impact, unless there is a clear intention to benefit one area at the expense of another.

Third, the economic impact is often exaggerated by assuming that an unrealistically large share of executive and player salaries remains in the local economy. The more a team's owner and players (i.e., those with very high incomes) live in and spend their income in the host city, the larger will be the economic impact. The extent to which players and their families reside in a team's host city year-round will vary significantly across cities. What will be true for most professional athletes, however, is that their high incomes will be conducive to very high savings rates. These savings are likely to go to national banks, money market funds at brokerage firms, pension accounts, stocks, and bonds, and therefore have little if any impact on the local economy.

Fourth, the promotional studies overstate the interconnections between the sports team and the rest of the city's economy. The greater these interconnections are, the larger will be the multiplier effect. Generally, these studies use a local area multiplier for sports spending of between 1.5 and 2, though some go considerably higher. These multipliers are based on local sales, not on local income generation. The problem with a local sales multiplier is that a sizable portion of the value of a sale is dependent on inputs imported into the area. The local income generation will reflect that portion of the sales that remains in the area; that is, the sales multiplier is based on gross value while the income multiplier is based on local value added. For example, suppose one buys a Samuel Adams beer at Yankee Stadium for $4.50. Of this, sizable shares go to the manufacturer in Boston, to the concessionaire, Volume Services Inc. (which is based in Spartanburg, South Carolina), and to George Steinbrenner and the other Yankees owners. A much smaller portion goes to pay the labor cost of the concessions worker and electricity usage at Yankee Stadium. Since Steinbrenner maintains his primary residence outside of New York City, travels widely, and saves a good portion of his income, and since the concessionaire probably remits most of its net sales to the home office (after paying the local personnel and other expenses), the local value added from this sale of beer is probably well below half of its $4.50 gross value.

Further suppose that on a typical day 10 percent of the crowd at Yankee Stadium comes from outside the greater New York metropolitan area and that half of this group came to New York principally to see the Yankees. Assuming an average attendance of 30,000, this means that 1,500 fans were spending new money in New York. If each of these fans spent an average of $10 on food at the game and 40 percent of this was local value added, then the direct (first-round) new money created per fan would be $4, and among the 1,500 fans the total new money would be $6,000. This is in contrast to taking $10 per fan for all 30,000 in attendance and using a sales approach (considering 100 percent of spending to impact on the local economy) which would generate first-round new money of $300,000, a fiftyfold difference. Now, using the $6,000 figure for new first-round income generated, the earners of this additional income will save some and spend the rest. If we continue to assume that 40 percent of spending results in local value added and the savings rate is 10 percent, then the round-two increase in local income resulting from food expenditures at the Yankee game will be $2,160, the round-three income increase will be $777.60, and so on. The total impact, after all successive rounds of spending, will be $9,375; this is 1.56 times greater than the first-round value added or 0.625 times the gross value of first-round spending by the out-of-town fans who came for the game ($15,000).[8] The extreme methodology used in some promotional studies would take the total first-round spending of $300,000, apply the 1.56 multiplier, and conclude that there was a $468,000 impact on the local economy from one day of food sales at the ballpark. We are suggesting that the correct methodology would find an impact of $9,375, a fiftyfold difference.

Finally, the local-area economic impact is also dependent on the fiscal impact of building or refurbishing a stadium or arena. Promotional studies, by making favorable assumptions regarding the terms of stadium financing and the conditions of its lease, usually conclude that there will be a salutary financial impact on local government budgets—an outcome which rarely obtains in practice (Zimmerman 1991). Indeed, since the new treatment of tax exemption for municipal bonds in the 1986 Tax Reform Act, it generally has become more difficult for stadium operations to yield a positive cash flow for the city treasury. In an apparent attempt to reduce the public subsidy to privately owned sports teams, this 1986 reform stipulated that beginning in 1990 stadiums whose debt service costs were more than 10 percent covered by private stadium revenues (e.g., rent, share of concessions or parking revenues, share of luxury-box income) would not qualify for tax-exempt bond issuance. In order to meet this requirement, the pattern of stadium finance has shifted. On the one hand, private money is raised up front from the long-term rather than annual sale of naming, concession, and pouring rights, as well as from the sale of permanent seat licenses and long-term luxury- and club-box leases. On the other hand, teams increasingly are gifted sweetheart leases with negligible or zero rent and little sharing from stadium revenues. The 1986 reform, then, rather than shifting some of the cost onto the stadium's economic beneficiary (the team owner), has perversely done the reverse.

Depending on the assumptions made and the methodology employed, then, one can get wildly different estimates of economic impact. For instance, two studies were made about the impact of the Colts on the Baltimore economy in 1984. One study found an impact of $30 million and the other an impact of $200,000. The former estimate is wildly unrealistic, but even at such a level the benefits would have to be weighed against the costs of constructing, financing, and possibly maintaining a new stadium.

There have been at least two promotional studies on the economic impact of Camden Yards, one by the state Department of Business and Economic Development and the other by the Department of Fiscal Services. The former estimated benefits at $110.6 million, with 1,394 jobs created, and the latter at $33 million, with 534 jobs created. Using a modest project cost estimate of $177 million, the cost per job created is $127,000 in the first study and $331,000 in the second. These estimates, though based on excessively optimistic assumptions, should be contrasted with the cost per job created of the state economic development program of $6,250 per job, a typical spending–job ratio for urban development expenditures (Zimmerman 1996).[9] Further, Camden Yards benefited from being part of the harbor redevelopment, from absorbing Washington, D.C. (the seventh-largest media market in the United States) by its location off the interstate in south Baltimore, from being the first example of its architectural genre, from the novelty effect of the park itself, and from housing a successful ball club.

It would be prudent both for teams and cities to anticipate that for aesthetic and economic reasons the Camden Yards/HOK design may begin to wear thin. The cookie-cutter stadiums of the 1960s and 1970s received enthusiastic reviews when they were built. Today they are scorned. The same fate awaits the old-fashioned ballpark design of the 1990s.

Mayors, under pressure not to lose a city's historic franchise and cajoled by local contractors, unions, lawyers, hotels, restaurants, and real estate interests, among other political powers, tend to look favorably upon new stadium construction.[10] They invoke images of city grandeur and new corporate headquarters moving to town. While it is conceivable that some cities are on the threshold of recognition and a sports team could lift them over the hump, such an effect is highly speculative and there is no case where it has actually taken hold in a significant way. Moreover, corporate relocations rarely occur to cities where the fiscal situation is deteriorating.

To the extent that a new stadium (1) is a central element of an urban-redevelopment plan and its location and attributes are carefully set out to maximize synergies with local business and (2) the terms of its lease are not negotiated under duress and are fair to the city, then the city may derive some modest economic benefit from a sports team. The problem, however, is that these two conditions rarely apply when dealing with monopoly sports leagues. Cities are forced to act hastily under pressure and to bargain without any leverage. Properly reckoned, the value of a sports team to a city should not be measured in dollars, but appreciated as a potential source of entertainment and civic pride.

TEAM RELOCATIONS AND PUBLIC POLICY

Are sports franchises, such as the Browns, Rams, or Oilers, so economically troubled that they need new stadiums for their survival? Definitively not.[11] Excluding the last two aberrant years in MLB, sports teams with very few exceptions are profitable or potentially profitable; indeed, well-managed franchises generally yield handsome returns to their owners.

On January 23, 1996, before the Senate Judiciary Committee, NFL Commissioner Paul Tagliabue was asked by Senator Arlen Specter why teams in the NFL required multi-million-dollar subsidies annually from their host cities. The commissioner responded that the short answer was rising player salaries. Senator Specter inquired what the long answer was because, he said, he didn't like the short answer. To be sure, municipal subsidies to NFL teams comfortably predate the emergence of modified free agency with salary cap in 1993. Football salaries have been in a catch-up mode over the last several years, making up for lost ground during the decades when no real free agency existed. Under the cap system, salaries will rise more slowly than revenues because stadium revenues, one of the most rapidly growing revenue sources in the NFL, are excluded from the 62-percent cap calculation.[12]

Generally, rising player salaries follow rising revenues and are a sign of economic success, not a cause of economic decline. Nevertheless, sports leagues have different economic characteristics than other businesses. Teams in a league compete on the playing field, but they must cooperate as business entities. Audiovox might want Motorola to go bankrupt, but the Cowboys do not desire the same fate for the 49ers. When leagues have insufficient revenue sharing among the teams or define revenue sharing too narrowly, then the drive of individual teams to maximize profits can begin to have deleterious effects on the cohesion and stability of the league.

What can public policy do about footloose franchises jilting their fans and blackmailing our cities? Some in Congress have suggested extending antitrust immunity as it pertains to franchise movements to the NFL, the NBA, and the NHL. On January 23, 1996, before the Senate Judiciary Committee, Commissioner Tagliabue asserted the primacy of cooperation among teams in a sports leagues and argued that a sports league is really a single economic entity. If the NFL is a single entity, the reasoning goes, then its teams are like branches in the same company and there can be no conspiracy among them to restrain trade.

Thus, Tagliabue believes that the proper judicial context for the NFL is to have an antitrust exemption, just like MLB. In the absence of a blanket exemption, he would settle happily for an exemption pertaining to franchise relocations. He believes that the tendency for clubs and cities to litigate would be diminished if this partial antitrust immunity were extended to the league. While he is probably correct that there would be less litigation, MLB's experience suggests that litigation would not disappear. There is, however, a striking irony in the fact that Mr. Tagliabue is now threatening to sue Mayor Lanier of Houston for supporting the Hoke bill, claiming it to be an act of interference in the planned move of the Oilers to Nashville. The NFL and Mayor Lanier had agreed to discuss a future NFL team for Houston on the condition that the mayor not interfere with the Oilers move. The only reason why the mayor's exercise of free speech is construed as interference is that the NFL has stipulated that its approval of the Oilers prospective move is contingent on the defeat of the Hoke bill. The representatives from Tennessee are being blackmailed by the NFL.

MLB's experience also suggests that there is another problem besides litigation, and that is the financial exploitation of cities. MLB has managed over the past twenty-three years to maintain franchise geographic stability, but it has also managed to play the stadium extortion game most effectively. Over the past two-plus decades MLB teams have not moved, but they have used threats to move, often supported by statements from the commissioner, in order to extract extremely lucrative stadium deals. If Congress extends partial antitrust immunity to the other team-sports leagues and does nothing else, it will make an already uneven playing field more imbalanced.

It is important to clarify that the 1984 decision of the Ninth Circuit Court of Appeals in the Raiders' I case did not state that sports leagues do not have a legitimate function in regulating franchise movements to promote league stability. It simply stated that the NFL's Rule 4.3 was too restrictive and it expressed concern that the league was trying to protect the Rams' monopoly in the Los Angeles market. The right of sports leagues to control franchise relocation was reaffirmed in the Ninth Circuit's 1986 decision in the Raiders' II case and the subsequent settlement between the NBA and the L.A. Clippers. To be sure, it was probably clear awareness of this judicial opinion that in 1995 led the NFL owners initially to deny the Rams' petition to move to St. Louis. It was not until a reported $46 million was preferred to the other owners (up from the earlier spurned $25 million) that the NFL permitted the move.[13] If the NFL had immunity in this case, the Rams probably would have moved anyway, but the extortion fee may have been even greater.

The root of the problem lies in the leagues' monopoly status, and the solution must attack the root. This can be done either by engendering competition or by regulating the abuse. Competition could be created by breaking up each of the leagues into two or more business entities. The leagues would be permitted to cooperate in setting playing rules and schedules, but not in setting their business practices. In competition, each league would attempt to occupy all the viable cities available before their rival, and the supply-and-demand situation would balance out.

Regulating the abuse could take several forms. There are two bills before committees in the House of Representatives (H.R. 2699, hereafter the Stokes bill, and H.R. 2740, hereafter the Hoke bill) that attempt to deal with the franchise-relocation issue.[14] Each bill extends partial antitrust immunity to the leagues relating to franchise relocation, but each bill also recognizes the need to circumscribe the discretionary power of the leagues in these matters.[15] In addition to establishing criteria which would govern a team's ability to move, the Stokes bill offers a right of first refusal to the host city or a local investor to buy the team. The bill stipulates that local governments would have the right to own a major league team, an opportunity that has always been denied by the sports leagues. The first-refusal provision in Stokes, however, carries little enforcement power. This is because the bill leaves the franchise price open to negotiation between the existing and prospective owners. Under these circumstances, the existing owner will want a price for the team commensurate with its value in the new city. Since the owner wants to move, the new city is by definition more attractive, either by virtue of its demographic characteristics or a new stadium with a favorable lease. Usually these factors can increase the value of a sports team by tens of millions of dollars. Thus, the Stokes bill does little more than give the right to a prospective local owner to buy an asset for substantially above its value in the local market. It will offer little protection to the existing host city.

The Hoke bill devises another mechanism for protecting host cities. It allows owners to preserve their "property right" to move their asset where they desire, but it allows for a vacated city to retain its team's name and obtain an expansion team within a three-year period. The Hoke bill also grants the sports leagues limited antitrust immunity for franchise relocations, but it circumscribes this power by requiring the leagues to provide expansion teams to the bereft cities. The leagues, thereby, will have a strong incentive and the muscle to limit team movements. The incentive comes from the fact that the league is allowing an individual owner to appropriate the extra value of a new city and stadium, while the league is left with a required expansion to a less-desirable city (the previous host city presumably has less market value since the owner wanted to move the team).

If passed, the Hoke bill would be the first legislative act to regulate the monopoly privilege and abuse of fans and taxpayers by professional sports leagues. I urge legislators to support it. There are, however, three areas where I believe that bill could be strengthened. First, there is absolutely no justification for excluding Major League Baseball from the protection provision in this bill. If Congress interprets present case law to mean that there is a blanket exemption for MLB, then excluding baseball from the provisions of this bill constitutes a legislative endorsement of this anomalous exemption. Legislators might want to review the August 1993 opinion of district court Judge Padova in *Piazza et al. v. Major League Baseball*, wherein Padova interprets the 1972 Supreme Court in *Flood* to limit baseball's exemption to the reserve clause. Moreover, several host cities in baseball are currently being threatened with the exodus of their team and, in the case of New York, there is discussion about investing $1 billion for a new stadium for the Yankees at the West Side Rail Yard in Manhattan. Host cities in baseball need the protection of the Hoke bill as much as those in other sports.[16]

Second, Section 4a of H.R. 2740 sets a price for a city's franchise recovery to be equal to the price of the last league expansion team. The difficulty here is that virtually all expansion sites have new facilities with high revenue-generation potential. A new facility make it possible for the owner to meet the league's exacting expansion-franchise fee. A team in an existing city will not generally be worth nearly as much as the expansion team, because the existing host city will not have a new facility. This will be true almost by definition, since it is almost certainly the reason why the owner wanted to move the ball club in the first place. Thus, for the bereaved host city to find an investor willing to pay an expansion fee price, the city will have to provide a new facility. A superior protective mechanism would provide for the recovery price to be set by an arbitration procedure which determined the value of a franchise in that city under existing conditions.

Third, since the bill provides for the possibility of city, county, or state ownership of sports teams, Section 8 should be modified to allow for the amendment of the National Labor Relations Act (NLRA) to cover collective bargaining for employees of public employers in sports leagues.

NOTES

1. Quoted in First Amended complaint, *City of Cleveland v. Cleveland Browns et al.*, Court of Common Pleas, Cuyahoga County, Ohio, p. 2.

2. The $200-million figure may quickly become obsolete. New York City Mayor Giuliani is supporting a proposal to build a new stadium for the Yankees in midtown on the West Side for an estimated $1.06 billion. This modest sum does not include the cost of land acquisition.

3. For instance, according to the *Wall Street Journal* (9 March 1995), "The 400 ushers and ticket-takers employed by the [Milwaukee] Brewers collectively earn about $300,000—one-quarter of the average $1.2 million salary for one ballplayer in 1994." See Robert L. Rose, "Stadium Workers Say Union Solidarity Doesn't Extend to Millionaire Players," *Wall Street Journal*, 9 March 1995, B1–2.

4. Some have pointed out that the presence of a major league sports team may induce certain local resident to travel less, and thereby spend more of their income locally. While it would be folly to deny that some may behave in this way, it is hard to believe (and to our knowledge no one has demonstrated) that the empirical effect here would be significant.

5. For instance, a study performed by the Cleveland Growth Association on the economic impact of the Cleveland Browns in 1995 found that out of an average game attendance of 70,160, only 4,780 or 6.8 percent were "nonlocal."

6. Hosting an All Star Game in baseball or the Super Bowl in football provide an additional financial fillip to the fortunate city.

7. The March 1996 Peat Marwick "Yankee Stadium Alternative Site Study" adopts an unusual bias in considering New York City as the local area for purposes of out-of-town expenditures but New York state as the relevant area for considering multiplier linkages. Similar to other promotional studies of its genre the Peat Marwick study obscures fundamental questions of methodology and substitutes endless numbers of computer-generated tables, intended, one supposes, to lend a scientific air to the report. The report *inter alia* leaves out the negative multiplier effects of higher taxes for financing construction and/or operating deficits; assumes unrealistically high prices for Permanent Seat Licenses (PSLs), club seats, and suites; assumes a 50-percent increase in attendance at Yankee games to persist indefinitely; and misapprehends the basic distinction between current and constant prices, along with a host of additional difficulties.

8. This is consistent with estimates cited by Crompton (1995, 29–30) of between 0.4 and 0.8 for the local multiplier (based on first-round gross spending) of vistor spending in U.S. counties.

9. A study by Deloite and Touche (Arizona Office of Sports Development 1993) of the new stadium being built for the Arizona Diamondbacks in Maricopa County for a projected $280 million (not including infrastructural costs associated with parking and land acquisition) estimates that the team and stadium will generate the equivalent of 400 full-time jobs. This comes to $700,000 per job.

10. For an interesting discussion of how new construction projects are viewed by different spheres of municipal employees, see Boardman, Vinig, and Waters (1993).

11. Each year, *Financial World* magazine puts out estimates of operating income for all the franchises in the NBL, NFL, NBA, and MLB based on figures and partial information provided by ownership. Their estimates tend to be conservative. For the 1994 season, *Financial World* estimated that the Browns had an operating income of $6 million, the Oilers had $2.8 million, and the Rams had an operating loss of $1.8 million. However, *Financial World* estimated that the Rams had an operating income of $5.5 million in 1993.

12. While it is true that individual teams can exceed the cap in some years by manipulating the timing of salary payments, eventually the same teams will be constrained to a tighter cap as the payments schemes catch up with them. The remaining NFL cap loophole (that it is not in effect for 1999) is expected to be closed when the current negotiations for a new collective bargaining agreement are concluded.

13. On January 23, 1996, before the Senate Judiciary Committee, Commissioner Tagliabue stated that the reason the Rams were allowed to leave Los

Angeles was because they filed a triple-damage antitrust suit. It is hard to believe that the NFL owners did not anticipate such a suit before their initial decision. Further, if the antitrust suit was the sole motivation for permitting the move, why did the relocation fee jump by over $20 million? Tagliabue also indicated that a disproportionate share of this relocation booty was given to the NFL's low-revenue teams. While this is a laudable use of the funds, it is still a payment to the NFL owners. Presumably, the greater use of relocation fees to aid low-revenue teams obviates the use of other league revenues for this purpose. In any event, it would make sense for the Congress to request details on the distribution of relocation fees and new revenue-sharing initiatives in the NFL.

14. Senator John Glenn has introduced a companion bill to H.R. 2699 in the Senate.

15. Senator Strom Thurmond's bill, the "Professional Sports Antitrust Improvements Act of 1996," extends partial immunity for relocation issues, but it provides no countervailing mechanism to circumscribe the potential abuse from granting the monopoly sports leagues this additional power.

16. Although it is difficult to imagine that the fledgling Major League Soccer will began to threaten U.S. cities in the near future, it would be prudent to include all professional team-sports leagues in this bill.

REFERENCES

Arizona Office of Sports Development. 1993. *Economic Impact Study of a Major League Baseball Stadium and Franchise.* Parsippany, N.J.: Deloite and Touche.

Baade, Robert A. 1994. Stadiums, Professional Sports, and Economic Development: Assessing the Reality. *Heartland Policy Study* 62 (April).

Baade, Robert A., and Richard F. Dye. 1990. The Impact of Stadiums and Professional Sports on Metropolitan Area Development. *Growth and Change* 21: 1–14.

Boardman, Anthony, Aidan Vinig, and W. G. Waters II. 1993. Costs and Benefits through Bureaucratic Lenses. *Journal of Policy Analysis and Management* 12: 532–555.

Crompton, John. 1995. Economic Impact Analysis of Sports Facilities and Events: Eleven Sources of Misapplication. *Journal of Sport Management* 9: 14–35.

Johnson, Arthur. 1993. *Minor League Baseball and Local Economic Development.* Urbana: University of Illinois Press.

Quirk, James, and Rodney D. Fort. 1992. *Pay Dirt: The Business of Professional Team Sports.* Princeton: Princeton University Press.

Rosentraub, Mark A. 1997. Stadiums and Urban Space. In *Sports, Jobs and Taxes: The Economic Impact of Sports Teams and Stadiums.* Washington, D.C.: The Brookings Institution.

Zimmerman, Dennis. 1996. *Limiting Tax-Exempt Bonds for Professional Sports Stadiums.* Washington, D.C.: Congressional Research Service.

Zimmerman, Dennis. 1991. Tax-Exempt Bond Legislation, 1968–1990: An Economic Perspective. In *CRS Report for Congress.* Washington, D.C.: Congressional Research Service.

3

Home Field Advantage?
Does the Metropolis or Neighborhood
Derive Benefit from a
Professional Sports Stadium?

Robert A. Baade

Among the noteworthy twentieth-century trends identified for the
United States has been the movement of people and economic activity
from urban centers to the suburbs. Business has followed the migration of its labor force, and as a consequence most American city centers have deteriorated economically in the latter stages of this century.
This urban economic malaise was further exacerbated in the 1980s by
President Ronald Reagan's vision of a nation less dependent on a federal government. One manifestation of Reagan's emphasis on greater
state autonomy was reduced federal revenue sharing. A less-gener-
ous federal government translated into more parsimonious state governments, and, following the dollar food chain, less financial support
for local governments. The erosion of the urban economic base compelled new economic strategies for cities, and mayors have responded
by devising policies that emphasize the urban core as a cultural destination. Mayors hope that their cultural entrepreneurship will reverse
the decades-old flow of people and money from city centers and serve
to reestablish them as the hubs of American life.

One aspect of this strategy has been the aggressive attempt by the
mayors of many large cities to relocate professional sports stadiums
from the suburbs to the central business districts. This relocation of

sports facilities has come at considerable public expense, and the advocates of sports subsidies rationalize their position on investment grounds. Subsidies for sports facilities do not force painful civic tradeoffs, apologists argue, but rather provide revenues in excess of the subsidies, thereby enabling rather than constraining the construction of schools, sewers, and roads. The purpose of this chapter is to evaluate this rationalization. Do professional sports teams and stadiums induce an increase in economic activity in either the metropolis or the neighborhood in which the stadium is located?

In addressing this issue, it is useful to first establish the incidence of stadium migration from the suburbs back to the city center and to discuss the reasons for this development. In the next section, the macroeconomic or metropolitan impact induced by the construction of a sports facility is analyzed. Scholars have studied the macroeconomic impact sufficiently enough that reliable evidence is available on the influence professional sports have exerted on metropolitan areas. There are reasons, however, to expect that, both in terms of magnitude and pattern, economic development at the neighborhood or microeconomic level may differ from that characterizing the metropolis, and the subsequent section of this chapter is devoted to analyzing the microeconomic or neighborhood impact. Particular attention will be devoted to a discussion of land values in a stadium's environs, a subject largely ignored by scholars to date.[1] Conclusions and policy implications are offered in the chapter's final part.

STADIUM MIGRATION: BACK TO THE FUTURE

Earlier in the twentieth century, stadiums were woven into dense urban fabrics. Rather than the stadium defining and shaping an area, the stadium was viewed as subordinate to a larger urban design and function. The existing city grid established the shape and location of many urban ballparks, lending an idiosyncratic character to many of them. For example the Baker Bowl, home to Major League Baseball's Philadelphia Phillies until 1938, was also known as the Hump because it was built on an elevated piece of ground to accommodate a railroad tunnel running under center field (Lowry 1992). Today only Fenway Park in Boston (1912) with its legendary "Green Monster," Tiger Stadium in Detroit (1912), and Wrigley Field in Chicago (1914) stand as representative monuments to past urban imperatives. As this is being written, a new ballpark for the Tigers is scheduled to open in the 2000 season in downtown Detroit, and discussions are under way to replace both Fenway Park and Wrigley Field.

In the post–World War II era, a rapidly expanding economy increased the personal incomes of most Americans to a point where former luxuries, such as automobiles and houses outside crowded cities, could be purchased by a majority of the population. As areas on the city's periphery were settled, businesses followed, in part to capitalize on emerging markets for consumer goods and to gain proximity to the labor force. In keeping with this suburban trend, stadiums followed the fans. Expressways were built to accommodate the automobile, and suburban stadiums were located in close proximity to expressways to facilitate fan travel to the ballpark. Automobiles required space, and the typical suburban ballpark was surrounded by a sea of asphalt. For most fans in the post–World War II era, their homes were connected to the ballpark by a seamless stream of concrete. Accommodating the automobile came at a price from the perspective of the neighborhood in which the stadium was located. Easing entry and egress to the stadium mitigated the spillover of pedestrian traffic and economic activity into the environs where the ballpark was located. On the way from the stadium to their automobiles, fans encountered car windows not store windows. Once in their cars, the strong current of the expressways did not allow easy contact with commercial entities lining the highways. Any commerce that did occur in conjunction with sports spectating, therefore, likely did so within the confines of the ballpark, unless excursions into the neighborhood or elsewhere were planned.

Professional sports has been undergoing an economic revolution inspired by a confluence of circumstances both inside and outside the professional sports industry. These changes have affected both the supply and demand for professional sports, which, in turn, have had implications for where and how professional sporting events are packaged and presented. Nowhere are these changes more apparent than in the design and location of stadiums and arenas. Financial imperatives have worked to all but eliminate the multipurpose, circular stadium built a few decades ago in cities such as Cincinnati, Pittsburgh, and Philadelphia to host both football and baseball. In addition, financial forces have reversed the trend toward locating ballparks in suburban areas with vast tracts of land suitable for providing inexpensive parking. Stadiums and arenas are coming back to the cities with promises of fan spending spilling over into the commercial corridors of the neighborhoods through which fans flow to reach transportation centers or remote parking lots. Cities have used this promise of increased economic activity to persuade citizens to lend financial support to an aggressive city strategy to remake their centers into cultural destinations. For example, Cleveland has developed the Gateway complex which serves as a home to the MLB Indians (Jacobs Field) and the National Basketball Association Cavaliers (Gund Arena) along with the Rock and Roll Hall of Fame to lure people back to the downtown. Atlanta, Baltimore, Indianapolis, Minneapolis, and Nashville, to name but a few, are other cities that have opted for placing stadiums in or near the CBD in an effort to help revitalize the area. Stadium construction in the NFL symbolizes the return to downtown or near-downtown locations. Barring unforeseen construction delays, thirteen new stadiums have been or will be built in the 1990s. Of those, only facilities in Jacksonville (the renovation was sufficient enough in scope to warrant calling it new), San Francisco, Tampa Bay, and Maryland (Washington Redskins) are located outside of what could be considered the CBD or CBD fringe. Approximately 60 percent of NFL stadiums were located in or near CBDs prior to the 1990s, or about 16 percent less than characterizes current construction trends. If the events conducted at the stadiums attract people from beyond the metropolitan areas in which they are located, then those who support public subsidies for these facilities promise metropolitan, state, and regional economies will benefit from such investments. Do metropolitan economies derive a boost from professional sports and their stadiums? If they do, then surely the neighborhood in which the stadium is located is the wellspring of those benefits.

TEAMS, STADIUMS, AND METROPOLITAN ECONOMIC IMPACT

The experience of a cross-section of cities across the United States over the past few decades strongly disputes the claim that professional sports teams and stadiums provide an economic boost for metropolises. Baade (1996) found no correlation between the real growth differential in real per capita personal income for cities experiencing some change in their professional sports industry and cities experiencing no such change or having no professional sports presence. Baade's analysis included all cities hosting a team in one of the four major professional sports (baseball, basketball, football, and hockey), and covered more than three decades of observations beginning in 1958. All else being equal, one would expect a professional sports host city to expand economically, if sports does attract more than local interest and dollars. The fact that evidence fails to support such a contention requires an explanation and several immediately come to mind.

First, the professional sports team may simply be too small to influence in any meaningful way a large, diverse metropolitan economy. For example, in debating the efficacy of using several hundred million dollars of public funds for subsidizing a new stadium for the NFL's Tampa Bay Buccaneers to replace a twenty-year-old facility, it was determined that the team's revenues ranked below more than seventy other enterprises in that city. In using an academic context to provide perspective, Noll and Zimbalist (1997) observed that the top ten universities in the United States received $2.8 billion in federal grant money in 1994, which was more than the combined revenue of the NFL and the NHL or the combined revenue of MLB and the NBA for that year. Second, and perhaps more important, consonant with elementary budget constraints, spending on professional sports spectating substitutes for time and money that could be spent on other goods or services. To the extent that the fan base is largely indigenous to the metropolitan area, net spending in the metropolitan area may increase, decrease, or stay constant even though gross spending on sports increases significantly. The distinction between gross and net spending changes is pivotal in precisely estimating the impact of professional sports. Some economic-impact studies supporting stadium subsidies use a gross measure of spending that occurs in conjunction with professional sports and then purport to capture the indirect impact through "multiplier analysis."[2] A measure of net spending changes, of course, requires substantially more data or more sophisticated modeling, and accounts in part for the use of estimates of gross spending to justify stadium subsidies. Given the paucity of data and the complex web of financial inflows and outflows that occur as a consequence of hosting a professional sports team, a reasonable estimate of the team's economic contribution can likely be rendered only through comparing the metropolitan economic landscape before and after the team or stadium. This after-the-fact audit in estimating the economic impact of professional sports has been favored by some economists (Noll and Zimbalist 1997).

Estimates on gross and net new spending differ substantially. For example, in a report estimating the economic impact of the Seattle Mariners on the city of Seattle, King County, and the state of Washington, prepared by Dick Conway & Associates for King County in 1994, net direct spending as a percentage of gross direct spending was identified as 44.3 percent for the city and county ($40.4 million out of $114 million for both the city and the state) and 32 percent ($29.1 million out of $114 million) for the state (Conway and Beyers 1994). The difference between gross and net total direct economic impact are more pronounced, since multipliers will compound differences in gross and net measures of direct economic impacts. Total net economic impact as a percentage of total gross economic impact as calculated by Conway & Associates was 23.9 percent ($42.9 million out of $179.7 million), 38.5 percent ($53.3 million out of $138.8 million), and 40.1 percent ($47.7 million out of $119.1 million) for the state, county, and city, respectively.

In relative terms, gross economic impact is arguably most pronounced in the neighborhood in which the stadium is located. In measuring the impact professional sports has on economies, circles could be drawn around the point where the event actually occurs, and it could be asserted reasonably that the magnitude of the impact, in relative terms at least, varies inversely with the size of each circle. Stated somewhat differently, the economic effect is thought to be most pronounced at "ground-zero," the exact location of the event. As the circumference of the circle expands, the net impact diminishes as the dollars spent on the sporting event are more completely offset by reduced spending elsewhere. Following this budgetary logic as it relates to leisure spending, the global impact of even the largest sporting events, such as the Summer Olympics, approximates zero if an increase in global net spending is not induced by the event. This is true since even those who come from great distances spend time and money at the Olympics in lieu of time and money they would have spent elsewhere. The impact locally, therefore, depends on the extent to which spending and respending occurs by those residing outside the environs where the event is held, or by local citizens who spend money on the sports event as opposed to spending their discretionary income outside their neighborhood. Theoretically, a local government might decide to subsidize sports if the audience is distinctly nonlocal. Within the neighborhood there are outflows associated with team and stadium activities, and so even at the local level professional sports might fail to provide much of an economic boost.

NEIGHBORHOOD ECONOMIC IMPACT

Stadiums dominate the neighborhoods in which they are located. The size of the facility and its design differentiate it from other local structures. In approaching New Orleans or Seattle by car from a certain direction, one cannot help but notice the Superdome and the Kingdome. In addition to their structural uniqueness, stadiums are also distinguished by the scale of human activity on game day. At first blush, it is not difficult to imagine that such frenetic activity substantially boosts the local economy. After all, are not fans spending money on parking, tickets, souvenirs, and concessions? First impressions, however, may be deceiving. The extent to which the stadium contributes to local economic activity depends on the extent to which the money remains and recirculates through the local economy. To help analyze and understand the extent to which the local economy is sparked by the presence of a professional sports stadium, the Kingdome in Seattle, Washington, and its relationship to its neighborhood host, Pioneer Square, will be discussed.[3]

Seattle typifies the contemporary economic relationship that U.S. cities hosting major league sports have with their teams, particularly as it relates to stadiums. Less than two decades after its construction, owners of the NFL Seahawks and the MLB Mariners declared the Kingdome economically obsolete. In the owners' opinion the Kingdome could not compete financially with the new breed of stadiums being built across the country. In citing a general shortcoming of multipurpose stadiums, the Kingdome's critics argued it failed to provide an environment that encouraged fans to return through compromising sight lines for individual sports to accommodate multiple sports and otherwise reducing the ambiance associated with single-sport structures (e.g., Wrigley Field in Chicago).

Based on the demographic characteristics, Pioneer Square has relatively few full-time residents with the financial wherewithal to buy tickets to professional sporting events. It follows that the sports events hosted by the Kingdome attract the majority of their fans from outside Pioneer Square. If the spending that occurs in conjunction with sports remains in the Pioneer Square economy, the local financial boost provided by the stadium could be substantial. The key, of course, is the extent to which the money spent by nonlocal fans is locally retained and spent again and again in the neighborhood. Those who assert the Kingdome provides a substantial economic boost for Pioneer Square likely focus their attention on the financial inflows only. Casual empiricism supports the assertion that the Kingdome represents a boon to Pioneer Square. On event days fans stream into the stadium and the environs and spend large amounts of money. A precise rendering of the economic impact, however, requires not only an accurate measure of the dollars spent on sports spectating and related activities, but a thorough identification of the money outflows that occur as a consequence of Kingdome events as well. The financial leakages from the neighborhood economy may well be substantial, and can be broadly categorized as (1) earnings repatriated by owners, players, and other team and stadium personnel to their residences; (2) the costs incurred to operate the stadium, including the opportunity costs; and (3) business losses incurred locally as a consequence of peak usage of local resources on game day. Stated somewhat differently, local business activity may be crowded out.

The Pioneer Square neighborhood, to be sure, experiences significantly more economic transactions as a consequence of the Kingdome. Assume for the moment that we think of Pioneer Square as a business entity, and that we identify the Kingdome as a part of Pioneer Square's stock of capital.[4] From this capital, stock income flows when tickets, baseball paraphernalia, and hot dogs are sold. The economic impact, however, is not equal to gross spending changes, any more than revenues are equal to business profits. Explicit and implicit costs arise as a consequence of conducting events at the Kingdome, and the economic contribution that the Kingdome makes to Pioneer Square is consonant not with gross financial inflows, but rather net financial inflows to the neighborhood. Two facts may well serve to vitiate the economic impact the operation of the Kingdome would at first blush appear to provide. First, the stadium may serve as little more than an economic conduit through which spending on Kingdome events passes from one set of nonresident hands to another. Second, the level and urgency of game-day activities may well strain local resources to the point where normal local business activity is crowded out. Should either of these effects be pronounced, the neighborhood in which the stadium is located derives far less stimulation than that suggested by the direct spending that occurs within the stadium's walls.

The first point can be illustrated through tracing player salaries. A stadium does not resemble the corner grocery, where the owners live above the store. Rather, the stadium owners and the stadium employees who receive most of the event revenues are in all probability not neighborhood residents. Thus, even if fans are not residents and their spending represents an infusion of funds, the boost provided is short lived because the nonresident owners and players appropriate that spending in the form of their profits and wages. Recent developments in professional sports as it relates to stadium construction may well be making the transfer of funds from one group of nonresidents to another more complete. In negotiations with their host cities, teams have more aggressively and thoroughly exploited the advantage imparted by an excess demand for teams. The new breed of stadiums have evolved into small walled cities that more completely compete with and capture the economic activity that used to spill out into the neighborhood. This stadium/mall concept has been encouraged by the leagues to help level the financial playing fields of league members. Furthermore, in their anxiety to attract or retain their teams, cities have been agreeing to more generous leases that allow teams to appropriate virtually all of the revenues from ticket sales, concessions, the sale of sports paraphernalia, parking, stadium advertising, and naming rights. The quid pro quo for these "sweetheart" leases is that the team dedicate one revenue source or another to satisfy public demands for a team "equity" stake in the ballpark project. Teams readily agree, since the present value of increased stadium earnings exceeds by a significant amount the present value of the dedicated revenue streams.

Owners have argued that stadiums are necessary to satisfy player demands for higher salaries. Suppose for the moment that this owner rationale is true. Today, for the NBA and NFL, two sports leagues that have instituted salary caps, the share of league gross revenues to which players as a group are entitled by agreement is 57.5 and 63 percent, respectively. It follows, therefore, that significantly more than half of the spending that occurs at the ballpark finds its way into the pockets of players. If players do not live in the community or otherwise do not spend on community goods and services, then more than one-half of the revenue that finds its way into the stadium on game day leaks from the neighborhood. In the case of Seattle it is a virtual certainty that few if any of the Seattle Seahawks' owners and players live in Pioneer Square. In fact, the market for players is national, and many of them do not establish their primary residences in the cities in which they play. Players invest their earnings internationally and are taxed nationally and, therefore, a substantial portion of what they earn leaves not only the Pioneer Square economy but the metropolitan economy as well.

The point made through tracing player salaries applies to taxes imposed by nonlocal governments. Ignoring for the moment "home rule," how much of the sales tax on sports clothing or excise tax on game tickets is retained by the local government? Much of it becomes a part of general revenues for the state, county, or city government imposing the tax, and the extent to which it is returned to the local government depends on institutional arrangements. The local governments which provide space for the stadium need to not only have a hand in shaping revenue sharing to ensure their costs incurred in providing space for the stadium are covered, but they need to understand the extent to which the stadium and team activities affect general tax revenues at higher levels of government from which they derive a share. Such an analysis is hardly trivial, and it must be undertaken if the neighborhood is to make wise decisions with regard to the use of their scarce land resources.

Opportunity and operating costs, as well as the likelihood that stadium activity will "crowd out" local economic activity, depend on the character of the neighborhood economy. Is there a natural synergy between the stadium and neighborhood, or will expenses mount and displacement and inactivity occur on a scale that ensures the cost of hosting the stadium exceeds the expected benefit? Stadiums require large tracts of land, not only for the structure itself but for parking if the stadium site or the institutional character of the metropolis or region makes it accessible primarily by automobile. Stadiums are not like shopping malls, where economic activity occurs throughout the course of a day, every day. Stadiums, particularly open-air football stadiums, spend more time waiting than working. How the community handles the "dead time" in the stadium and its attendant areas is critical to the ability of the community to use the facility to its economic advantage. Of course, local governments can benefit directly and substantially from increases in property taxes fostered by an increase in land assessments attributable to the construction and operation of a stadium. It should be noted, however, that one benefit often conferred on professional sports teams is property-tax abatement or the inclusion of the stadium in a tax increment financing (TIF) district. These issues aside, property-tax increases could potentially benefit the neighborhood, and therefore warrant analysis.

STADIUMS AND LAND VALUES IN CONTIGUOUS AREAS

The amount of land required by a stadium, including automobile parking, alters the character of the neighborhood and its economy. Whether the economic impact measures positive or negative depends on several things, such as the intensity with which and purpose for which land was and will be utilized. Land use and designation, in turn, will affect land values. Underutilized land or vacant land may be converted to more productive uses and land values in the stadium environs can be expected to rise as a result. It is also plausible that land could be converted from more-efficient to less-productive uses. For example, warehouses or light industry may be converted from those uses to parking lots, at some cost to the local economy, to accommodate the peak automobile traffic characteristic of sports events.

Not only is there some question with respect to the character of economic development induced by the sports facility, but the timing and duration of the impact are uncertain as well. A large public or private project encourages conjecture about the economic impact on the surrounding area. Optimism about economic prospects for the micro area fuels increases in local real estate prices, some of which may be scaled back when a clearer picture of how the stadium has really influenced economic activity emerges. A new stadium or team attracts people who might not otherwise attend a game. This novelty effect translates into greater-than-normal crowds, and the secondary economic activity that spills out into the neighborhood is likely greatest when the stadium is newest. As the bloom wears off the stadium rose, the secondary economic activity associated with stadium pedestrian traffic diminishes and the value of the neighborhood real estate may grow at a slower rate, become negative, or move in lockstep with team fortunes. Whatever the change, it is important to distinguish between the immediate and longer-term consequences of stadium construction and operation.

From a metropolitan or macroeconomic perspective, the public subsidization of a stadium diverts resources from more-preferred to less-preferred uses. Indeed, the fact that the stadium would not be built in the absence of public financial support is prima facie evidence that the stadium is not a preferred use of the land on which it is built. If this is true, then it follows that economic well-being for the metropolis and, perhaps, for the neighborhood, is adversely affected by diverting resources away from preferred uses. The infusion of funds into a neighborhood, therefore, may accelerate development of that micro area's economy, but at the expense of the larger economy unless there is a public-goods or externality argument that exists and can be invoked to justify the reallocation of economic activity from one part of the metropolis to another. What would the property values have been in the neighborhood in the absence of the stadium development? This is a particularly difficult question to answer if the stadium development is accompanied by other significant construction. A response, therefore, depends on the ability to separate the impact of the stadium on property values from that of other developments that occur simultaneously, and on an understanding of the variety of conditions and circumstances that characterize the local and metropolitan economies and impinge on property values. There is always the possibility, for example, that development in the stadium environs may have been well under way, and stadium construction diverted development in another direction that renders the land utilized by existing owners less valuable than it would otherwise have been. What is not clear is whether the path of accelerated development blazed by the stadium is the best and, therefore, preferred use of the land. Some would argue that condemnation hearings and litigation exist to make such determinations. Fair market value, however, is not properly established by a condemnation decree reflecting current market conditions and uses of the land restricted to those compatible with the construction of a sports stadium. Rather, fair market value is defined by the development of the land that would utilize it to its "best" advantage or purpose as determined by its salient character over the long term. Also relevant to establishing fair market value is an estimate of what the land would have been worth had development been allowed to follow its "natural" course (that which induced the current owner to purchase the property).

This analysis recognizes that the infusion of hundreds of millions of dollars into a neighborhood economy is an investment of sufficient magnitude and scope to stimulate greater interest in real estate in the stadium's environs. In most cases there is a discernible speculative burst in land values that occurs in the stadium's neighborhood. In Table 3.1, information on the changes in local real estate price changes associated with stadium site selection in several cities is presented.

Several common threads can be identified from the information recorded in Table 3.1. First, the downtown or edge-of-downtown real estate is going to be significantly more expensive than suburban real estate. Second, real estate prices in the stadium district, in general, increase by roughly 100 to 150 percent after the selection of the site. Third, the square-foot price for real estate in the environs of a downtown stadium site is roughly $15 to $20 per square foot. It is useful to elaborate on the spe-

Table 3.1
Real Estate Price Developments in Neighborhoods in Which Stadiums Were Constructed in Selected Cities in the U.S.

City, Stadium (Team)	Year built; cost (millions); capacity and location	Land acquisition costs (millions)	Costs per square foot before site announcement	Cost per square foot after site announcement
Baltimore, Camden Yards (Orioles)	1992; $210; 48,262 Downtown	$100 for 20 properties in 1990	Not available	$15-20 per square foot[a]
Cincinnati, Riverfront Site (Two stadiums, Bengals and Reds)	2000; $180; 70,000 Downtown	$27.93	Not available	$20.37 per square foot
Denver, Coors Field (Rockies)	1995; $214; 50,200 Downtown	Not available	Not available	Real estate prices have nearly doubled in lower downtown (LoDo)
Detroit (Two Stadiums, Tigers and Lions)	2000; $435; 42,000 (Tigers), Downtown	Not available	$4.60 per square foot	$13.80 per square foot
Raljon, Maryland, Jack Kent Cooke (Washington Redskins)	1997; $250.5; 78,000 Suburban	$4.10	$0.47 per square foot	$0.47 per square foot

Table 3.1 (*continued*)

City, Stadium (Team)	Year built; cost (millions); capacity and location	Land acquisition costs (millions)	Costs per square foot before site announcement	Cost per square foot after site announcement
San Diego (Padres)	2000; $400; Downtown	Not available	$8.27 per square foot	$20.67 per square foot[b]
San Francisco (Giants)	2000; $300; Downtown		$6.00 per square foot	$15-$30 per square foot[c]
Seattle (Two Stadiums, Mariners and Seahawks)	1999; $363.5; 45,611 (Mariners)	Not available	Not available	Property value increases will be slightly greater than inflation[d]

[a]Baltimore City warehouse prices in 1995. See David Harrison, "Stadium Sites Count Weeks to Takeover," *Baltimore Business Journal*, 28 October 1996. It is significant that values for the property were established by making reference to warehouse prices in Baltimore overall rather than prices specific to the micro area.

[b]These estimates are the highest that I have seen published, and are based on estimates of the value of the more than 111 acres of the site designated for the new stadium owned by San Diego Gas and Electric (see http://www.sandiego-online.com/issues/april98/ballpark.stm).

[c]Cost per square foot before and after refer to lease rates. See Kenneth Howe, "A Grand Slam in the Gulch: New Stadium Causing Boom for Real Estate—Bust for Tenants," *San Francisco Chronicle*, 24 March 1998.

[d]Peter K. Shorett, "Stadium to Boost SODO Area Values," *Seattle Daily Journal of Commerce*, 22 November 1996.

cifics of the stadium real estate markets for each of the seven cities identified. Brief summaries follow in alphabetical order.

An October 28, 1996, *Baltimore Business Journal* article (Harrison 1996) reported that the condemnation of the twenty Camden Industrial Park properties in 1990 at a cost of $100 million proved a bonanza for some of the Industrial Park occupants but a disaster for others. Notable among those commercial concerns harmed was Parks Sausage, which used the $9-million state condemnation payment to build a much larger plant on Parks Circle in the northwest part of the city. Parks eventually declared bankruptcy and attributed its demise to the new plant's higher debt service. It is noteworthy that some of the condemned property is used for parking lots, which presumably will employ fewer people at lower wages than the light industry that occupied Camden Industrial Park prior to the construction of Orioles Park. Full-time jobs were replaced by part-time jobs if the businesses failed to reestablish themselves in the Baltimore area. It should also be noted that the Maryland Stadium Authority had to compensate the Orioles for the reduction in parking spaces made available to them as a consequence of the construction of the new stadium for the NFL Baltimore Ravens. In conjunction with this, it is also noteworthy that plans for a football stadium on its current site were developed nine years before a football team was adopted by Baltimore, but the condemnation of businesses necessary to create additional parking spaces for the Orioles made it difficult for businesses faced with likely condemnation to sell their property if they wished to move to another site. The nine-year wait proved advantageous from the state's point of view, since the property appraisals at the height of the 1987 real estate market boom were substantially higher than the appraisals in 1995.

Cincinnati considered two parcels of land for the construction of two stadiums, one for the MLB Reds and one for the NFL Bengals. An October 10, 1998 article in the *Cincinnati Enquirer* (May 1998) reported that records from the Hamilton County Auditor's office indicated that the Broadway Commons site (northern fringes of downtown) would cost $51.4 million, which is approximately the same as the riverfront site which is the location of the current Riverfront Stadium in which both the Bengals and the Reds play. It is noteworthy that a portion of the Broadway Commons site, which was rejected on November 3, 1998, by voters in Cincinnati as a site for the new stadiums, recently sold for more than four times the value Hamilton County auditors placed on the property (18.2 acres sold for $26.4 million, in contrast to the auditor's assessed valuation of $6.05 million). This has significant implications for at least two reasons. First, it is not the stadium that lends value to the land, but rather the other way around. Two, the government's appraisal of land values often substantially underestimates the market value of the property. Underassessment is not news to anyone who knows even a little about the land-valuation process, but it clearly indicates that the value of the land is a debatable issue and not one that should be determined by government appraisals that depend on current assessments alone.

In Denver the value of land for the purposes of building a stadium was established in a unique transaction where Denver Broncos owner Pat Bowlen agreed to pay $5 million for 6.75 acres of land that constitutes the only two remaining private parcels of land within the site selected for the new stadium for the Denver Broncos. The land is being purchased by Bowlen for slightly less than $17 per square foot, and is in keeping with the values identified for other cities in this study (Flynn 1998). Again, the point needs to be emphasized that because the official assessed value of the property is often less than what is paid is not indicative of the fact that the stadium provides a windfall that property owners would not receive in the absence of stadium construction, but rather only brings assessed values closer to true market value. Condemned property is still likely to bring less than fair market value because the affected property owners will likely discount the value of the property by what it would cost for the legal resources necessary to get fair market value for the property. Furthermore, property that is likely to be condemned discourages potential investors which, as anyone who has participated in an auction will attest, likely diminishes the price at which the property is sold.

The situation in Detroit, where separate stadiums are being built for the MLB Tigers and the NFL Lions, suggests, as do the previous examples, that sometimes there are substantial differentials among the official assessed values, the parcel price negotiated by the owner and the government, and the true market value of the property. Phil Linsalata (1997) of the *Detroit News* noted with regard to the sale of the downtown YMCA to the Stadium Authority that the tentative price is about five times the assessed value of $990,800. The president of the Greater Detroit YMCA, Reid Thebault, noted that the $5-million price is close to fair market value. Thebault, however, also noted that "part of the deal is nonmonetary." In a 1997 article, *Detroit News* columnist Mark Puls opined that property values on the west side of downtown Detroit have more than tripled since the stadium development was announced. The question, of course, is what information Puls used to determine that before the announcement property sold for $220,000 an acre.

Jack Kent Cooke Stadium in Raljon, Maryland, is of limited usefulness in that it is a suburban stadium. There is one piece of information that is useful, however. Jack Kent Cooke Stadium is advertised as a privately financed stadium, but the state of Maryland contributed $78 million to the project for access roads, parking lots, and other facilities around the stadium.

Although it was not part of the sample included in Table 3.1 because it is an arena and not a stadium, the Target Center in Minneapolis is noteworthy on several levels. First, the government purchased the land on which the Target Center was built for $15.4 and contributed $5.7 million for roadwork. Second, contrary to predictions by the Twin Cities Metropolitan Council, the Target Center has had an adverse impact on area economic activity. Third, competition among arenas in the Twin Cities coupled with cost overruns that tripled production costs forced a buyout by the Minneapolis Community Development Agency (MCDA), which purchased the Target Center for $54.6 million. The Target Center has been appraised at $63.1 million, while the city has invested $75.7 million in the facility.

Tax-increment financing may be used to help finance the construction of a $411-million downtown stadium in San Diego near San Diego Bay and the city's convention center. This is an interesting proposal, since the proposed TIF could offer some insight into the micro-area economic impact induced by a stadium. The stadium's economic impact will determine the ability of the stadium to sustain any increase in land values realized during the speculative phase of stadium land-value adjustments. Current projections are that $40 to $80 million could be raised through redevelopment of the stadium district.

San Francisco's China Basin/Multimedia Gulch is experiencing a surge in real estate prices. Some would attribute the significant rise in prices to the new $300-million stadium being constructed for the MLB Giants. The increase in land values, however, is the result of a combination of circumstances, including the continued expansion of internet business activity (350 companies currently located there employing 35,000 people), the huge 313-acre Mission Bay project (includes a university campus, entertainment, shopping, and housing), and the ballpark for the Giants (Howe 1998). It would be very difficult to identify what fraction of the increase in real estate prices is attributable to the stadium, but no such ambiguity exists with regard to the fears expressed by residents about the stadium's impact on the course of economic development. Anticipating development skewed toward bars and fast-food restaurants, in December 1997 Multimedia Gulch residents successfully lobbied for zoning legislation that restricted the operation of businesses that develop in concert with stadium construction. In particular, bars, large fast-food restaurants, music clubs, and video-game parlors have been restricted by the legislation.

Increases in real estate prices and the anticipated congestion that commonly accompanies game day has changed the economic character of Multimedia Gulch. The high rents are forcing many small businesses to look elsewhere, and the search for more reasonably priced real estate is likely to push up real estate prices in neighborhoods nearby. The extent to which land values increase nearby will provide a reasonable measure of the extent to which an expanding nonsport business presence in Multimedia Gulch is responsible for the increase in real estate prices there.

The impact of the two new stadiums being built in Seattle for the MLB Mariners and the NFL Seahawks is unclear. There could be an increase in the demand for real estate in the south of the dome (SODO) area, but traffic congestion is likely to mitigate any positive effect on land values. Demand for real estate in SODO has been strong without the stadiums because the businesses located in SODO by their natures require close proximity to downtown Seattle. In the absence of improved access to the area, redevelopment opportunities will be compromised. If new transportation links are provided, will the redevelopment that occurs be attributable to the new stadiums or the additions to the transportation infrastructure?

CONCLUSIONS

Those who support public subsidies for professional sports facilities justify them on economic grounds. Do sports facilities provide benefits in excess of the costs incurred by the metropolis or the neighborhood? Empirical evidence fails to support the proposition that sports infrastructure contributes meaningfully to the metropolitan economy, but what about the neighborhood? The intense economic activity characterizing game day creates the impression that even if the metropolis does not derive measurable economic gain, the neighborhood benefits from the presence of the stadium. A more careful analysis, however, casts doubt on the proposition that the mere presence of a stadium confers substantial positive economic benefit on the neighborhood. Financial leakages, peak usage of community resources on game day, and the exercise of elementary budget constraints for both consumers and producers conspire to negate the privately induced economic impact on the neighborhood.

Can the local government expect increases in tax revenues that approximate local costs incurred from the presence of a stadium? Since taxes to a substantial extent are derived from economic activity, if the stadium does not expand the tax base, tax revenues are unlikely to increase. However, evidence indicates that real estate prices in a neighborhood rise as a consequence of a stadium, and one could contend that rising land assessments yield an increase in property taxes which may benefit the local economy. To be credible, this argument tacitly assumes that the present value of property-tax revenues generated by the stadium exceed the present value of property taxes that would have been collected had the land been put to its best alternative use. This may not occur for several reasons, and the fact that stadiums are not privately financed suggests building a stadium may not represent the optimal use of the land. Furthermore, cities often provide tax relief as part of the package of incentives to attract or retain a professional sports franchise. If a substantial portion of local real estate is effectively taken off the books through TIF or outright tax exemptions, a stadium may drain rather than fill local coffers.

The policy implications are clear. Before a community commits scarce resources, particularly land, to a sports facility, a careful cost–benefit analysis should be undertaken. An arena or stadium may well involve costs that are lost in sports hyperbole buttressed by game-day excitement. A precise rendering of the economic costs and benefits conferred by stadiums may make "not in my backyard" a rational neighborhood response to those who seek a home for a professional sports team.

NOTES

1. Timothy Chapin, a doctoral student at the University of Washington, is attempting to fill this void with a dissertation devoted to the subject. The tentative title of Chapin's dissertation is "Sports Stadia as (Possible) Urban Revitalization Tools: An Assessment of Impacts at the Microarea Level."

2. See, for example, the work of Baade, Hamilton, and Kahn, and Austrian and Rosentraub in Noll and Zimbalist (1997).

3. The ensuing discussion borrows heavily from Baade (1999).

4. Representing the neighborhood as a business admittedly captures only a portion of a community's character and quality of life, but such a representation provides some useful insights.

REFERENCES

Baade, Robert A. 1999. Metropolitan versus Neighborhood Economic Impact Induced by Professional Sports Teams and Stadiums: What's the Score? W. E. Upjohn Institute for Employment Research, Kalamazoo, Michigan.

Baade, Robert A. 1996. Professional Sports as Catalysts for Metropolitan Economic Development. *Journal of Urban Affairs* 18: 1–17.

Conway, R. S., and W. B. Beyers. 1994. Seattle Mariners Baseball Club Economic Impact (mimeograph).

Flynn, Kevin. 1998. Bowlen to Pay $5 Million for Lots. *Rocky Mountain News*, October 22, sec. F, p. 4A.

Harrison, David. 1996. Stadium Sites Count Weeks to Takeover. *Baltimore Business Journal*, 14: 1.

Howe, Kenneth. 1998. A Grand Slam in the Gulch: New Stadium Causing Boom for Real Estate—Bust for Tenants. *San Francisco Chronicle*, 24 March, p. C1.

Linsalata, Phil. 1997. In Detroit: One-Third of Stadium Land Bought. *Detroit News*, 16 January, p. E2.

Lowry, Philip. 1992. *Green Cathedrals*. New York: Addison-Wesley.

May, Lucy. 1998. Bedinghaus Puts Broadway Land at $54.1M. *Cincinnati Enquirer*, 10 October, p. B01.

Noll, Roger, and Andrew Zimbalist, eds. 1997. *Sports, Jobs and Taxes: The Economic Impact of Sports Teams and Taxes*. Washington, D.C.: The Brookings Institution.

Puls, Mark. 1997. Land Near Stadiums Explodes in Value. *Detroit News*, 8 August, p. C8.

Shorett, Peter K. 1996. Stadium to Boost SODO Area Values. *Seattle Daily Journal of Commerce*, 22 November, p. 1.

III

CITIES AND SPORTS FRANCHISES

Bruce J. Schulman's From Cotton Belt to Sunbelt: Federal Policy, Economic Development, and the Transformation of the South, 1938–1980 *(1991) traces the social and economic transformation of the old south to the new south, from the agrarian economy of the post–Depression era to the new era of high-tech companies in North Carolina's Research Triangle and petrochemical companies in Texas. Atlanta has become the transportation hub of the southeastern United States. Houston fancies itself as the golden buckle of the Sun Belt. It follows that these cities should have professional sports teams in every sport. Hockey teams in Dallas and Atlanta? Although hockey is not a sport schoolkids play in the winter, these cities had to be current. Besides, if a company such as UPS moves from New York City to Atlanta, the employees should be able to have the same amenities they enjoyed in the snowbelt cities. Every Sun-Belt city of any size is now in the queue for whatever sports franchise is ready to move. All the so-called fast-track cities such as San Antonio, New Orleans, Miami, Atlanta, Dallas, Houston, San Diego, and Jacksonville, have either NBA, MLB, or NBA franchises. Some have all three.*

What makes a city a candidate for big-time sports? Why is Phoenix, Arizona, a big-league town? Phoenix, once known as a sleepy desert town, is now the fastest growing American city. Why? Because of air conditioning, retirees, space, and scenery. Thirty years ago there was barely any activity at night. Now they have nighttime baseball. At one point in time the only thing residents shared in common were air conditioners, now they have the Phoenix Suns, the Arizona Diamondbacks, and the Phoenix Cardinals. It has a lot of space, a growing population base, and a highly effective pro-growth regime. For this reason, Phoenix is a great case study for the pro-growth machine. In Chapter 4, Richard Temple Middleton IV captures the politics of stadium building in this desert city.

New Orleans is a Sun-Belt city with a fascinating history. The "Big Easy," with its Mardi Gras, Bourbon Street, and Cajun culture has always been able to attract visitors. For generations it has always sold itself as a tourist city. Yet it must remain competitive. The Superdome, once called the eighth wonder of the world, is getting old. The city is being challenged by other southern cities for tourist dollars. Since it lost the New Orleans Jazz professional basketball team to Salt Lake City, Utah, the city has carefully guarded its sports asset, the New Orleans Saints. In Chapter 5, Robert K. Whelan and Alma H. Young take a different look at the city's fight to stay competitive in the stadium-building business. They examine the politics and the planning of a new stadium for a minor league team in Jefferson Parish, the suburban parish adjacent to the city, and a new arena to be built in downtown New Orleans next to the Superdome.

In Chapter 6, Lynn W. Bachelor examines how Detroit and Toledo use solution sets to dictate how to approach downtown development challenges. Detroit is an important case study because of the unique challenges it faces in redevelopment. The return of the Detroit Lions from Pontiac and the relocation of the Detroit Tigers are being promoted as corporate largess and civic responsibility. These new stadiums will change the entire skyline of downtown Detroit. Bachelor's work on the Toledo Mud Hens, the AAA farm club of the Detroit Tigers, relates to some of the themes Arthur T. Johnson develops in Chapter 7, on minor league franchises.

One would not think of a minor league franchise as big business or a magnet for economic development. This is particularly true in baseball. Minor league baseball is becoming popular because it is marketing itself as a form of family entertainment. Toledo will support their Mud Hens and Providence will support their Pawtucket Red Sox because the players are one step from the "big show." Teams are also drawing crowds by repackaging themselves as budget-conscious fare for families. Hollywood has gotten into the marketing of minor league teams with such movies as Bull Durham, a story about the reality of minor league life. The issue of minor league teams is raised by both Whelan and Young's review of New Orleans and Bachelor's discussion of the Toledo Mud Hens. Johnson's chapter addresses the economic-development issue more directly. He suggests that minor league franchises are evolving into big businesses and exerting influence on the redevelopment thinking of city leaders.

Edward I. Sidlow and Beth M. Henschen add a comparative perspective in Chapter 8. They revisit Detroit and add Chicago, Baltimore, and Cleveland in their case studies. They show the differences and similarities in stadium-building politics. Camden Yards in Baltimore has become one of the architectual models for new baseball parks. Comiskey II is a great structure. It was constructed after the team threatened to move the franchise to St. Petersburg, Florida. A new stadium for the Chicago White Sox may stimulate more calls for a new park for the Chicago Cubs. In all of the cases Sidlow and Henschen reviewed, politics played a deciding role.

Last, Neil J. Sullivan presents a strategy for playing the stadium game in Chapter 9.

REFERENCE

Schulman, Bruce J. 1991. *From Cotton Belt to Sunbelt: Federal Policy, Economic Development, and the Transformation of the South, 1938–1980.* New York: Oxford University Press.

4

The Politics of Stadium Development in Phoenix, Arizona

Richard Temple Middleton IV

The construction of municipal public sports stadiums to increase and enhance the economic growth of cities can be traced back to the turn of the twenty-first century. From the opening of a 20,000-seat facility in San Diego in 1914 to Pasadena's Rose Bowl in 1922, cities of various sizes have recognized the viability of building sports stadiums to encourage athletic competitions and attract sporting events and teams to their locale (Riess 1998, 4). With the proliferation of professional sports leagues, many cities seized the opportunity to attract lucrative teams to their cities by building facilities to accommodate them. Many municipalities, in an effort to "keep up with the Joneses," began building stadiums for "the sake of maintaining the city's reputation as a major league city" (Rich 1998, 1). Perhaps a more-common phenomena has been the promise of community economic growth being forwarded by sports entrepreneurs and politicians alike in an effort to persuade taxpayers to subsidize the exorbitant costs of sports arenas. Such optimists argue that sports franchises bring millions of dollars to the local economy, along with new jobs.

Analyses of the economic benefits of sports stadiums and franchises have produced surprising results. Many economists and political scientists question the actual benefits of sports stadiums and teams on local economies (Baade and Dye 1990; Rosentraub et al. 1994; Quirk and Fort 1992; Baade 1994; Baim 1994; Johnson 1986). According to economist Andrew Zimbalist (1998), sports teams are "not big business," "have only a small positive economic effect [on cities], similar to that of a new department store," and "most public stadiums and arenas do not cover their own fixed and operating costs" (pp. 18–19). The dreams of politicians and entrepreneurs of newfound economic vigor in the local economy, as supported by economic studies, seem to be just that—a dream.

Despite a plethora of studies that indicate sports teams and stadiums do not lead to an increase in economic growth, cities have continued to build new facilities, often at the approval of taxpayers. Many municipalities have held special elections in which voters have approved the use of taxpayer money to finance new stadiums (Denver in 1998, San Diego in 1998, and Austin in 1998). In most instances, attraction or retention of sports teams for civic pride proves to be paramount to citizens, as opposed to the potential for economic growth. However, a growing number of locations have voted down measures to use taxpayer money to subsidize the costs of building new arenas (Birmingham in 1998, Charlotte in 1996).

An interesting case of state and county efforts toward building an MLB sports facility is Bank One Ballpark in Phoenix, Arizona. With the enactment of a statute by the Arizona legislature, the construction of a major league baseball park became a priority for the Maricopa County (which includes the city of Phoenix and twelve other communities) Board of Supervisors. The Maricopa County Stadium District, which was created by the county's Board of Supervisors, was given the power to levy a tax to fund construction of a major league baseball stadium. The city of Phoenix, which had unsuccessfully attempted to build a ballpark over the previous two decades, played no part in the financing of the stadium. Rather, the state of Arizona and the county of Maricopa were the two major actors responsible for MLB coming to downtown Phoenix. The attraction of the new franchise and subsequent construction of the ballpark was considered by many in Phoenix to be one more piece to the puzzle in the city's effort to invigorate the economy in the "Sports Hub of the Valley." The case of Bank One Ballpark in Phoenix demonstrates that even state legislatures remain prominent actors in the procurement of major league sports franchises.

This section of the chapter examines the politics behind constructing a major league baseball park in Phoenix, Arizona, by discussing the city's background, its leadership structure, and its attempt to establish itself as a major league sports town. Second, this chapter investigates the economic-development strategy employed by the city of Phoenix and Maricopa County. In this endeavor, the chapter focuses closely on how construction of a major league baseball stadium and landing of an MLB franchise is part of the city and county's overall economic-development strategy. The final section focuses in detail on the public- and private-sector actors who played a major role in MLB's arrival in metro Phoenix. This analysis involves the investigation of actors from the state level to the grassroots organizations supporting and opposing public subsidization of the new ballpark. Before beginning this analysis, however, this chapter briefly explores the rise and decline of public favor toward public financing of sports stadiums. This analysis is useful because it allows for a juxtaposition of the Phoenix experience to that of other major metropolitan areas.

THE RISE AND DECLINE OF PUBLIC FAVOR
FOR FINANCING STADIUMS

States and municipalities, along with sports entrepreneurs, have utilized numerous strategies in an effort to finance construction of stadiums. These have included the use of public and private subsidies as well as complete public-based funding. With the proliferation of public financing of sports stadiums, voters and politicians have begun to debate the legitimacy of using public monies for stadium construction. Politicians and sports entrepreneurs have argued that new stadiums catalyze economic growth in the communities in which they are constructed. In addition, proponents have claimed that public financing of stadiums is an effective means of lowering individual burdens for widespread economic gains. No matter the credibility of these arguments, cities and states have continued to consider the use of public monies for construction of sport stadiums.

The process of publicly subsidizing stadiums in Cleveland, Cincinnati, and Baltimore, as analyzed by Veronica Kalich (1998), exemplifies the arduous nature of publicly financing stadium construction. In Cleveland, financing of a new stadium for an NFL franchise, which was to cost $175 million (with a possible $21-million overrun), was to be covered by funds generated from the extension of a local tax increase passed the previous year. The plan included a 0.5-percent increase in the sales tax, an excise tax on liquor ($3 per gallon), and a 4.5-cent-per-pack increase in cigarette taxes. In March 1996 voters in Cincinnati were presented with a tax-increase proposal that would increase the sales tax from 5.5 percent to 6 percent and generate $50 million annually, of which $35 million would go toward the stadium project. Supporters of a new stadium in Cincinnati argued that such a project would create nearly 7,000 new jobs and $170 million in spending on the local economy.

Support of stadium construction in Cincinnati and Cleveland did not come without much debate on the merits of using public funds for the projects. Backed by a coalition of Cleveland's mayor, area restaurants, and local fans, proponents of a new stadium argued that the likelihood of Cleveland securing an NFL franchise to replace the loss of the Browns to Baltimore was contingent upon their approving a tax extension. Voters opposed to the tax increase, however, grouped themselves in an effort to defeat the proposal. In Cincinnati, antitax forces formed the Citizens for Choice in Taxation group, supported by a $40,000 campaign fund to protest the proposed sales-tax increase and funding for the stadium. Their efforts focused on creating public skepticism toward proponent's claims that a new stadium would prompt economic benefits to the community. Despite public discontent, voters in Cincinnati passed a tax increase with 59 percent in favor and 41 percent against. In Cleveland, public support was even larger, with the tax increase supported by 72 percent.

Public financing of a new stadium for the city of Baltimore, Maryland, unlike the cases of Cincinnati and Cleveland, was debated as a priority of the state legislature. The state of Maryland created a stadium authority in 1986 whose responsibility was to issue bonds to service the debt on the construction of a new stadium and institute a sports lottery to pay the debt service. The state legislature had to approve the outlay of funds for stadium construction in addition to funds to pay for roads and infrastructure. Opponents of the use of public funds for the construction of a Baltimore stadium formed a special interest group called Citizens for Legitimate Investment Priorities (CLIP). Their primary goal was to convince legislators that public monies should be spend on other projects than a single stadium in Baltimore. Despite being backed by numerous public-interest groups, the state senate approved a $270.5-million funding package by a vote of 25–22 (Kalich 1998, 216).

The trend toward public financing of stadium construction has continued with voters in cities such as Dallas, San Francisco, and San Diego all approving some form of public financing. There has been, however, a countermove by voters in many areas voting down the use of any public funds for stadium construction. In November 1997 voters in metropolitan Pittsburgh turned down a referendum that would have partially funded new football and baseball stadiums through a sales-tax increase. Proponents of the stadium spent millions of dollars to convince voters that the plan would keep the teams in Pittsburgh and create thousands of new jobs. The plan, which called for a half-cent sales-tax increase, was designed to raise nearly $700 million over seven years. The ownership group with the Steelers offered 27 percent of the estimated $185 million cost of a new stadium. The Pirates pledged $35 million toward the estimated $185 to $200 million cost of a new baseball stadium. Despite the efforts of proponents, voters in Allegheny County, in which Pittsburgh is located, voted 58 percent against to 42 percent in favor.

Public discontent with the use of public monies for construction of sports stadiums has grown more evident over time. According to Charles Mathesian (1998), voters have begun to send a clear message: "They don't want to pay for new professional sports stadiums. But that doesn't mean they don't want them" (p. 22). Simultaneous with the Pittsburgh referendum, voters in Minneapolis approved a $10-million limit on financial assistance the city could provide toward building a new ballpark for the Minnesota Twins or for construction of any other professional sports facilities. In 1996 voters in Milwaukee and Seattle rejected stadium taxes to finance construction of new sports facilities. Voters in Birmingham, Alabama, were presented in 1998 with a proposal to use funds collected via public subsidies for the construction of a 70,000-seat stadium. Proponents of the arena argued that the city, which had recently lost the Southeastern Conference championship football game to Atlanta due to the deteriorating conditions of the city's Legion Field, needed the facility to compete for lucrative sports tournaments and professional franchises. Despite the pleas of those in support of public financing of the proposed facility, voters in Birmingham turned down the measure.

CITY BACKGROUND: PHOENIX, ARIZONA

The city of Phoenix (population 1,218,823) is the sixth-largest city in the United States. Phoenix sits in sprawling Maricopa County, Arizona, which includes thirteen communities (among them Tempe, Mesa, Scottsdale, and Avondale). Maricopa County has consistently led the nation in population growth over the past decade. The county has seen a 32-percent increase in population over an eight-year period to reach its estimated 1998 population of 2,803,300. It is the nation's fifth-largest county in terms of population size, and also the fourteenth largest in the continental United States in land area (Greater Phoenix Economic Council 1999).

Over the past decade Phoenix has come to represent a model U.S. city. It has received countless national awards and recognition for its economic vitality, business climate, tourist appeal, and casual lifestyle. Phoenix is known as the golf capital of the world, is home to more five-star/diamond resorts than any other location, considered the airline hub of the southwest, is home to several of the nation's largest corporations, and is near to scenic Arizona destinations like the Grand Canyon and Sedona. Among the major corporations that call Phoenix home are Motorola, Bank One Arizona, America West Airlines, and Best Western Hotels (Greater Phoenix Economic Council 1999).

The city of Phoenix has slowly evolved from a tourism- and resource-based economy to a major center for high-tech manufacturing, customer-service operations, distribution, and professional services. As a part of this evolution, the greater Phoenix area has experienced dramatic increases in the number of available jobs. The city experienced an employment growth rate of 174 percent over the past twenty years (compared with 50 percent nationally) (Greater Phoenix Economic Council 1999). *Fortune* (1998) magazine has credited greater Phoenix with having the fastest-growing large labor market in the nation for the past four years. According to *Fortune*, the region has created 378,650 new jobs since 1990 (*Fortune* 1998).

The city of Phoenix operates under a mayor–manager form of government. The Phoenix City Council is comprised of a mayor and eight council members elected by the people on a nonpartisan ballot for four-year terms. The mayor is elected at large, while council members are elected by voters in each of the eight districts they represent. The mayor and council serve as the legislative and policy-making body of the municipal government. Together they enact city ordinances and appropriate funds to the administrative staff. The city manager works with the mayor and council to assist them in developing policies and programs. Responsible for overseeing more than 13,000 city employees, the city manager is also responsible for the efficient operation of all city services as set forth by the city council. The current city manager, Frank Fairbanks, was appointed by the Phoenix city council in April 1990. He answers to Mayor Skip Rimsza (elected in 1994) and the city council for the day-to-day management and operation of the city.

Mayor Skip Rimsza prides himself in calling Phoenix the "Best Run City in the World" (City of Phoenix 1997). As such, the city has adopted a credo of providing "Seamless Service" to its customers, the citizens of Phoenix. This approach to governance takes the approach of reducing bureaucratic red tape for citizens. According to Mayor Rimsza, Phoenix prides itself on providing efficient and courteous service to its citizens.

PHOENIX'S ATTEMPT TO ESTABLISH ITSELF AS A MAJOR LEAGUE CITY

The city of Phoenix's attempt to establish itself as a major league city—economically speaking—began during a post–World War II transition period. By the early 1940s Phoenix had reached its apex as a farming and distribution center. During the war Phoenix rapidly turned into a fledgling industrial city. With the arrival of thousands of soldiers in Phoenix, large industry learned of this new labor pool and started moving branches to the city. In addition, smaller plants were started by private capital and local initiative. By the end of the 1940s Phoenix had a wealth of technology to fall back on.

During its growth into one of America's prominent cities, Phoenix has been fortunate to have a community that has supported development efforts. Since 1950 the residents of Phoenix have shown their faith in city government by approving bond issues totaling about $3.5 billion for improvements in urban facilities and services. In 1988 the residents of Phoenix approved one of the largest general-purpose municipal-bond elections ever. Among the projects financed by these bonds was the development of Phoenix Sky Harbor International Airport, which serves almost 25 million commercial passengers a year and is among the fastest-growing airports in the country; building of the twenty-story Phoenix City Hall; opening of the central library in 1995; and construction of the History Museum and Arizona Science Center in 1996 (City of Phoenix 1997c).

Professional sports franchises have also played a role in Phoenix's effort to establish itself as a major league city. The city is currently home to numerous major league sports teams. Among these are the NBA Phoenix Suns, the NFL Arizona Cardinals, the WNBA Phoenix Mercury, the NHL Phoenix Coyotes, the AFL Arizona Rattlers, and the MLB Arizona Diamondbacks. The city is also home to a number of minor league teams, the WCHL Phoenix Mustangs and the CISL Arizona Sandsharks. In 1996 Phoenix became headquarters of the Western Professional Hockey League. The league, founded by savvy sports entrepreneur Rick Kozuback, has flourished into one of the premier minor hockey leagues in the Southwest and Southeast.

Phoenix's attempt to establish itself as a major league sports town has also been evidenced by the city's relationship with the Cactus League. The Cactus League, which serves as a spring training module for several MLB teams, has been hosted by Phoenix (as well as other Arizona cities) since the mid-1950s. Local residents, civic leaders, and state politicians have argued that the Cactus League serves as a major tourist attraction and has a "direct economic impact on the state" (Geiger 1999). Because the city of Phoenix serves as one of the host cities for the lucrative Cactus League, the state of Arizona has a vested interested in ensuring that Phoenix has high-quality baseball facilities.

Phoenix has undertaken a concerted effort to display an image that it is receptive to major league sports franchises. The city was very proactive in working with private investor Jerry Colangelo to construct America West Arena in the city's downtown area. As a part of this public–private partnership, the city committed $35 million toward capital construction and $12 million to be responsible for land assemblage. The remaining cost, $105 million, was contributed by the Phoenix Suns of the National Basketball Association—owned by Colangelo. The Suns have underlying use of the arena, while the city retains the land and improvements to the arena (Geiger 1999). The city administration's major impetus behind building America West Arena was a need to move the Suns from the city's Veterans Memorial Coliseum into an arena that could offer revenue-generating luxury skyboxes, a trend that was just beginning in professional basketball.

The city of Phoenix also added to its major league status in the late 1980s by successfully wooing the St. Louis Cardinals of the NFL from Busch Stadium to Sun Devil Stadium on the campus of Arizona State University. The city's coup came after the Cardinal's battle with the city of St. Louis over building a new stadium strictly for football. When the team announced it was interested in leaving St. Louis, Phoenix, as well as five other cities, expressed interest in landing the team. In the spring of 1988 the Cardinals announced plans to leave St. Louis for Phoenix. Less than a decade later, the city landed the Phoenix Coyotes of the National Hockey League and the Phoenix Mercury of the Women's National Basketball Association, additional indicators of Phoenix becoming a major league sports town.

ECONOMIC DEVELOPMENT STRATEGY: THE CITY OF PHOENIX AND MARICOPA COUNTY

The city of Phoenix enjoys a healthy economy that has attracted national and international attention. Phoenix's economic success story is largely a result of a progressive economic-development strategy. The city's economic-development strategy is premised on strategic partnerships with numerous economic partners, including the Greater Phoenix Chamber of Commerce, Phoenix Community Alliance, Downtown Phoenix Partnership, Greater Phoenix Convention and Visitors Bureau, Arizona Department of Commerce, and Greater Phoenix Economic Council. These partnerships have created a synergy whereby new investments in the local economy have resulted. In addition, such partnerships have contributed to a positive job-growth rate that has spanned the last fifty years (City of Phoenix 1997b).

In Phoenix, the mayor and city council set policy relating to the city's role in economic-development activities. The Community and Economic Development Department is the lead actor in the city's efforts to strengthen the local economy. Under the direction of the mayor and city council, the department focuses on (1) creating employment opportunities, (2) enhancing they city's business environment, (3) increasing city revenue, and (4) improving the quality of life (City of Phoenix 1997b). The city has also demonstrated a recognition of the importance of creating employment opportunities for its residents and generating revenue for city services.

While Phoenix's economic-development policies take into account a public input network, the most influential actors are arguably the numerous appointed boards and commissions, community agencies, and local organizations that work with the city council and city management. For example, the Phoenix Commission on the Economy reviews city council issues and makes recommendations to the council concerning the development of a vital Phoenix economy from the perspective of private industry. The commission has aided the city in developing policy positions on retail development, commercial industrial development, and regulatory issues (City of Phoenix 1997b). The Greater Phoenix Economic Council, a cooperative effort of Maricopa County and thirteen communities within it along with more than 150 private-sector business partners, serves as the region's official economic-development authority. The council provides assistance to corporate entities seeking to relocate or expand to the greater Phoenix area (Greater Phoenix Economic Council 1999).

The city of Phoenix's economic-development strategies are also corroborated by those of Maricopa County's board of supervisors. The county government consists of a board of supervisors with five members who work to provide services and resources to county residents. The county's economic-development strategy is based upon (1) attraction of business and retention of established organizations, (2) implementing programs directed at improving the region's business climate, (3) promoting professional sports, tourism, and small-business development, and (4) providing strategic information to businesses to foster decisions (Maricopa County Economic Development Strategy 1997). Under the direction of the county administrative officer, David Smith, the Maricopa County board of supervisors has been able to achieve an upgrade in its bond ratings, lower tax rates, and implement a quarter-cent sales tax for construction of a major league baseball stadium (Smith 1999).

BANK ONE BALLPARK, MAJOR LEAGUE BASEBALL, AND ECONOMIC DEVELOPMENT IN THE CITY OF PHOENIX

Beginning in the mid-1980s, the city of Phoenix undertook a downtown development strategy focused on enhancing the city's economic development. Attraction and retention of professional sports franchises has been a key strategy in the city's efforts to revitalize its downtown area. As a result of a push for downtown development, Phoenix has seen more than $1.5 billion in public and private investment poured into downtown development projects over the past fifteen years (Downtown Development 1999). Of the projects recently completed in downtown Phoenix, two of the most lucrative were oriented toward professional sports: the $100-million America West Arena, and the $370-million Bank One Ballpark. These two "trophy-case" projects have contributed to the nearly 4 million visitors who visit downtown Phoenix annually (Frienden and Sagalyn 1989).

According to Jerry Geiger (1999), deputy director for the city's Community and Economic Development Department, Phoenix's economic environment and overall development objectives have mirrored that of other major cities across the country. Major league sports franchises have become just one piece to the puzzle of the city's economic-development plans. Attracting a major league baseball franchise to Phoenix had long been a goal that had somehow eluded the city. When the city made it a conscious strategy to reinvigorate the downtown area in an effort to combat the exodus of downtown businesses to more suburban settings, former mayors Paul Johnson and Terry Goddard pushed for a new baseball ballpark in downtown Phoenix. However, the city was never successful in achieving this goal.

Supporters of a new ballpark argued that the stadium would serve to offset the impact of corporate abandonment of downtown Phoenix. The city was faced with the reality of losing one of its downtown corporate citizens when the Dial Corporation, one of the city's larger employers, announced that it would leave its office tower in downtown for industrial-type space in Scottsdale, Arizona. According to Dan Dever of the Greater Phoenix Economic Council, many corporate entities in Phoenix had begun to follow the national trend toward abandoning downtown high-rise offices for "midrise suburban markets." By the early 1990s the city of Phoenix had begun to realize it faced the tough challenge of recovering from a massive 1980s overbuilding binge that saw a 19.6-percent downtown vacancy rate in the face of corporate flight to the suburbs (Fatsis 1997).

HOW MAJOR LEAGUE BASEBALL CAME TO PHOENIX

In early 1990 a series of events began to unfold which would threaten Phoenix and the state of Arizona's economic vitality and image as a major league sports destination. The Cleveland Indians, one of several teams that conducted their spring training in the Cactus League, made a surprising revelation that they were considering moving their spring training operations to Florida's Grapefruit League. Subsequent to the announcement by the Indians, a number of other teams training in the Cactus League announced they too would consider moving their operations to Florida if the Indians left. These threats led many state legislators to believe the Cactus League was in jeopardy of losing all of its teams. This was a stark reality for many politicians, as the Cactus League was estimated to have a $220-million annual economic impact on Maricopa County, roughly the equivalent to having a Super Bowl every year (Geiger 1999).

As a consequence of the announcements made by the teams in the Cactus League, the Arizona legislature passed an act (Title 48, Chapter 26, Arizona Revised Statutes) that allowed for the formation of a stadium district by the board of supervisors of each county having a population of more than 1.5 million, or any county in which a major league baseball organization established or sought to establish a spring training operation. This legislation, according to Jerry Geiger (1999), was intended to provide a mechanism to stabilize the Cactus League. The two counties in which Cactus League play took place, Maricopa and Pima, formed stadium districts as a result of the Arizona statute (the Maricopa County Stadium District was formed in September 1991). The enabling legislation allowed for the stadium district to invoke a car-rental surcharge as a source of funding for the stadium district to generate bonding capacity. From the revenue raised, the Maricopa County Stadium District contributed over $66 million to several cities within the county toward Cactus League facilities (Maricopa County Stadium District 1997). These new facilities gave reassurance to the county that the Cactus League would stay in Arizona for years to come.

In addition to its goal of improving MLB spring training facilities in the county, the Maricopa County Stadium District also had as its goal the construction and maintenance of a new MLB stadium. A statute passed by the Arizona legislature in 1990 had already authorized counties meeting the same criteria as mentioned to form a tax-levying district for the purpose of building a stadium. A number of stipulations, however, were put in place before the stadium could be financed. One requirement was that an MLB franchise had to be awarded within the district. Second, the district board of directors was to require financial participation from (1) the county or municipality in which the stadium was to be located, (2) a private party, or (3) a combination of both, which equaled or exceeded one-half of the amount to be expended by the district. Further, the Arizona legislature stipulated that the stadium could not be used for National Football League games (Geiger 1999).

Much of the financial matters behind constructing an MLB ballpark in downtown Phoenix had been resolved by the time a franchise was awarded to wealthy Phoenix entrepreneur Jerry Colangelo in March 1995. The Maricopa County Stadium District revealed plans for a quarter-cent stadium tax well before the district knew an MLB franchise would be awarded within the county. On February 17, 1994, the district entered into an agreement with the Arizona Professional Baseball Team Limited Partnership to provide the financing for a portion of the cost of land acquisition and construction of a new ballpark. It was not until later, in March 1995, that Colangelo was awarded an MLB franchise. Upon receipt of the franchise, the stadium district was legally authorized to invoke the quarter-cent sales tax to raise $253 million toward a new ballpark, and wasted no time by announcing an April 1995 beginning date for the tax. Doing so would prove to be controversial, however, because unlike in most states and municipalities, the stadium tax proposal was not put to a popular vote of the people.

The financial plans behind financing an MLB ballpark in downtown Phoenix called for the stadium district to spend $238 million garnered from a quarter-cent sales tax that was not to sunset before April 1998. The district was originally obligated to borrow up to $15 million more for project costs, bringing the total public financial burden to $253 million. The franchise owned by Jerry Colangelo, the Arizona Diamondbacks, relieved the district of this $15-million obligation. As a result, the Diamondbacks franchise promised to contribute a total of $111 million toward the ballpark. As a part of the plan, the Diamondbacks franchise would be responsible for managing the new stadium, play in the stadium for thirty years, and, if sold, pay the district $5 million. From the Diamondbacks' use of the $349-million ballpark, the district would also receive a minimum of $1 million in license fees annually, 5 percent of suite license revenues, 5 percent of premium seat sales, $325,000 annually from stadium naming rights, as well as more than $1 million in other revenues (Maricopa County Stadium District 1997).

Supporters of the new ballpark attempted to garner public acceptance of the tax through a number of economic-impact studies. According to the Downtown Phoenix Partnership, the construction of the ballpark would create over 3,000 full-time jobs over a two-year construction period and generate $12.2 million in fiscal revenue for the state of Arizona. Further, the stadium would serve as a catalyst toward reinvigorating the downtown area (Downtown Phoenix Partnership 1998). The ballpark-financing plan was promoted by the Maricopa County Stadium District as one that would "protect the taxpayer" (Maricopa County Stadium District 1997). According to the stadium district, the cap placed on the amount of tax dollars that could be spent on the construction of the stadium would protect taxpayers from overruns in costs. Further, once the stadium was constructed the district could not require the public to pay for general operations and maintenance expenses associated with the stadium. Perhaps in a pleading fashion, the district noted that the financial agreement had been nationally recognized as "among the best of recent baseball deals" (Maricopa County Stadium District 1997).

To say that the stadium-financing plans proffered by the stadium district were controversial is a major understatement. The case of Phoenix represents one of the most polemical and contentious examples of community dissent toward public financing of a major league ballpark. Efforts to halt the enactment of the stadium district's quarter-cent sales tax became commonplace in Phoenix. In March 1995 opponents of the tax, spearheaded by grassroots activist Art Kaufman and Ernest Hancock, launched ballot efforts at the state and county levels and even took one issue to the courts. Among their goals were to force a statewide vote amending the law by which the stadium tax was enacted and to get the court to decide exactly how the public could challenge actions of the stadium district. According to Hancock, the state of Arizona had "created an entirely new branch of government . . . immune from the people" (Flannery 1995). Shared sentiment spread throughout the community, as many people were infuriated over the stadium district's refusal to put the quarter-cent sales-tax idea to a popular vote. In fact, preliminary polls had demonstrated that, if put to a vote, the stadium tax would fail. According to local activist Art Kaufman, the state of Arizona should have amended the statute, giving the stadium district the right to tax by requiring a public vote of approval before any county could do so (Flannery 1995).

The assaults on the Maricopa County Stadium District began to come hard and heavy shortly after the tax was levied. A local resident, seventy-three-year-old Herb Knauss, took his complaint about the sales tax to federal court, claiming that invoking a tax without allowing him a vote violated his U.S. constitutional rights. Knauss also took the time to design, print, and distribute thousands of prank postcards, which he sent to the Maricopa County board of supervisors insisting that the stadium be labeled the "Maricopa Tax Dome" (Davis 1995). In a span of only six months, local Arizona courts had thrown out over four cases contesting the tax. Some opponents of the tax even went to extremes to get their point across. Stadium-district member Mary Rose Wilcox was shot by a man who claimed he was "trying to stop the political dictatorship of Jerry Colangelo, supervisors, and legislators in pushing the baseball stadium tax" (Miller 1997). The fallout from the tax was also said to be responsible for the electoral defeats of district members Ed King and Jim Bruner. Threats to life and limb of Diamondbacks owner Jerry Colangelo, as well as head of the Downtown Phoenix Partnership Margaret Mullen, were also common. Colangelo was forced to install bulletproof glass in the windows of his Bank One Ballpark office, while Mullen was shot at and received numerous death threats (Miller 1997).

With the stadium tax a reality, construction on what many consider to be one of the most elaborate yet ostentatious ballparks ever conceived began on November 16, 1995, and was completed in March 1998. The ballpark, whose naming rights were bought by Bank One, features approximately 48,500 seats, an unprecedented retractable roof, a natural-grass playing surface, a swimming pool in the stands, a 10,500-square-foot interactive baseball theme park, a 2,000-square-foot

Hall of Fame, a children's playland in center field, and 110 picnic tables, and is the only major league facility in the United States to have a McDonald's restaurant on the inside (Maricopa County Stadium District 1999). In all, private investor Jerry Colangelo and Maricopa County Stadium District officials felt they hammered out a good deal. One stadium district member had the following to say about Bank One Ballpark:

It's still a good deal. Negotiating for sports teams is a dreadful task. More cities want them than are available and politicians loath to put taxpayer money at risk. It combines to reduce the public's leverage when its negotiators sit across the table from professional sport-franchise moguls. . . . Rightly or wrongly, cities fall all over themselves for professional sports franchises. We just didn't have to fall all over as much as the others. (Miller 1995)

CONCLUSION

The case of Bank One Ballpark in Phoenix, Arizona, demonstrates that state legislatures remain dominant players in the procurement of major league sports. After years of being unsuccessful in garnering public support for financing a major league baseball park, the city of Phoenix received the help it needed when the state of Arizona enacted a critical piece of legislation. By passing a statute permitting for creation of a special stadium district, the state of Arizona provided the county in which Phoenix sits, Maricopa County, the ability to tax its residents for the purpose of generating revenue to go toward a public–private stadium-financing partnership. This stadium district was given full taxing power as a legal subdivision of the state. In essence, this allowed the district to levy a tax without a vote of public approval. The notion that the state of Arizona would allow a county to have such power for financing a professional sports stadium raises important questions about democratic decision making. The levying of a tax toward constructing a major league ballpark would have been voted down by the people of Maricopa County, according to many polls. As such, one can question the legitimacy of the county stadium district's option to place such external costs on the citizens in light of the majority's obvious opposition. This case will continue to reverberate throughout the community and nation for a long time to come.

REFERENCES

Arizona Revised Statutes, Title 48, Chapter 26, 4201 (1997).
Baade, Robert A. 1994. Stadiums, Professional Sports, and Economic Development: Assessing the Reality. *Heartland Policy Study* 62 (28 March): 1–39. Detroit: Heartland Institute.

Baade, Robert A., and Richard F. Dye. 1998. Best Cities for Business Survey. *Fortune* (November).

Baade, Robert A., and Richard F. Dye. 1990. The Impact of Stadiums and Professional Sports on Metropolitan Area Development. *Growth and Change* 21: 1–14.

Baim, Dean V. 1994. *The Sports Stadium as a Municipal Investment*. Westport, Conn.: Greenwood Press.

City of Phoenix. 1997a. *City of Phoenix 1997 Annual Citizen's Report*. City of Phoenix. Arizona.

City of Phoenix. 1997b. *Community and Economic Development Report 1997*. City of Phoenix.

City of Phoenix. 1997c. *History of the City of Phoenix*. City of Phoenix.

Davis, Bill. 1995. Stadium Hit With Federal Lawsuit. *Scottsdale Tribune*, 15 June, p. B3.

Downtown Phoenix Partnership. 1998. Economic and Fiscal Impact of Bank One Ballpark and Arizona Diamondback Report 10 (10 September).

Fatsis, Stefan. 1997. Phoenix Looks to Hit Home Run. *Wall Street Journal*, 28 March, sec. B, p. 12.

Flannery, Pat. 1995. Stadium Tax under Fire, Again. *Phoenix Gazette*, 1 March, p. 1B.

Fortune Magazine. 1998. Best Cities for Business Survey. 23 November, p. 142.

Frienden, Bernard J., and Lynne B. Sagalyn. 1989. *Downtown Inc.: How America Rebuilds Cities*. Cambridge: MIT Press.

Geiger, Jerry, Deputy Director, Community and Economic Development Department, Phoenix, Arizona. 1999. Telephone interviews with author, February.

Greater Phoenix Economic Council. 1999. *Greater Phoenix Fact Book*.

History of Phoenix. City of Phoenix, Arizona. http://www.ci.phoenix.az.us.

Johnson, Arthur T. 1986. Economic and Policy Implications of Hosting Sports Franchises: Lessons from Baltimore. *Urban Affairs Quarterly* 21: 411–433.

Kalich, Veronica Z. 1998. A Public Choice Perspective on the Subsidization of Private Industry: A Case Study of Three Cities and Three Stadiums. *Journal of Urban Affairs* 20: 199–219.

Maricopa County Stadium District. 1997. *Maricopa County Business Strategies Report* (July). Maricopa County, Arizona.

Maricopa County Stadium District. 1997. *Summary of Bank One Ballpark Transactions Report*. Maricopa County, Arizona.

Mathesian, Charles. 1998. The Stadium Trap. *Governing* 11: 22–24.

Miller, Eric. 1997. No-Vote Tax Built Ballpark, Bitterness. *Arizona Republic*, 23 November, p. A1.

Miller, Eric. 1995. How Stadium Deal Stacks Up. *Arizona Republic*, 18 June, p. A1.

Quirk, James, and Rodney D. Fort. 1992. *Pay Dirt: The Business of Professional Team Sports*. Princeton: Princeton University Press.

Rich, Wilbur C. 1998. Professional Sports, Economic Development and Public Policy. *Policy Studies Review* 15: 1–2.

Riess, Steven. 1998. Historical Perspectives on Sport and Public Policy. In Wilbur C. Rich, Professional Sports, Economic Development and Public Policy. *Policy Studies Review* 15: 3–15.

Rosentraub, Mark S., David Swindell, Michael Przybylski, and Daniel R. Mulling. 1994. Sport and Downtown Development Strategy: If You Build It, Will Jobs Come? *Journal of Urban Affairs* 16: 221–239.

Smith, David. 1999. County Administrative Officer, Maricopa County, Arizona. http://www.maricopa.go.

Zimbalist, Andrew. 1998. The Economics of Stadiums, Teams and Cities. *Policy Studies Review* 15: 17–29.

5

The Politics of Planning and Developing New Sports Facilities: The Case of Zephyrs Park and the New Orleans Arena

Robert K. Whelan and Alma H. Young

The relationship of professional sports to urban development is a topic which has occupied both academics and policy makers in recent years. Across North America, big-city mayors and governors (and provincial premiers) have struggled with difficult choices in providing new sports facilities for professional teams. An academic literature has emerged, which usually urges caution and analysis in the development of these facilities (Danielson 1997; Johnson 1993; Rosentraub 1997; Zimbalist 1992 are examples). Yet in the real world, stadiums and arenas are often built without caution and analysis. If there is cautious criticism and analysis these concerns are often ignored. Why is this the case?

This chapter will consider the politics of planning and development in the construction of two facilities in the New Orleans metropolitan area in the 1990s: a new minor league baseball stadium in Jefferson Parish (the suburban parish adjacent to New Orleans), and a new arena in downtown New Orleans, adjacent to the New Orleans Superdome.

There are three points that we will make. First, the election cycles of politicians are such that the construction of public facilities is almost always desirable from the perspective of local officials. In the long run, a stadium may not be an economic success. In the short run, politicians get credit for the construction of the facility. Second, regional competition and cooperation are more subtle phenomena than their usual characterizations in the literature. Everyone knows about franchise shifts from one metropolitan area to another—the most famous examples are the 1957 relocation of the Brooklyn Dodgers and the New York Giants to Los Angeles and San Francisco (Sullivan 1987), and the "flight by night" of the Baltimore Colts to Indianapolis. Some students characterize the moves of a franchise from city to suburb (as in the New York Giants and Jets move to the Meadowlands) as franchise shifts, although they remain within the same metropolitan area. Recently, we have seen some variations on this theme, as teams move from suburb to city (the Minnesota Twins moved from Bloomington to Minneapolis), and as teams build "old-fashioned, city" stadiums in suburban locations (such as The Ballpark at Arlington, Texas). In our case, we see the forces of regional competition at work in a highly fragmented metropolitan area. Third, planning and evaluation are not required in stadium development. When they occur, planning and evaluation studies are often ignored. Why is this the case?

To present the New Orleans case, we will first discuss the existing sports facilities in the New Orleans area. These include the Superdome, the Municipal Auditorium, the University of New Orleans (UNO) Kiefer Lakefront Arena, Privateer Park (UNO baseball field), and Fogelman Arena (Tulane's arena). After the discussion of existing facilities, we will present two complex and interrelated case studies: the development of Zephyrs Park in Jefferson Parish, and the construction of a new arena in downtown New Orleans. Finally, we will try to reach some conclusions from these cases about the politics of planning and urban development.

EXISTING FACILITIES

First and foremost, there is the Louisiana Superdome, which was built using state bond authority in the 1970s. The bonds were repaid by the imposition of a hotel/motel tax in New Orleans (Orleans Parish) and Jefferson Parish, the large suburban parish which borders New Orleans to its west. Mayor Moon Landrieu and former governors John McKeithen and Edwin W. Edwards were instrumental in getting the Dome built. Patronage resulting from the construction of the Dome (e.g., concessions contracts) was used to reward their political supporters, including African-American politicians who were supporters of these white political leaders.

The Superdome has been most successful as a football arena, where it is home to the New Orleans Saints (NFL) and Tulane University football teams. The Sugar Bowl and the Bayou Classic (between Southern University and Grambling University) games are annual events which fill the dome and bring large numbers of tourists to the city. Several Super Bowls have been held in New Orleans, and the city is said to be a favored site in NFL opinion because of its good weather, the availability of many hotel rooms, and the proximity of the hotel rooms to the Superdome and to restaurants and entertainment.

Other sports have not been so successful in the Superdome. The large 70,000-seat stadium makes basketball spectators remote from the action. In a smaller configuration (25,000 seats), the Dome is an excellent basketball facility, as it was for the 1999 NCAA regionals. In the larger configuration, it will again host the Final Four in 2003. Although several successful NCAA Final Four tournaments have been held at the Superdome, the NBA was not successful. Although the NBA New Orleans Jazz held some individual-game attendance records, overall the team was not supported well. The franchise left New Orleans for Utah in 1979 after five years of mediocre fan support.

The Superdome facility is poorly suited for baseball in the opinion of MLB people. Major league rules will not accept the short foul lines in the Superdome baseball configuration. The transition from artificial turf to concrete in foul ground is also unacceptable by major league standards. One informed observer compared Dome baseball to "shooting marbles in a bathtub." The fiscal reality of today's major league baseball is such that New Orleans is considered far too small to support a team, with only 1.3 million people in the metropolitan area. A minor league team (AAA) based at the Dome in the late 1970s was a failure at the box office. The franchise was moved, and the city was not represented in professional baseball for fifteen years. During that time, New Orleans was the largest U.S. city without professional baseball of any kind.

We have written about other aspects of the Superdome on several other occasions. The Superdome is often credited with the revival of Poydras Street and the skyscraper development of New Orleans in the 1970s. It has been the site of many conventions, including the 1988 Republican Party National Convention. But the fact is that the city has built, and extended, the Ernest N. Morial Convention Center as its major convention facility in the last two decades. This supplants the Dome's convention function. Second, the Dome is a limited venue for concerts and entertainment. The economics are such that only events such as the Essence Fest (a large summer music festival oriented to an African-American audience) or star performers (such as Celine Dion, Michael Jackson, Bette Midler, and the Rolling Stones) can succeed at the Superdome.

Besides the Superdome, other arena facilities exist in New Orleans. There is the Kiefer Arena, built primarily for the University of New

Orleans, with state monies. The arena opened in 1983, and it has 11,000 seats. In addition to UNO sports (basketball, volleyball), the arena hosts concerts and other performances. As a medium-size arena, it does not attract the biggest events, but it has brought in performers like Sting, Madonna, and Ray Charles.

There is also the Municipal Auditorium, the old sporting venue in downtown New Orleans. It was the site of boxing matches and college basketball games in the 1950s and 1960s, and it is still the site of Mardi Gras balls. In the 1990s the auditorium was, briefly, the temporary site of the land-based Harrah's Casino. The failure of the temporary casino was attributed by some to the fact that people are afraid to come downtown at night. After minor league hockey arrived in New Orleans in 1997, several thousand people on game night come downtown to that same old Municipal Auditorium facility to watch the New Orleans Brass (ECHL) play. The Mardi Gras balls, always a priority in New Orleans, present a problem for the hockey team, which must endure long road trips during Mardi Gras season.

There is Fogelman Arena, Tulane University's on-campus basketball facility. The arena seats 3,600, which is very small for a major college program in Division One. In the early 1990s, Tulane filled its arena to capacity while it had several excellent teams. More recently, the team has not done as well, and attendance has declined to averages of 2,400 in 1997–1998, and 1,700 in 1998–1999.

In review, it is clear that any new major indoor facility would have major impacts on the existing facilities—possibly positive, possibly negative, or possibly some combination. These facilities are also all located in central city New Orleans: The Municipal Auditorium and Superdome are downtown; the Kiefer Arena, on the UNO East Campus, is located on the Lake Pontchartrain Lakefront; and the Fogelman Arena, on the Tulane campus, is located uptown.

THE MINOR LEAGUE BASEBALL STADIUM

In 1993, minor league baseball returned to New Orleans when the Denver Zephyrs AAA franchise relocated because of the creation of the Colorado Rockies (National League) club (Whitford 1993). The team was owned by John Dikeou, a Denver-based parking entrepreneur. At the time there was a dispute between Dikeou and New Orleans Saints owner Tom Benson, who wanted to purchase Charlotte's AA baseball franchise and move it to New Orleans. Organized baseball rules give priority to the higher classification. Benson had $100,000 down on a Double A franchise, and he had a lease to use UNO's baseball stadium. It cost the Zephyrs ownership dearly to buy off Benson's legal challenge. AAA rules require a 10,000-seat stadium. Since no such stadium was immediately available, the New Orleans Zephyrs played at the University of New Orleans baseball field, Privateer Park.

Privateer Park is a beautiful field, kept immaculately by UNO head coach and groundskeeper Tom Schwaner. The Zephyrs contributed heavily to the improvement of Privateer Park, by installing new lights, an electronic scoreboard, and new seating. However, Privateer Park could not have been a modern AAA league facility without substantial improvement. Even with new seats, the overwhelming majority of seats lacked chair backs, a creature comfort demanded by many fans. Bathroom facilities were inadequate, both in number and quality, and there are experts in baseball marketing who think that numerous, clean restrooms are vital to a franchise's economic success (Wolff 1998). Some people were afraid to attend games at the lakefront. The structure of contemporary minor league baseball is such that New Orleans needed a new baseball facility if it wanted to be a part of professional baseball. A minor league baseball stadium was part of a 1990 report by the Jefferson Parish Economic Development Agency (JEDCO) on facility needs for economic development.

In 1992 Jefferson Parish legislators tried to obtain state help in financing a new baseball stadium. This effort was spearheaded by former State Senator Hank Lauricella, a Jefferson Parish and power structure figure. Lauricella had longtime sports connections, since he was a star single-wing tailback on General Robert Neyland's University of Tennessee teams in the early 1950s. This first attempt failed because Orleans Parish legislators wanted the stadium in New Orleans. In 1993 New Orleans Mayor Sidney Barthelemy and Louisiana Governor Edwin Edwards crafted a successful political deal: Jefferson Parish got its minor league baseball stadium and New Orleans got a new downtown arena. Under the Stadium Bill (House 2013, Act 640, 1993), Jefferson Parish received $20 million for a baseball stadium and $6 million for a football training facility for the New Orleans Saints, owned by Edwards's political ally and contributor, Tom Benson. The first bonds issued by the State Bond Commission, in the fall of 1993, were for planning studies for these facilities. The second issue of bonds, in 1994, included the actual baseball stadium. The construction of the facilities was financed by an extension of the hotel/motel tax in New Orleans and Jefferson Parish, which had paid for the Superdome bonds. This tax was scheduled to expire in 2001, and was extended for the refinancing period. While New Orleans always provided the great majority of these revenues (85%), Jefferson Parish hotels contributed a significant minority (15%). This gave an economic rationale, as well as a political reason, to build a stadium in Jefferson Parish.

In the first planning phase, Hellmuth Obata Kassabaum (HOK), a nationally recognized recreational- and sports-facility architectural firm, was retained to draft the program of requirements for the new stadium. HOK is the firm which is responsible for the planning of several of the newer successful major league parks, such as Camden Yards in Baltimore. The plan considers such amenities as parking (3,350 total spaces) and seats (10,000 comfortable seats with good sightlines), as well as toilets and concession stands. The new stadium was planned with adequate ticket windows and, of course, the inevitable luxury suites. Their planning feasibility study cost $210,000, and included $12,700,000 in costs for the stadium. The actual building, including options such as a scoreboard, would bring cost to $19,647,000.

The baseball stadium project was beset by the inevitable delays which occur with public-sector projects of this type. Feasibility studies are never completed as quickly as desired. The coordination of many diverse public and private entities is necessary in a project of this type. There was really no single agency designated for the coordination of the stadium project, although the Superdome Commission, as the owner of the new stadium, came closest.

From the perspective of Jefferson Parish authorities, the baseball stadium was "a central piece, but only a piece of an overall development plan for a 150 acre tract referred to as the LaSalle Development" (Evans 1994). This planned development also includes the New Orleans Saints training facility and other recreational uses for the general public. A feasibility plan for the LaSalle tract had been adopted by the Jefferson Parish Council in 1991, following a study by Economics Research Associates (ERA) of Chicago. HOK were then selected to develop a master plan and to design the stadium. The parish owns the property on which the stadium was built. This property is leased to the state, via the Superdome Commission, which built the baseball stadium and football training facility. The remaining green space is leased back to Jefferson Parish.

The sale of bonds took longer than expected, with the actual sale of bonds for construction of the stadium not occurring until August 1995. In January 1995, Rob Couhig, a Jefferson Parish attorney and political activist, bought the Zephyrs franchise from John Dikeou. This gave the team local ownership with connections to local and state politicians. Along the way the sale was delayed when New Orleans legislators walked out of a meeting, leaving it without a quorum, because of Jefferson Parish support for rechanneling arena bonds to the convention center. Sherman Copelin, a legislative leader from New Orleans, was quoted as saying, "I am not convinced we ever need to build a new stadium. I don't know if the attendance demands it" (Anderson 1995). The attempt at redirecting arena funds failed, and the baseball stadium and the arena was saved. Couhig and his partners signed a ten-year lease with the Superdome Commission in 1995 to play at the new stadium. Groundbreaking for the stadium finally occurred on November 30, 1995.

A new stadium is often expected to have wider positive impacts on a neighborhood or city. In the case of the Zephyrs Park, there has been hope that the stadium will stimulate development along Airline Highway, the old road into New Orleans. The location of a new stadium on Airline provided a contrast to the large numbers of run-down trailer parks, bars, and motels on that part of the street. For example, stadium development might stimulate the construction of a new hotel, which could draw some of its clientele from visiting teams and sports-minded tourists.

Another problem causing delay was caused by a city–state dispute after the election of a new governor, Murphy (Mike) Foster, in 1995. This dispute resulted in the parish paying for sewer and water lines on parish-owned land to the state-owned baseball stadium, and the state buying thirty acres from two private companies for the parish recreation park.

To review, a state agency (the Superdome Commission) paid for the stadium and owns it. The State Department of Transportation and Development controls Airline Highway outside the stadium, because it is a state highway. Thus, the state government was responsible for transportation improvements and planning. The land on which the stadium is built is owned by Jefferson Parish. The parish wanted to buy thirty adjacent acres for a public park. The thirty acres, in turn, were owned by two private companies: the Kansas City Southern Railroad and Robco Inc., a local development firm. This is complicated enough—two levels of government, and the private sector. In a project of this type, many other outside people—consultants, engineers, lawyers, and architects—are involved. And in this era of term limitations the cast of characters is always changing in state and local government. Thus, we have new governors, new parish presidents, new state legislators, and new parish council members. As Pressman and Wildavsky (1973) observed many years ago, with this many blocking points, it's a wonder that anything gets done!

In spite of the delays, the stadium was constructed in time for the 1997 season. Team owner Rob Couhig touted the stadium "as an economic engine for East Jefferson" (Mulé 1996). Once the stadium was opened, the whole story changes, both on the field and off. The new stadium was an instant success, with the Zephyrs drawing over 500,000 fans in their first two seasons. These are among the highest figures in the minor leagues (sixth overall in 1997, for example). The successful attendance is based on several factors. First, there is location. The new ballpark is located in close proximity to a middle-class, largely white population in Jefferson Parish. Moreover, the stadium is generally accessible by highway to anyone in the metropolitan area. Second, there is the facility itself. The park is pleasant, with good seating, easy parking, and plenty of concessions and bathrooms. You can sit on the grass in left field if you want an inexpensive evening at the ballpark, or you can rent the hot tub in right field if you want to be sybaritic. Third, there is promotion. As in most successful minor league franchises, there are promotions almost every evening. There are fireworks after every Friday night game. Many spectators attend because going to the game is a "social" event.

Finally, there is on-the-field success. After 1996 the Zephyrs changed their major league affiliation from the Milwaukee Brewers to the Houston Astros. On the surface, this is a change from a mediocre team to a successful one. There is more to it than that, however (many successful major league teams are not concerned with winning at the minor league level). Houston is only 350 miles from New Orleans, and many New Orleans fans attend major league games there. The Astros AA fan team is currently located at Jackson, Mississippi, which is less than 200 miles from New Orleans. There is a certain synergy which occurs: It's easy to move players around, the major league team plays exhibitions against the minor league teams, fans can follow all three teams, and so on. The Astros have provided a high-quality team. Indeed, the Zephyrs won the first AAA World Series in 1998.

The Zephyrs have had several players with local connections since they affiliated with the Astros. Former LSU star Russ Johnson played third base for New Orleans, and former UNO pitching ace Joe Slusarsky was a Zephyrs reliever. Best of all, the fans have had the opportunity to watch several players who are already in major league lineups or rotations, such as Richard Hidalgo and John Halama, and several prospects who seem likely to be future stars, such as former Rice University slugger Lance Berkman.

THE NEW ORLEANS DOWNTOWN ARENA

In the case of the baseball stadium in Jefferson Parish, it is clear that the project was part of economic-development plans for the LaSalle Tract. The idea of a baseball stadium and bringing minor league baseball back to the New Orleans area had been around for some time. The arena is somewhat of a contrast. Both authors lived in New Orleans during the time span covered; one of them worked on the Metrovision (the downtown economic-development entity) strategic plan for economic development in the late 1980s. Neither of us ever heard of an arena as part of the city's downtown plans before the 1992 legislation. No one had expressed dissatisfaction with existing facilities (the Superdome and Kiefer Arena) and there was no suggestion that anyone needed something between the two.

The filed 1992 legislation included plans for a 12,000-seat, $35-million arena to be located on an open area next to New Orleans City Hall. The 1993 legislation provided for a 20,000-seat, $85-million arena to be built on a site between the Superdome and the Pontchartrain Expressway. Thus, the site (an old railroad property) serves as a further buffer between the Central Business District and the impoverished neighborhoods of Central City to the west (Reichl 1998; Cook and Lauria 1995). The original proposed site was located in the Central Business District, adjoining public and private offices and the hospital complex. As downtown New Orleans receives further infusions of development capital, it seems that adjoining neighborhoods are walled off from development. The original announcement included the possibility of $30 million of federal money being used to renovate the nearby Union Passenger Terminal. The original announcement also included the possibility of a new hotel and a new office tower flanking the basketball arena (Donze and Roesler 1993). The arena was to be financed, like the ballpark, through a refinancing of Superdome bonds and a continuation of the hotel/motel tax in Orleans and Jefferson Parishes.

When plans for the arena were unveiled by Governor Edwards and Mayor Barthelemy, a National Basketball Association franchise, more jobs, and $200 million more in the downtown New Orleans economy were mentioned as benefits. Barthelemy's support was based on "hopes of revitalizing the Central Business District with the underlying goal of attracting a professional basketball franchise" (Bell 1993). Governor Edwards cited a study by Tulane University economist William Oakland which predicted the creation of between 4,500 and 8,500 new jobs and nearly $20 million in annual tax revenue from a new arena. In Oakland's view, the arena would make a significant impact without an NBA team.

The issue of the NBA team (or NHL franchise) has been prominent since the start of the arena. A 1994 consultant's report by the Peat Marwick accounting firm said that the building would only be affordable if it had an NBA team as the prime tenant. Otherwise, the consultants warned that the arena could lose $1 million a year (Anderson 1994). The arena did have influential opponents. Even though Tulane University was a prospective tenant, uptown State Senator (and Tulane supporter) John Hainkel labeled the arena as a "pork barrel building with no tenants" (McClain 1995).

Like the baseball stadium, preliminary drawings and designs were developed by HOK, the Missouri sports-architecture firm. In this instance, New Orleans architects Arthur Q. Davis, Faia and Partners were part of the architecture team.

The need for the arena has never been justified by its supporters. Furthermore, there has never been any discussion of the impacts on the Kiefer Arena. During the late 1980s and early 1990s, Kiefer was consistently among the top-grossing arenas in its size category. The new downtown arena creates a situation in which one state-owned facility competes with another statewide facility. Moreover, as a nationwide trend, revenues from live performances and concert tours have dropped. This leaves a smaller pie to be split by more facilities.

Overall, the major economic problem with the new arena is that it lacks a prime tenant. Efforts to relocate the NBA Minnesota Timberwolves to New Orleans failed during the 1994–1995 season. In 1996 a flurry of rumors suggested that the NBA San Antonio Spurs might move to New Orleans. These rumors were just that. To the best of our knowledge, there has never been an effort to bring an NHL franchise—existing or expansion—to New Orleans.

In 1997 minor league ice hockey arrived in New Orleans. As usual, the arrival occurred with some controversy, as competing groups sought local rights for franchises in different hockey leagues. Ultimately, an investment group headed by Ray Nagin, a top executive for Cox Communications, won an East Coast Hockey League franchise for New Orleans. The new franchise, called the New Orleans Brass, was supported in its efforts by Mayor Marc Morial. The Brass played their first two seasons at the Municipal Auditorium, as mentioned.

City–state government relations were complicated during the arena project, too. The city gave the state some land for the arena site, which will be run by a state agency (the Superdome Commission). In exchange, the city controls bookings in the arena for twenty days a year, keeping the rental revenue, and 20 percent of concession revenues on those dates. This satisfies a state constitutional requirement that the city be compensated for the land. The state also paid the cost of moving a heliport.

The $84 million originally projected for the cost of building the new arena is substantially lower than that of other NBA and NHL arenas opened in the 1990s. Part of the reason for lower projected costs is because of shared facilities with the Superdome. No new parking has been built for the arena. Fans will use existing parking at the Superdome and the New Orleans Centre (a shopping mall). The arena will use the Superdome's air conditioning and heating systems. Some existing Superdome equipment, such as the basketball court and hockey goals, are owned by the Dome. Much of the office space needed by arena staff will be located at the Dome. Finally, land acquisition costs were low, because the state and city already owned much of the site. Two pedestrian bridges will connect the Dome and the arena.

Competition involving several players in the political economy of New Orleans sports occurred over which hockey franchise would play in the new arena. In late 1997 New Orleans Saints owner Tom Benson filed an application and a $500,000 deposit to bring an International Hockey League (IHL) franchise to New Orleans. Rob Couhig, the owner of the New Orleans Zephyrs, headed a group which also wanted to bring an IHL team to New Orleans. The Brass owners, after beginning play in the Municipal Auditorium, wanted to move their team to the new arena. Ultimately, the Dome's management firm chose the Brass to be the tenant and to have a ten-year lease for use of the new arena.

Three other issues surfaced as the arena held its grand opening on October 27, 1999. First, there are questions about the financing. Was the $84-million amount too low? Will the new arena include luxury boxes and amenities desired by professional sports owners? If so, who will pay for them? Second, the arena has no name. The management is looking for a corporate sponsor, who will pay from $400,000 to $700,000 a year. This will defray some of the costs. Third, the arena and its prime tenants (the ECHL Brass and Tulane University) are still discussing contract terms.

The major economic problem with the new arena is that it lacks a prime tenant. The Brass hockey team will play in the new arena in the 1999–2000 season. This will surely be a plus, but to succeed the arena needs a prime NBA (or NHL) tenant, selling out the arena forty nights a year and providing the skybox revenues so vital in the structure of today's sports economies. Tulane University has scaled back its plans to play in the new arena. Instead of playing their entire basketball schedule at the arena, Tulane will play three to six games at the arena, with the remaining home games on campus. In 1998, New Orleans Saints owner Tom Benson was awarded an Arena Football League franchise. The indoor football league operates in the spring and summer months, and will play in the new arena starting in 2000. With these sports uses, plus concerts and other events, it is possible that the arena may not be a liability for Louisiana taxpayers. A greater possibility exists that the New Orleans Arena may be another arena or stadium without a prime tenant, to be used as a means of blackmail by NBA owners.

CONCLUSIONS

From the perspective of downtown development, it is clear that the arena could succeed as a complement to the Superdome and the adjacent New Orleans Centre hotel–retail–commercial complex.

First, in review, it is clear that the arena and the baseball stadium are clearly the result of ad hoc political deal making by state and local Louisiana politicians. At this stage Zephyrs Park is an aesthetic and economic success. The arena should be fine as a facility, but its long-term economic prospects may not be bright. But this is irrelevant from a political perspective. Politicians like construction projects because they provide jobs, and contractors are often political donors. Consulting firms, architecture firms, and engineering firms—all involved in projects of this type—are also sources of campaign funds. As recreation and leisure activities become larger parts of the local economy, leaders in that industry have more political importance. Tom Benson of the Saints is a longtime supporter of Governor Edwards, who crafted the deal that "saved" the Saints in 1985 and brought Benson in as owner. Benson has made hundreds of millions as the Saints owner for the last fifteen years. Rob Couhig, the Zephyrs owner, ran for Congress in 1999, using his baseball success as a large part of his campaign advertising. Ray Nagin and the other owners of the Brass are strong supporters of New Orleans Mayor Marc Morial.

Second, regional competition is more subtle than the usual portrayal in the literature. These cases illustrate how this is so in relation to other metropolitan areas and within the New Orleans metropolitan area. The baseball case suggests that New Orleans has accepted its status as a second-rung city. The construction of a stadium for AAA baseball means that New Orleans has given up its dream of major league baseball. Of the fifteen other cities in the Pacific Coast league, only Nashville is mentioned as a major league expansion possibility. On the other hand, the arena indicates that New Orleans is still pursuing its dreams of a return to the NBA. Within the region there is always economic competition between central city and suburbs. In this case, a deal was crafted in which each major jurisdiction received a facility that it wanted. This may not be true regional cooperation, but it could be said to be a step in the direction of economic development in a metropolitan area that is highly fragmented on the basis of race and income.

Third, in these cases planning and evaluation were minimal. Some economic-development studies for Jefferson Parish mentioned the possibility of a minor league ballpark as an economic stimulus for East Jefferson. Planning studies for the arena were minimal. As part of this process, no public agency was asked to study the economic, physical, and social impacts of the facility. For example, the role of the planning-department staff in Orleans and Jefferson was minimal. When any sort of evaluation was undertaken, it was by a private firm. When warnings were sounded (such as Peat Marwick's concerns about the arena), they were ignored. Perhaps we could have legislation (state or national) which might require economic and environmental impact statements for projects over a certain size (Persky, Felsenstein, and Wiewel 1997). As it stands, in Louisiana (and in many other places in North America) the politics of development are such that new facilities can be built without much thought as to their ultimate costs.

REFERENCES

Anderson, Ed. 1995. Jeff Stadium Jeopardized by N.O. Lawmakers Protest. *Times Picayune*, 16 June, B3.

Anderson, Ed. 1994. The Game Plan. *Times Picayune*, 15 August, A1.

Bell, Kevin. 1993. New Sports Arena Pitched by Edwards, Barthelemy. *Times Picayune*, 25 February, A1.

Bingham, Richard D., and Robert Mier, eds. 1997. *Dilemmas of Urban Economic Development: Issues in Theory and Practice*. Thousand Oaks, Calif.: Sage.

Cook, Christine, and Mickey Lauria. 1995. Urban Regeneration and Public Housing in New Orleans. *Urban Affairs Review* 30: 538–557.

Danielson, Michael. 1997. *Home Team*. Princeton: Princeton University Press.

Donze, Frank, and Bob Roesler. 1993. Sports Development Plans Revived. *Times Picayune*, 20 February, A1.

Evans, Robert. 1994. Letter to State Treasurer Mary Landrieu. 16 March.

Johnson, Arthur T. 1993. *Minor League Baseball and Local Economic Development*. Urbana: University of Illinois Press.

McClain, Randy. 1995. Arena Is a Go, Proponents Say. *New Orleans City Business*, 8–14 May, 1.

Mulé, Marty. 1996. Z's Show Off Stadium Work. *Times Picayune*, 13 December, B3.

Persky, Joseph, Daniel Felsenstein, and W. Wiewel. 1997. How Do We Know That "but for the Incentives the Development" Would Not Have Occurred? In *Dilemmas of Urban Economic Development Issues in Theory and Practice*, edited by Richard D. Bingham and Robert Mier. Thousand Oaks, Calif.: Sage, 28–45.

Pressman, Jeffrey L., and Aaron B. Wildavsky. 1973. *Implementation*. Berkeley and Los Angeles: University of California Press.

Reichl, Alexander J. 1998. Reconstructing Community in New Orleans Public Housing. Paper presented at the annual meeting of the American Political Science Association, Boston. September 1–4.

Rosentraub, Mark S. 1997. *Major League Losers: The Real Costs of Sports and Who's Paying for It*. New York: Basic Books.

Sullivan, Neil J. 1987. *The Dodgers Move West*. New York: Oxford University Press.

Whitford, David. 1993. *Playing Hardball: The High-Stakes Battle for Baseball's New Franchises*. New York: Doubleday.

Wolff, Miles. 1998. *The Season of the Owl*. Durham, N.C.: Baseball America.

Zimbalist, Andrew. 1992. *Baseball and Billions: A Probing Look Inside the Big Business of Our National Pastime*. New York: Basic Books.

6

Stadiums as Solution Sets: Baseball, Football, and Downtown Development

Lynn W. Bachelor

The concept of solution sets emphasizes the continuity and replication of policy solutions and a policy process in which the availability of a "solution" precludes analysis of problems. In Detroit in the 1980s, large-scale industrial projects with significant levels of intergovernment funding were the primary components of economic-development solution sets, which had important regime-maintenance functions for public officials seeking to demonstrate their capacity to govern and the effectiveness of their policies through the replication of these policies. In the 1990s the composition of Detroit's governing coalition has changed, and entertainment (in particular, sports stadiums and casinos) has replaced manufacturing as the centerpiece of the city's economic-development solution set.

This strategy for urban revitalization resembles earlier industrial policies in several ways. First, stadium projects, like the assembly plant projects of the 1980s, have generally been proposed by a few top private and public officials (members of the governing coalition) and presented for "ratification" by the public and its representatives. Second, financial packages for both types of projects have involved a mix of public and private funding (but without the federal assistance which was available in the 1980s). Third, both offer uncertain economic payoffs and have been promoted more for their intangible benefits than for their economic impacts (although economic impact studies have frequently been presented in support of both types of projects). Enhancement of the image of a city and the reputation of its mayor are the most immediate payoffs from stadiums, so these projects are driven by the same incentives that earlier led to support for assembly plants, convention centers, and other large, visible uses of public money. The economic benefits from stadiums are even more uncertain than those from industrial projects—most jobs are seasonal and pay less than manufacturing employment, and the multiplier effects are smaller. Fourth, major league sports teams, like large corporations, have made effective use of relocation threats (made more credible by actual relocations, such as the move of the Cleveland Browns to Baltimore) and their attendant symbolic costs for public officials. Finally, the financial benefits of stadiums to team owners and the political benefits for public officials encourage the preservation of a "growth machine" type of regime. In Detroit, the election of Dennis Archer as mayor, and the presence of a "new generation" of corporate leadership (the sons and daughters of team owners), conveys the impression of a new regime. The continued appeal of an approach to economic development very similar to that developed by the previous mayoral administration suggests that the priorities of the new leadership closely resemble those of their predecessors.

The current appeal of sports stadiums, in cities of all sizes in all regions of the United States, supports an argument of the imitativeness of economic-development policy making and the limited options available to local officials for promoting revitalization. It appears that the smokestack chasing for which city and state officials were criticized in the last decade has been replaced by the pursuit of major and minor league franchises, driven by many of the same forces: (1) capital mobility of teams and corporations; (2) informational asymmetry, which promotes generation of a corporate surplus—public officials lack information on relocation options of the team or corporation and the minimum level of incentives necessary to prevent relocation, while private-sector officials know exactly what government is capable of offering and ask for it; (3) public officials have limited bargaining power because of the absence of alternative development proposals for stadium or plant sites; (4) large projects like stadiums, arenas, assembly plants, or corporate headquarters generate media attention and political payoffs for public officials; and (5) team owners stand to gain significant financial rewards in the form of higher profits and reduced construction and operating costs from public funding and new lease arrangements.

In the mid-1990s, public–private partnerships for the construction and operation of sports stadiums have become a solution set for many cities. Since 1991, twenty-three sports arenas or stadiums have opened at a cost of approximately $4 billion, and $7 billion in future spending is projected (Laing 1996, 24). Teams as well as cities copy each other's projects: Shortly after a plan was "finalized" for a new baseball stadium for the Detroit Tigers, the football Lions began negotiating with city and county officials for a new facility. The Lions' contribution to the joint stadium project was less than half the Tigers', and public costs (state, county, and city downtown development authority) were more than two and a half times those for the baseball stadium alone; still, the public sector contribution, 48 percent of total estimated costs of $505 million, is significantly less than for most recent stadium projects, largely because of the $140-million contribution of Tigers owner Mike Ilitch (who also owns Little Caesars Pizza, the Detroit Red Wings hockey team, and the Fox Theater, a focal point of the entertainment district being developed adjacent to the stadium site).

Like other stadium projects, this one was announced by a small group of top government and private officials amid media rhapsodies about its role in revitalizing downtown Detroit. "Detroit comeback," proclaimed a banner headline on the front page of the *Detroit Free Press*; the accompanying article took note of the participation of "two generations of two powerful Detroit families" in negotiating the "deal" with Wayne County Executive Edward McNamara and Detroit Mayor Dennis Archer (Lam and Fricker 1996, 1A). Most economic benefits will go to the two sports teams, which will receive all revenue from advertising, ticket sales, luxury and club seats, naming rights, parking, and concessions; the city's "payback" was described as "development expected near the project and a new image for downtown" (p. 9A). Like the earlier assembly plants, the stadium project offered selective material benefits to the team owners and symbolic benefits to public officials, a "win–win" solution for the governing coalition. As a solution set, it borrowed both from Detroit's past experience—for example, utilizing the bonding capacity of the Downtown Development Authority (DDA)—and other cities' experience with stadiums, with initial media discussions of the project referring extensively to the positive impacts of stadiums in Baltimore and Cleveland (Phillips 1996).

The industrial projects of the 1980s were promoted as being in the public interest because of their alleged impacts on employment. In testimony in a court case challenging the city government's taking of property for a General Motors assembly plant, Detroit Mayor Coleman Young observed, "To the degree that it is in the public interest to provide adequate services to our people . . . . it is necessary to have a tax base, and the basic ingredient of a tax base is jobs and manufacturing. . . . It is clearly in the interest of any society to have its citizens employed" (Jones and Bachelor 1993, 125). Pelissero, Henschen, and Sidlow (1991) found that Chicago's governing coalition used a similar justification for their support of sports stadiums: "The governing coalition in some ways seemed to be selling a potential gain for itself as one that would serve the general welfare of the community" (pp. 125–126).

The differences between sports and industry as economic development tools are relatively minor: (1) Stadiums cost less than major assembly plants—the average stadium can be built for $200 to $250 million, while the Chrysler Jefferson assembly plant cost $1.2 billion; (2) physical size and complexity—assembly plants are much larger, requiring more land and networks of road and rail access not necessary for stadiums; and (3) the economic impact of assembly plants, while considerably less than projected by their promoters, dwarfs that of stadiums, because stadium jobs are temporary, pay less, have less of a multiplier effect, and there are less of them than in a major assembly plant.

A comparison of cities and teams reveals significant variations in levels of public and private contributions to stadium projects, but no well-defined patterns. The proportion of public funding has neither systematically increased nor systematically decreased over time, nor have total project costs escalated significantly. While details of these solution sets may have been influenced by local economic and political conditions, their basic structure is similar.

PARTICIPANTS

Stadium projects typically arise from discussions among top-level public and private officials. In Indianapolis, for example, two mayors and "an informal group of business, professional, governmental, civic, and philanthropic leaders in the community" have been credited with developing that city's emphasis on amateur sports as an economic-development strategy (Kotler, Haider, and Rein 1993, 41; Schaffer, Jaffee, and Davidson 1993, 26). Both corporate and progressive regimes have promoted stadiums as development tools, according to Pelissero, Henschen, and Sidlow (1991, 118); the membership of such "sports development coalitions" has included city and state government officials, their political supporters, franchise owners (who are often "the first to advance sports stadium agenda items by complaining about their current playing facility or threatening to move"), large corporations, developers, financial institutions, sports spectators, team fans, and others who "make their livelihood from sports and stadium-related products" (pp. 118–119).

In Detroit, two of the area's wealthiest families played a central role in the stadium project: the Ilitch family, owners of Little Caesars Pizza, the Tigers, and the Red Wings; and the Ford (as in Ford Motor Company) family, owners of the Lions, who had moved their team to suburban Pontiac from Detroit in 1974. "Peak bargaining" between high-level public and private officials characterized negotiations: The Lions' William Clay Ford Jr. invited deputy Wayne County executive Michael Duggan to lunch in November 1994 to discuss bringing the team back downtown. Ford's motive was financial—the team's lease arrangement at the Pontiac Silverdome seriously limited revenues and made it difficult to compete for free-agent talent. Unable to obtain a better deal at the Silverdome, Ford then contacted Duggan and Detroit Mayor Archer to see whether "Wayne County and Detroit could meet the Lions' price" (Pepper 1996). In early 1996, when negotiations with the Silverdome had broken down, Lions officials approached Wayne County again, initiating the discussions which culminated in the announcement of the joint stadium project nearly six months later. The process, and the relationship, recalls the origins of the GM Poletown project in 1980: a letter from GM chairman Thomas A. Murphy to Detroit Mayor Coleman Young pledging to build an assembly plant if detailed site criteria requirements, ranging from tax abatement to zoning changes, were met (Jones and Bachelor 1993, 4). For stadiums, as for industrial projects, policy results from public-sector responses to demands initiated by the private sector.

FUNDING

Another defining characteristic of both industrial and stadium projects as economic development solution sets has been their reliance on a mix of public and private funding sources. Grants, loans, and loan guarantees from federal agencies were a major source of funding for large-scale development projects in Detroit in the 1980s, but are no longer available. Financing has become more creative: Sales of naming rights to stadiums are common, resulting in facilities such as the TWA Dome, Coors Field, Molson Centre, United Center, and Marine Midland Arena. In St. Louis, personal seat licenses for the privilege of buying season tickets were sold for as much as $4,500 apiece, raising $70 million (Laing 1996, 24); the Carolina Panthers raised $150 million from the sale of seat licenses (Lam 1995, 1B). Public funding choices are more limited, with most projects relying heavily on revenue bonds and various types of sales taxes. The public share of spending for many stadiums has been well above 50 percent: 64 percent in Milwaukee, 74 percent in Denver, 86 percent in Seattle, 90 percent for Baltimore's Camden Yards, and 100 percent for St. Petersburg's Thunderdome (Lam 1995, 1B). The public share of Detroit's joint stadium project, 48 percent, is low in comparison to most recently completed facilities. Yet it is significantly higher than the public-sector proportion of industrial projects: Chrysler invested $1.2 billion in its new Jefferson assembly plant, while estimates of the public cost ranged from $436 to $264 million (approximately one-third) (Jones and Bachelor 1993, 220, 226). It is also worth noting that the public sector's share of the joint stadium project was considerably greater than for the one stadium which was first proposed (that stadium, for the Tigers, was to have cost $240 million, of which the Tigers were to have contributed $145 million) (Lam and Fricker 1996, 1A).

The joint project had an announced cost of $505 million: $240 million for the Tigers' stadium, $225 million for the Lions' stadium, $20 million for parking facilities, and $20 million for a Lions headquarters and practice facilities. The Tigers remained committed to $145 million, the Lions would contribute $70 million, and another $50 million was to be raised from corporate contributions. The public sector's $240-million share was to be divided among the state of Michigan ($55 million), Wayne County ($100 million), and the Detroit Downtown Development Authority ($85 million) (Lam and Fricker 1996, 1A).

None of these public financing mechanisms were automatic or implemented without some controversy. Use of $55 million in state strategic fund money had been proposed in 1995 for a new Tiger Stadium, and was challenged unsuccessfully in the courts by the Tiger Stadium Fan Club. Wayne County's contribution of $100 million was to be derived from the sale of surplus county land ($20 million) and bond sales, with the $80 million in bond debt to be repaid over thirty years by revenues from an additional 1-percent county hotel tax and an additional 2-percent county rental-car tax; the tax increases had to be approved by county voters in the November 5, 1996 election.

Downtown Development Authority funding required revision of the DDA's Tax Increment Financing and Development Plan by extending the boundaries of its Downtown Development Area to include the two stadiums and incorporate development and financial plans for the project. This was a critical element in project financing, because the DDA's tax increment financing authority permits increased tax revenues from development in areas under its jurisdiction to be used to support new development projects. Tax increment financing had also been an essential component of financial packages for the Chrysler Jefferson and GM Poletown assembly-plant projects in Detroit in the 1980s; the Detroit Economic Development Corporation and Local Development Financing Authority were authorized to use tax increment financing in those projects, which were not located within or adjacent to the boundaries of the DDA.

The complex financial arrangements that characterized Detroit's industrial projects were also evident in the financing plan agreed to by the DDA, Wayne County, the City of Detroit, the Tigers, and the

Lions for the joint stadium project. The financing arrangements out-lined in the Memorandum of Understanding between the DDA, the teams, and Wayne County, and included in amendments to the DDA's Tax Increment Financing Plan and Development Plan, suggest that its contribution would be larger than the $85 million initially mentioned in newspaper reports: a $40-million contribution to Tiger Stadium (as provided in an agreement signed with the Tigers in 1995), and $70 million to the Lions Stadium, of which $40 million would be raised through the sale by the DDA of its ownership rights in the new Tiger Stadium to the Detroit/Wayne County Stadium Authority; in addi-tion, the DDA is obligated to reimburse the city of Detroit for the issu-ance of $15 million in bonds (Downtown Development Authority 1996a, 191–193).

The use of special public–private authorities had facilitated imple-mentation of project plans for Detroit's earlier industrial projects, so the creation of a Detroit/Wayne County Stadium Authority to develop and operate the new stadiums is indicative of another linkage between past and present solution sets. In a complicated jurisdictional arrange-ment, the stadium authority will own the stadiums and lease them to Wayne County, which, in turn, will sublet them to the DDA; the DDA will then enter into separate concession agreements with the Tigers and the Lions for the operation and management of Tiger Stadium and Lions Stadium respectively (Downtown Development Authority 1996a, 191–193).

BENEFITS OF STADIUMS

Despite a growing body of research suggesting that stadium projects have a minimal impact on employment or economic growth (e.g., Baade 1996; Rosentraub et al. 1994; Euchner 1993), proponents of the Detroit stadiums emphasized their direct and indirect economic consequences for the downtown area and the city as a whole. These predictions were generally echoed by the media, although some columnists expressed concerns about possible cost overruns (these criticisms had also ap-peared in investigative reports on the Poletown and Chrysler assem-bly-plant projects).

A new Tiger Stadium alone, according to a 1995 study, would have a direct impact of $66 million in its first year of operations, and $1.3 billion over a twenty-year period; its indirect impact was projected to be $118.8 million in its first year and $2.4 billion over twenty years (Michigan Consultants 1995). These calculations were based on pro-jected annual attendance of 2.45 million, and included team spend-ing, off-site spending by customers, off-site spending by visiting teams and media, and special-event spending (including restaurants, hotels, retail, off-site parking, and taxis). Promotional materials for the 1996 county tax election claimed the two stadiums would have a $200-million annual economic impact. The DDA's resolution supporting modification of its downtown development plan was less specific, claiming that "the Stadia project will provide jobs for the jobless, help stabilize and increase property values in the DDA District, and encourage and increase business activity and investment in the City of Detroit's downtown area" (Downtown Development Authority 1996a). According to Wayne County officials, impact studies were done by the teams but not by the county.

Given this level of uncertainty about economic payoffs, it is not surprising that the intangible benefits to Detroit's image received more media attention. Such symbolic benefits were a defining characteristic of the solution sets formulated for industrial projects in Detroit in the 1980s (Bachelor 1994, 614). A similar pattern has been evident for stadium projects in other cities. As Rosentraub (1996) observed in a rejoinder to Baade's (1996) analysis demonstrating the absence of economic returns on public funds invested in these projects, "[No] stadium or arena can affect development patterns, even at the neighborhood level." Rosentraub (1996) then identified the nature of intangible benefits resulting from Cleveland's Gateway Project:

Downtown Cleveland is, once again, an entertainment and recreation center for the region. Is downtown Cleveland a more exciting place? Is there a greater sense of excitement and civic pride? Are people who long ago gave up on downtown returning for recreation? Are young people looking at Cleveland as a center of their region? The answer to each of these question is yes. Are these benefits or returns worth the hundreds of millions of dollars spent by taxpayers to subsidize professional sports? In a city with a full set of urban challenges, is the new image created by these public investments worth the commitments if there is no direct economic impact? Is the myth or illusion of activity created by the glamour from sports and downtown crowds worth what the public sector spent? Those are questions only the residents of Cleveland and Cuyahoga County should answer. (pp. 26–27)

For many Clevelanders, whose city was demeaned for years as "the mistake on the lake" and known for having its river catch fire, the answer is probably that the change in image has been worth the price.

Detroit, like Cleveland, has suffered from a negative reputation among the national media, and the value of image was accurately captured by a *Detroit News* headline, "City basks in glow of favorable headlines in U.S." (Detroit News 1996). The article reported comments from the *New York Times* and *Wall Street Journal* which credited Mayor Dennis Archer with initiating the revitalization of Detroit. Another article emphasized the benefits to Detroit's image, concluding with comments from a former St. Louis economic development director:

There are intangible benefits . . . corporate recruiting, community attitude and reintroducing people to a city. We experienced it in St. Louis. . . . Often the barriers to development and investment in a city are as mythical and hard to quantify as the direct economic benefit of the new stadium itself. But as people come downtown and get comfortable there, they are more likely to come down again, hang out and spend time. Eventually people may even choose to live there. (Linsalata 1996b)

On November 5, as Wayne County voters approved the two tourist-tax increases for the new stadium, Michigan voters, by a narrow margin, authorized three casinos in Detroit. While specific locations have yet to be identified, they are likely to be in or near downtown, and to dwarf the stadiums in their economic and symbolic impacts on the city.

RELOCATION AND COMPETITION

In many cities threats of relocation by sports teams have prompted bidding wars much like those which characterized earlier competition for industrial facilities. Neither the Lions nor the Tigers, however, made even veiled threats to move their teams in order to get a better deal. Even without such threats, the recent experience of other cities was an inevitable part of the policy-making environment of Detroit officials. In November 1995, six weeks after plans for the new Tiger Stadium were announced, Cleveland Browns owner Art Modell made a deal with Maryland officials to move his team to Baltimore. Baltimore, in turn, had been courting NFL teams since losing the Colts to Indianapolis in 1984; a Maryland delegation had attended every NFL owners meeting since 1987, renting a hospitality suite, serving Chesapeake Bay crab to owners and league officials, and presenting the package of a new $200-million stadium, luxury boxes, club seats, restaurants, and a lease that would deliver almost all stadium revenue to the team (Diemer and Koff 1995). Detroit officials familiar with the success of Cleveland's Gateway project involving new facilities for the MLB Indians and NBA Cavaliers could not help but empathize with the loss of the Browns, and perhaps feel a sense of "there but for the grace of God go we."

Detroit was fortunate to have team owners with a commitment to stay in Detroit or in the Detroit area. Tigers owner Mike Ilitch has a substantial investment in an entertainment district being developed adjacent to the proposed stadium location. The Ilitch family, through Olympia Entertainment, operates the Detroit Red Wings hockey team (which plays downtown in Joe Louis Arena) and the Fox Theater (located across Woodward Avenue from the proposed stadiums); the headquarters of Little Caesars Pizza, also owned by the Ilitch family, is nearby. In October 1996 Olympia Development Corporation, a division of Olympia Entertainment, announced plans for a $6-million "entertainment avenue," with a mix of sports bars, themed restaurants, microbreweries, and music cafes next to the Fox Theater (King 1996). No specific tenants were mentioned, but two months later it was announced that it would include a Hard Rock Cafe with a Detroit/ Motown theme and a guitar on the roof which would light up when home runs were hit at the baseball stadium across the street. At the time of the initial announcement, financial commitments for the stadium project had not all been completed, so the plans for the entertainment district are indicative of the Ilitch family's ongoing interest in downtown development.

Lions owner William Clay Ford Sr. reportedly wanted to keep the team in Pontiac, and had to be convinced by his son of the economic advantages of the move downtown (Pepper 1996). According to media reports and those involved, no other locations were considered, and serious discussions between the Lions and Detroit and Wayne County officials did not begin until Pontiac and the Silverdome had rejected their final proposal (Pepper 1996; Johnson 1996). The Ford family has had a significant presence in downtown Detroit for many years through the Renaissance Center, a skyscraper complex on the riverfront, the building and financing of which was spearheaded by Henry Ford Jr. in the 1970s. In the fall of 1996, however, Ford sold the Renaissance Center to General Motors for a fraction of its original cost, and in December announced that the 2,500 Ford Motor Company office workers employed there would be relocated to suburban Dearborn, adjacent to Ford world headquarters (Bradsher, 1996, A10). In return for a $40-million contribution from Ford Motor Company, however, "Ford" will be part of the name of the new Lions stadium, and a giant Ford insignia on the stadium dome is likely (Hughes 1996).

The low probability of relocation, and the strength of the team owners' commitment to Detroit, may also have helped to reduce the level of public-sector funding demanded for the stadium project. Of course, the owners themselves stand to reap major financial gains from their investments. Sports-finance analysts have estimated that the new stadiums could double the value of the Detroit Tigers and increase the worth of the Lions by as much as $90 million, as well as increasing the Lions' annual revenues by $10 million (Durfee 1996). Revenues from concession sales, luxury suites, and parking, as well as increased attendance, all figure into the economic gains. For Ilitch, this could mean the first profits he has reaped since buying the team in 1992. According to experts, a new stadium could increase attendance by more than 1 million fans annually, even if the team's performance did not improve (Durfee 1996).

These projections are, in true solution-set fashion, drawn from the experience of other teams, although analysts acknowledge that the impact on the value of a franchise is affected by the nature of the deal and specific cost-sharing and lease agreements. The Baltimore Orioles baseball team was reportedly worth $70 million before moving into its new park at Camden Yards, and was sold two years later for $172 million (Durfee 1996). The Baltimore Ravens (formerly the Cleveland Browns) will retain $65 million from personal seat license fees in their new stadium, as well as all revenue from luxury suites, premium seats, concessions, and in-park advertising and 50 percent of all revenues from nonfootball events held there; they will pay no rent for the term of their thirty-year lease other than a 10-percent tax on all tickets, and will be responsible for covering operating and maintenance expenses of the facility. It has been estimated that the value of the franchise will appreciate by 50 percent after the first season in the new stadium (Laing 1996, 25). More generally, four of the top ten most valuable baseball franchises have new stadiums, and new facilities are considered to have helped the Phoenix Suns, Chicago Bulls, and Detroit Pistons (who have moved twice, from downtown Detroit to the Pontiac Silverdome, and then to the Palace in suburban Auburn Hills) move to the top of Financial World's list of most valuable basketball franchises (p. 24).

Political benefits to public officials are probably comparable to the economic gains which accrue to corporate members of the governing coalition, but they are impossible to quantify. Detroit Mayor Dennis Archer received extensive favorable local and national media coverage in the wake of the announcement of the stadium project. The Detroit Free Press observed that more than $2.1 billion in investment (in addition to the approximately $500 million for the stadiums) had been pledged to Detroit since Archer became mayor in 1994 (Oguntoyinbo 1996, 9A). Articles in the New York Times and Wall Street Journal praised Archer for building business support, in contrast to the confrontational approach favored by his predecessor, Coleman Young, and credited him with beginning Detroit's economic revival (Detroit News 1996). Councilman Mel Ravitz, although critical of Archer for working too closely with corporate leadership, spoke positively of his relationship with the city council, and Wayne County officials noted that communications and cooperation between the city and the county had improved under Archer (Ravitz 1996).

After President Clinton's reelection and the success of both the stadium tax and casino legislation, Archer's name was mentioned for a possible cabinet position; the mayor, however, said his loyalties were in Detroit and he would decline such an offer (Linsalata 1996a). Since the election, land acquisition for the stadiums has moved ahead fairly smoothly and most media attention has focused on casino prospects, with Archer again playing a central role. Two days after the election, Archer made it clear that his office would decide where casinos would be located, ruling out locations on the riverfront or near the two stadiums, and who would operate them (Linsalata and Wilson 1996a). Nationally recognized casino operators such as Harrah's expressed interest in a Detroit location, and Wall Street analysts were reportedly willing to invest up to $600 million in casinos and related hotels (Linsalata and Wilson 1996b).

TOLEDO: NOT READY FOR THE MAJOR LEAGUES

The attractiveness of professional sports facilities as an economic development strategy is not limited to "major league" cities like Detroit and Cleveland. Attracting or retaining a minor league team has been an important objective for public officials in many smaller cities, who have used the same arguments in support of their cause as officials in larger metropolitan areas.

The Detroit Tigers' AAA farm team, the Toledo Mud Hens, recently expressed an interest in a new ballpark, initiating a heated debate among city, county, and state officials, the local media, and the team. Toledo's central business district, like Detroit's, is struggling, and some officials viewed the construction of a downtown stadium to be essential to the CBD's immediate and long-term future. Both the city of Toledo and Lucas County have pledged millions of dollars in support of building a new Jeep manufacturing plant, and cannot afford to commit significant amounts of financial support to the construction of a stadium.

Toledo's economic development solution set, then, is a hybrid of the manufacturing model pioneered by Detroit in the 1980s and the entertainment theme of the 1990s. Casinos are not part of the mix in Toledo, but with a minor league hockey team playing in an old arena, Toledo, like Detroit, may be negotiating with two teams. The package provided for the Mud Hens, in this context, could set the parameters for funding of a hockey arena. Unlike most professional teams, however, the Mud Hens are publicly owned by a nonprofit arm of county government and run by a five-member board of directors who are accountable to the Lucas County Recreation Center advisory board and the Lucas County Commissioners. Moving the team would not be possible unless it was sold to a different owner.

Nevertheless, metaphors of competition with other teams and cities abound in the planning study prepared by consultants for the Toledo

Regional Sports Facility Committee (KPMG 1997). Charts and tables in the study compared Toledo and the Mud Hens to other AAA baseball teams and cities with respect to attendance, population, and market characteristics, and noted the impact of new stadiums on average attendance levels for other teams. The report also presents a detailed analysis of the inadequacies of the existing facility, Ned Skeldon Stadium, recalling the criticisms of Detroit's Tiger Stadium made by team management and other promoters of a new stadium for that team. The report's financial analysis of the proposed stadium relied heavily on comparisons with the experience of other AAA baseball teams, as did its economic and fiscal analysis and assessment of funding options. Rather than proceeding from an examination of needs and problems particular to the Mud Hens and Toledo to an analysis of how a new stadium could address these needs and problems, the report relied upon making connections between the costs and benefits of other stadium projects and projected costs and benefits of a new stadium for the Toledo area. It was presented, in other words, as a solution set: a set of policies developed in one context and applied to another.

This policy package unraveled when Lucas County voters rejected a temporary quarter-cent sales-tax increase to cover part of the cost of a $37-million downtown stadium. City, county, and Mud Hens officials went back to the drawing board to formulate alternative financing options that would permit the project to be built without a local tax increase. Their discussions revealed the difficulties of coordinating actions among organizations with different agendas and priorities, and the tensions inherent in a development strategy that mixed industrial and entertainment projects: county officials reacted negatively to a suggestion by Toledo's mayor that state funding for the stadium should be transferred to help the city cover cost overruns associated with development of the site for a new Jeep assembly plant (Baessler 1998). Subsequently, the location of the proposed stadium also became an issue when the Mud Hens board presented a plan for a stadium in East Toledo, across the Maumee River from the downtown area, instead of the warehouse district site that had been the initial choice.

CONCLUSIONS

Detroit's stadium project is now one of several developments proposed or underway in or near downtown. In this context, estimation of its impact is difficult. The entertainment district being developed around the Fox Theater, the stadiums, and the casinos will replace abandoned buildings and vacant lots with glittering new facilities, and promise to bring thousands of people back downtown. Together they convey a sense of positive momentum to a city that has been "down" for decades. Whether this momentum could be sustained without any one of the projects is difficult to determine, but their combined effect is impressive. This effect, like that of the earlier industrial projects, is more symbolic than economic, lifting the spirits of city residents and improving its image among potential residents and investors.

Toledo, like Detroit, hoped to improve its image and gain a sense of positive momentum from major development projects. So far it has been less successful. The Jeep project has encountered cost overruns and negative publicity from the resistance of a few residents to property acquisition and possible eminent-domain proceedings. No consensus has developed on a site for a new stadium, no new financing plan has been proposed, and a split has emerged between the Mud Hens board and the county commissioners over the membership of the board and ambiguities in the team's financial situation. Without any tangible progress on these major projects, other development initiatives may also suffer. Jeep and the Mud Hens are an important part of Toledo's image, and the costs will be more than financial if officials are unable to repair their solution set and get them back on track.

Public subsidies for professional sports stadiums, even more than business incentives, confirm the validity of Wolman's (1988) conclusion that political factors significantly shape the decision processes of public officials. Stadiums and sports teams offer fewer, lower-paying jobs, with smaller multiplier effects than manufacturing facilities. The association of a city's name with its sports teams, however, elevates the level of potential political costs and benefits associated with these projects. Mayors fear the damage to their reputations and political influence that may result from losing a team to another city, and anticipate taking credit for keeping it in a new, publicly supported stadium. Perhaps because the economic and fiscal payoffs are so minimal and uncertain, political costs and benefits assume greater importance. Evaluation of stadium projects must also take into consideration the absence of more economically attractive alternatives for the development of stadium sites, which, in both Toledo and Detroit, were comprised of vacant lots and abandoned buildings. A stadium provides an attractive alternative to these eyesores and their negative visual and symbolic impact on a Central Business District. Even if it generates few jobs and minimal tax revenues, it can diminish the political costs of urban decay. Like other large economic-development projects, stadiums provide city officials with a tangible response to the public demand to "do something" to revitalize their communities. For these reasons, despite the drawbacks and risks evident in the experiences of Detroit and Toledo, stadiums are likely to remain attractive solution sets.

REFERENCES

Baade, Robert A. 1996. Professional Sports as Catalysts for Metropolitan Economic Development. *Journal of Urban Affairs* 18: 1–17.

Bachelor, Lynn W. 1994. Regime Maintenance, Solution Sets, and Urban Economic Development. *Urban Affairs Quarterly* 29: 596–616.

Baessler, J. 1998. County Ponders Finance Options for Downtown Mud Hens Roost. *The Blade* 3 (September): 17–18.

Bradsher, Keith. 1996. Ford Returns 2,500 Jobs to Suburb in a Blow to Detroit's Economic Hopes. *New York Times*, 11 December, A19.

Detroit News. 1996. In Detroit: City Basks in Glow of Favorable Headlines in U.S. *Detroit News*, 23 August, A1.

Diemer, Tom, and Stephen Koff. 1995. Baltimore Still Hasn't Forgotten the Pain of Losing Its NFL Team. *The Plain Dealer*, 6 November, 1A, 8A.

Downtown Development Authority. 1996a. Tax Increment Financing Plan and Development Plan for Development Area No. 1 (resolution). Detroit, 10 September 10.

Downtown Development Authority. 1996b. Tax Increment Plan and Development Plan for Development Area No. 1. Detroit, 10 September.

Durfee, Doug. 1996. The Payoff: New Parks Mean Bonanza for Teams. *Detroit News*, 22 September, A12.

Euchner, Charles C. 1993. *Playing the Field: Why Sports Teams Move and Cities Fight to Keep Them*. Baltimore: Johns Hopkins University Press.

Hughes, John. 1996. It's Official: Ford Will Pay $40 Million to Name New Football Stadium. *Detroit News*, 12 October, 1A.

Johnson, Tim, Director for Marketing and Communications, Wayne County Department of Jobs and Economic Development. 1996. Telephone interview with author, 10 December.

Jones, Bryan D., and Lynn W. Bachelor. 1993. *The Sustaining Hand*. Lawrence: University Press of Kansas.

King, R. J. 1996. Ilitch Family Unveils Plan for Avenue of Fun. *Detroit News*, 10 October, A1.

Kotler, P., D. H. Haider, and I. Rein. 1993. *Marketing Places*. New York: Free Press.

KPMG Peat Marwick LLP. 1997. Development Planning Study for the Renovation of Ned Skeldon Stadium or a Proposed New Class AAA Baseball Stadium in Toledo, Ohio. Draft Report, July.

Laing, Jonathan R. 1996. Foul Play? *Barron's*, 19 August, 23–27.

Lam, Tina. 1995. Public's Share for New Stadium Relatively Low. *Detroit Free Press*, 19 September, 1B.

Lam, Tina, and Daniel G. Fricker. 1996. Detroit Comeback. *Detroit Free Press*, 21 August, 1A, 9A.

Linsalata, Phil. 1996a. Cabinet Post for Archer? No, but He'd Be Flattered. *Detroit News*, 8 November, A1.

Linsalata, Phil. 1996b. New Stadium Can Help Detroit's Image. *Detroit News*, 21 August, A6.

Linsalata, Phil, and Melinda Wilson. 1996a. Mayor Archer Says New, Single Floor Buildings Will Be Built; His Office Will Decide Ultimate Locations. *Detroit News*, 8 November, A1.

Linsalata, Phil, and Melinda Wilson. 1996b. Wall Street Bullish on Detroit: Brokerages Willing to Invest Up to $600 Million in Casinos, Hotels. *Detroit News*, 12 November, A1.

Michigan Consultants. 1995. *Detroit Analysis: Economic Impact of a New Tiger Stadium*. Lansing: Michigan Consultants.

Oguntoyinbo, Lekan. 1996. Other Projects. *Detroit Free Press*, 21 August, 9A.

Pelissero, John P., Beth M. Henschen, and Edward I. Sidlow. 1991. Urban Regimes, Sports Stadiums, and the Politics of Economic Development Agendas in Chicago. *Policy Studies Review* 10: 117–129.

Pepper, Jon. 1996. A "Miraculous" Deal Gets Done. *Detroit News*, 1 September, 1A.

Phillips, Cheryl. 1996. Kansas City, Cleveland Say Side-by-Side Stadiums Work for Them. *Detroit News*, 21 August, A7.

Ravitz, Mel. Member, Detroit City Council. 1996. Personal interview with author, 2 October.

Rosentraub, Mark S. 1996. Does the Emperor Have New Clothes? A Reply to Robert A. Baade. *Journal of Urban Affairs* 18: 23–31.

Rosentraub, Mark S., David Swindell, Michael Przybylski, and Daniel R. Mullins. 1994. Sport and Downtown Development Strategy: If You Build It, Will Jobs Come? *Journal of Urban Affairs* 16: 221–239.

Schaffer, W. A., B. L. Jaffee, and L. S. Davidson. 1993. *Beyond the Game: The Economic Impact of Amateur Sports*. Indianapolis: Chamber of Commerce.

Wolman, H. 1988. Local Economic Development Policy: What Explains the Divergence between Policy Analysis and Political Behavior? *Journal of Urban Affairs* 10: 19–28.

7

Minor League Baseball: Risks and Potential Benefits for Communities Large and Small

Arthur T. Johnson

The chapters in this volume demonstrate that publicly financed sports facilities are the basis on which communities compete with one another in their pursuit of sports teams. To fund or not to fund a new stadium or significant renovations to an existing stadium is a public-policy decision local (and state) officials in communities seeking to retain or attract a team must address. This is true not only for cities dealing with major league sports teams, but also for communities operating in the secondary sports markets, especially that of minor league baseball.

Minor league baseball franchises are located in more than 150 communities, large and small, in the United States and Canada.[1] It is an industry swathed in myth and nostalgia. Marketing strategies adeptly use these positive feelings for the sport of baseball in general and minor league baseball in particular to sell the product of minor league baseball as family entertainment. This has generated a growth industry in the 1990s. For example, the sale of licensed merchandise of minor league teams was more than $170 million from 1991 to mid-1996. Retail sales of merchandise bearing the names of teams in minor league baseball totaled more than $46 million in 1995. Several teams playing in small communities such as Hickory, North Carolina, and Wappingers

Falls, New York, were among the top twenty-five teams in sales (National Association of Professional Baseball Leagues [NAPBL] 1996b).

Attendance at minor league games has increased each year from 1986, when attendance was 18,456,808. In 1991 attendance reached 26,590,096, and in 1998, 35,427,012 fans attended minor league baseball games.[2] Five minor leagues (from short-season A to AAA leagues) and twenty-seven teams set attendance records in 1998.

The construction of modern new stadiums to house minor league teams is in part responsible for this growth in attendance. From 1985 to 1989, nineteen new minor league stadiums were constructed, and from 1990 to 1996, forty-nine new minor league stadiums were constructed (National Association of Professional Baseball Leagues 1996c). Since 1996, several more new stadiums have been opened, including those in Akron, New Orleans, Oklahoma City, Rochester (New York), and Charleston (South Carolina). At the beginning of 1999 a number of communities—ranging from Missoula, Montana, and Round Rock, Texas, to Brooklyn, New York—had committed funds for new minor league stadiums. By the year 2000 more than half of all minor league teams will be playing in stadiums constructed since the late 1980s.

New minor league stadiums provide fans with a variety of concession and novelty stands, clean facilities, family-friendly accommodations, and even luxury suites. Minor league stadiums cost between $2 million and $25 million to construct. An exception, the stadium built for the Buffalo Bisons, cost in excess of $40 million, partly because it was designed to be expanded for major league baseball when Buffalo receives a major league franchise. Renovations of minor league stadiums also often range in the millions of dollars. For example, Pawtucket, Rhode Island, and Everett, Washington, are investing more than $15 and $5 million dollars, respectively, in stadium renovations as the decade comes to an end.

Such sizable investments are often justified with the promise of significant economic impact. As chapters in this book and other academic analyses (Okner 1974; Baim 1992; Quirk and Fort 1992; Rosentraub et al. 1994; Baade 1996) demonstrate, it is unlikely that significant economic impact will be created to recoup the public's financial investment. This is especially true for minor league stadiums, because a minor league team's attendance, payroll, number of employees, tourist potential, and media coverage are much smaller than those of a major league team (Rosentraub and Swindell 1991; Johnson 1993). In addition, the host community's economy is less likely to capture the revenue generated by a minor league team than is a larger city hosting a major league team.

Proposals to invest public funds in new minor league stadiums, therefore, often prove to be controversial. Boosters' promises of economic growth and other positive benefits are met with disbelief and arguments for other priorities. The public official must understand the nature of the industry in order to evaluate the arguments presented, and must understand the role minor league stadiums can play in a community's life. This chapter, updating previous research (Johnson 1993), provides insight into the business of minor league baseball to suggest the types of risk that officials accept if they invest in a stadium, and describes how a minor league stadium might be of value to a community even if it is not a significant economic growth engine.

GOVERNANCE OF MINOR LEAGUE BASEBALL

The governance of the minor leagues, the ownership of teams, and the potential for franchise relocation create a level of risk for any investment in a minor league stadium of which local officials should be aware. The minor leagues are organized according to the level of the players' skills. Leagues are classified from highest to lowest: AAA (three leagues including the Mexican League), AA (three leagues), A (seven leagues), and Rookie Advanced (two leagues). The National Association of Professional Baseball Leagues governs these fifteen professional baseball leagues. Each league has its own officers, who manage their league's affairs under the jurisdiction of their league's by-laws, the National Association Agreement, and the Professional Baseball Agreement (PBA).

The PBA governs the relationship between the major leagues and the minor leagues as well as certain specified actions of minor league clubs, the minor leagues, and their governing bodies. It defines the Player Development Contract (PDC), which identifies the obligations of a major league team and its affiliate minor league teams, including responsibility for player salaries, player assignments, travel and per diem expenses, uniforms, equipment, and the manner of team travel, among many other issues.

The current PBA was signed by the National Association and Major League Baseball in fall 1997. It replaced a PBA signed in December 1990 after intense and often bitter negotiations. The 1990 PBA imposed upon minor leagues payments to the major leagues that did not previously exist, denied them payments previously made by Major League Baseball, and reduced subsidies for certain operating expenses. The current PBA did not introduce significant changes and was negotiated without the rancor that accompanied the 1990 negotiations.

The 1990 PBA guaranteed only 119 Player Development Contracts for future years. This fact and statements made by major league team owners fueled speculation that major league owners would seek to reduce their costs by reducing the number of minor league teams with which they affiliate. This has not occurred and does not appear likely in the near future. Nevertheless, it is essential for local officials to understand the way minor league baseball is governed in order to understand that minor league officials and team owners do not control their own destiny. Local officials must recognize that while the minor leagues appear to be flourishing, the future is clouded by the uncertainty of major league team owners' future actions and their desire to reduce operating costs.[3]

Neil Sullivan (1990), in his review of the historic relationship between the minor leagues and the major leagues, establishes the fact that on several occasions throughout the twentieth century the minor leagues were in a position to operate independently and to challenge the major league's dominance. He describes the history of the minor leagues as being scarred by the major league's successful efforts to keep minor leagues subordinate. "The majors have continually made decisions about personnel policies, franchise relocation, expansion, and broadcasting that were indifferent or damaging to the minors" (p. viii).

Table 7.1
Minor League Franchise Relocations, 1988–1998

Leagues	1988	1989	1990	1991	1992
AAA*					
American Association					
International		1			
Pacific Coast	1				
AA					
Eastern		4			1
Southern	1	1		1	
Texas					
A					
California	1	1		1	
Carolina		1			
Florida State	2	1			1
Midwest				1	
South Atlantic	1			1	1
New York--Penn	2	2			
Northwest			1		
Totals	8	11	1	4	3

*In 1998, realignment of AAA leagues resulted in the dissolution of the American Association and its teams being assigned to one of the two remaining leagues.

The PBA also dictates specific stadium standards for each league level. These standards apply to existing stadiums as well as to new stadiums. They apply to all aspects of a stadium, from field lighting, plumbing fixtures, parking, and sound systems to team laundries, clubhouses, and concession stands. Communities have had to decide to either finance required renovations or lose their teams. The cost of new stadiums and renovations is in part driven by the required standards. Because the supply of minor league teams is controlled, the demand for teams exceeds the supply. Thus, teams accompany their stadium demands with credible threats to relocate. In fact, major league team owners may pressure their minor league affiliates to relocate so that their minor league players can experience the best playing conditions.

PBA stadium standards are a partial explanation for the boom in stadium construction and the frequency of franchise relocation. Table 7.1 reports franchise relocations from 1988 to 1998 and reveals instability, especially at the A and AA levels. A closer examination of these relocations reveals no relationship between the sizes of communities losing and attracting teams. That is, a team may just as likely move

Table 7.1 (*continued*)

1993	1994	1995	1996	1997	1998	Totals
1						1
						1
	1				1	3
1	1	1		1		9
1		1		1	1	7
						0
3	1		1			8
1					1	3
2	2				1	9
1	2	1	1			6
2		1	1			7
1	5	1	1			12
		1		1		3
13	12	6	4	3	4	69

from a larger to a smaller community as from a smaller to a larger community. For example, teams from Riverside, California (estimated population 226,000), Albany, Georgia (estimated population 78,000), and Nashville, Tennessee (estimated population 533,000), lost teams to Lancaster, California (estimated population 96,000), Salisbury, Maryland (20,000), and Wilmington, North Carolina (56,000), in the mid-1990s. However, many fear the increasing cost of operating minor league teams will make it more and more difficult to operate in smaller markets in the future (Lingo 1998, 14). For example, according to the NAPBL, more than one-third of its teams experienced operating losses in the 1998 season. Of these teams, nearly three-fourths were A level or Rookie league teams, which normally are found in the smaller markets.

Relocation is made more likely by the fact that team ownership is by business groups who view a team as an investment, rather than a hobby or a civic commitment. Several investment groups and individuals own more than one team. The value of teams has escalated since the mid-1980s, so that today minor league teams at all levels are worth several million dollars. For example, Northwest League franchises (Rookie Advanced) are estimated to be worth $1 to $5 million; the Fort Wayne franchise (A level), which sold for $1 million in 1991, sold for a reported $4.75 million in 1998; the New Britain franchise (AA level) sold for a reported $7.5 million, despite having the lowest attendance in its league in 1998; and the expansion fee for AAA teams which began play in 1998 was $7.5 million dollars. The stadium arrangement is the last fixed cost (relative to labor, equipment, and travel costs, most of which are defined by the PBA) for the team owner. Recent team purchases are likely to be heavily financed, so owners attempt to negotiate the least-costly stadium arrangement in order to minimize operating expenses.

Local officials, therefore, must prepare for difficult negotiations over lease terms and stadium conditions. Failure to resist team demands may result in annual operating deficits for the stadium or an inability to meet debt-service payments. Minor league team owners in the past have resisted leases beyond five or ten years, but with the rising cost of stadiums, communities have been more successful in negotiating longer-term commitments in an effort to protect their stadium investments.

THE VALUE OF MINOR LEAGUE TEAMS TO A COMMUNITY

Communities should not expect to recoup their stadium investment on a dollar-for-dollar basis. For the reasons noted, the economic impact of minor league teams is minimal. They are a seasonal operation (approximately seventy-five or fewer home games from April to August), and are comparable to a small business in the community. Even so, minor league teams and their stadiums can be contributors to a community's economic well-being and quality of life.

Investment in minor league stadiums may be worth it from a public-policy perspective if a project is developed as part of a community-development plan and linked to specific objectives. A development logic must drive the project; simply building a stadium on the belief and hope that "if you build it, they will come" is not likely to be a wise policy choice. Three objectives for a minor league stadium appear to be reasonable.

Stadiums can be used to advance economic-development objectives through redevelopment activity, or new development opportunities by virtue of their location. Such stadiums can be given specific purposes, such as anchoring downtowns or opening new land for development. Locations must be selected with care to ensure that the necessary infrastructure is available, accessibility is reasonable, and synergistic activity exists or is planned. For example, a minor league stadium in South Bend, Indiana, was located to open up an industrial corridor for redevelopment and was designed as part of a larger entertainment strategy to attract people downtown. The Harrisburg, Pennsylvania, stadium was located to stimulate the redevelopment of a dilapidated island park and to attract suburbanites downtown. A stadium in Hoover, Alabama, was located so as to open up land for new development and to provide a base for future annexations, and a stadium in York County, South Carolina, provided a reason to put infrastructure in place that will eventually be used to support growth along a corridor that was projected for future development, thereby accelerating the expected development. More recently, the cities of Akron, Rochester, Trenton (New Jersey), and Portland (Maine) have sought to use minor league stadiums as catalysts for redevelopment.

Perhaps other projects could accomplish these goals, but it is often the case that the popularity of a sports stadium creates an environment that will gain approval that alternative projects could not achieve. If that is the case, then promoting a stadium project to achieve economic development objectives may be a wise policy decision.

Thus, a stadium by itself will not trigger significant development, but based on an appropriate development logic, a stadium can assist in achieving specific development goals. Without such a development logic or an appropriate plan, the economic benefits that a stadium is capable of producing either will not be realized or will be too diffuse to have a meaningful impact.

A second objective may be to enhance a community's image. A minor league team is capable of promoting a community's name throughout the region in which it plays. Its stadium can serve as a symbol of the community's commitment to growth, quality of life, and a number of positive goals. Hoover, Alabama, constructed its stadium in an effort to be accepted by Birmingham as a serious metropolitan partner. The Frederick, Maryland, stadium was built in conjunction with other projects in an effort to create the image of Frederick as an attractive destination city for the region of West Virginia, Washington, D.C., Pennsylvania, and Maryland.

Local officials also want residents to possess a positive image of their home town. They hope that a team and its stadium will create civic pride and a sense of positive identity. In order to achieve this, local officials must aggressively exploit the team and the stadium. Local government agencies, the mayor's office, economic development agencies, and tourist bureaus must energetically promote the team and stadium in their promotional literature and presentations. A variety of community events can be planned around the stadium and the team to create a positive image. Local officials must persuade the business community to participate in these efforts. The chamber of commerce and other business organizations must become partners to promote a positive image of the community, within and beyond its borders.

For example, the city of Harrisburg printed brochures containing city information with action pictures of the newly acquired Harrisburg Senators on their front cover and mayor's reports noting the success of the Senators and City Island, the stadium's location. The city's July Fourth celebration focused on the riverfront, City Island, and the team. Recently, the city bought the team to prevent it from relocating.

When a publicly funded stadium is built to house a sports team, the community and team are joined in a partnership. The success of the stadium is dependent on the success of its primary tenant, the team. The team, carrying the city's name, is an agent of the city. Thus, if enhancement of image is a local government's goal, it must take an active role in ensuring that the stadium and the team help achieve that goal.

A third potential objective for a stadium is to provide additional recreational amenities for residents and to contribute to the community's quality of life. Minor league baseball is marketed as low-cost family entertainment. Some stadiums rival shopping malls in attracting teenagers. Families come to minor league games for a night out, often staying only a few innings. For the baseball fan, minor league baseball provides the opportunity to watch the game "up close" and to identify future stars.

The stadium must be more than where a team plays seventy games. It must be conceptualized as a community resource that provides different types of recreational opportunities. If the stadium is developed and utilized in this manner, the impact of the team's relocation or demise will be minimized. The team's lease for use of the stadium must permit nonteam events to take place in the stadium and must balance the interests of the community with those of the team. The stadium may be used for amateur sports events, different types of concerts, holiday gatherings and parades, exhibits, and trade shows, among other activities. For example, the Lackawanna County Stadium Authority (Scranton–Wilkes-Barre) erects an ice skating rink in the outfield of its stadium during the winter for community ice skaters. South Bend, Indiana, in an effort to generate closer community identity with the stadium, used stadium revenues to fund small neighborhood grants.

CONCLUSIONS

In sum, an increasing number of communities, large and small, are making multi-million-dollar investments in minor league stadiums. One should not expect an investment in a minor league baseball stadium to generate significant economic impact. On the other hand, such an investment can be a public-policy decision with positive outcomes. If a development logic drives the stadium decision, the stadium may be used to promote economic objectives of the community, enhance the community's image, or improve the recreational infrastructure of the community.

A sports stadium is one of only a few possible projects capable of bringing thousands of citizens together in one place. Sports gatherings are capable of promoting civic identity and pride. A sports team is capable of generating community excitement and enthusiasm more than the typical economic-development project. Partly for these reasons, it is less important that a stadium return the public investment to a community dollar for dollar. What is important is that the primary beneficiary of the investment, the team owner, accept responsibility as a major partner with the community, meet the civic obligations resulting from that partnership, and cooperatively pursue community objectives. This should be as important a part of the stadium agreement as the lease's financial terms. For example, Buffalo and other communities have written into their stadium agreements with teams affirmative-action goals and other "understandings" about hiring minority employees.

Without clear goals for a minor league stadium and a strategy to achieve those goals, it is doubtful whether a community's investment in minor league baseball will be "worth it." The measure of the wisdom of such public-policy decisions is not the success of the team in attracting fans, but what a stadium and the team contribute to the host community.

NOTES

1. This chapter focuses only on those minor leagues governed by the National Association of Professional Baseball Leagues. It does not address the relatively new phenomenon of independent leagues. Local officials should understand the differences between independent league teams and NAPBL teams. Independent leagues are not governed by the NAPBL and have no affiliation with major league teams as do NAPBL teams. Teams in independent leagues, therefore, can sell player contracts to any major league team, whereas teams governed by the NAPBL can neither sign players nor control their contract assignments, which is done by their major league affiliates. Independent leagues reappeared in 1993 and have had varying degrees of stability. Since 1993, seven leagues have failed. In 1996 nine independent leagues existed with fifty-six teams, and drew 3,454,557 fans ("Independent Leagues" 1996, 45). In 1998 seven leagues with forty-seven teams finished the season, and in 1999 six leagues are expected to operate. Team relocations are numerous. For example, since the Western League's inception in 1995, seven franchises either relocated or failed. Four new teams are expected in 1999. The league operates with eight teams.

2. Attendance figures include attendance at Mexican League games. Mexican League attendance in 1991 was 2,419,567; in 1998 it exceeded 3.1 million fans. Attendance figures are provided by the National Association of Professional Baseball Leagues (1996a) and *Baseball America* (1998, 18).

3. In 1998, legislation was signed into law which provides for a partial repeal of baseball's antitrust exemption. The legislation, to be known as the Curt Flood Act, explicitly states that it does not apply to "anything related to the business of minor league baseball" or the PBA. The legislation addresses the narrow issue of labor relations at the major league level, but otherwise preserves Major League Baseball's antitrust exemption. As such, it most likely will strengthen the exemption and preserve the existing relationship between Major League Baseball and the minor leagues.

REFERENCES

Baade, Robert. 1996. Professional Sports as Catalysts for Metropolitan Economic Development. *Journal of Urban Affairs* 18: 1–17.
Baim, Dean. 1992. *The Sports Stadium as a Municipal Investment*. Westport, Conn.: Greenwood Press.
Baseball America. 1998. *Baseball America*, 26 October–8 November, 18.
Independent Leagues—Standings, Leaders. 1996. *Baseball America*, 30 September–13 October, 45.
Johnson, Arthur T. 1993. *Minor League Baseball and Local Economic Development*. Urbana: University of Illinois Press.
Lingo, Will. 1998. Diehards Keep Game Going in Small Towns. *Baseball America*, 9–22 November, 14.
National Association of Professional Baseball Leagues. 1996a. 1996 NAPBL Club Attendance, 2 October, Mimeographed.

National Association of Professional Baseball Leagues. 1996b. Minor League Baseball Logos Produce $46-Million in Retail Sales, 6 May. Mimeographed.

National Association of Professional Baseball Leagues. 1996c. New Ballparks Constructed Since 1985. Mimeographed.

Okner, Benjamin. 1974. Subsidies of Stadiums and Arenas. In *Government and the Sports Business*, edited by Roger Noll. Washington, D.C.: The Brookings Institution, 325–347.

Quirk, James, and Rodney D. Fort. 1992. *Pay Dirt: The Business of Professional Team Sports*. Princeton: Princeton University Press.

Rosentraub, Mark S., David Swindell, Michael Przybylski, and Daniel R. Mullins. 1994. Sport and Downtown Development Strategy: If You Build It, Will Jobs Come? *Journal of Urban Affairs* 16: 221–239.

Rosentraub, Mark S., and David Swindell. 1991. Just Say No? The Economic and Political Realities of a Small City's Investment in Minor League Baseball. *Economic Development Quarterly* 5: 152–167.

Sullivan, Neil. 1990. *The Minors*. New York: St. Martin's Press.

8

Building Ballparks:
The Public-Policy Dimensions of
Keeping the Game in Town

Edward I. Sidlow and Beth M. Henschen

The nation is experiencing a stadium "binge." By some estimates, American cities and states spent at least $1 billion on new facilities in the early 1990s to lure professional teams to relocate or to keep the teams they have, and as the twenty-first century begins, as many as forty-five stadiums and arenas will have been built at a cost of more than $9 billion (see, e.g., Lever 1995; Laing 1996; Brady and Howlett 1996).

The extraordinary public costs of the "sweetheart deals" that so many wealthy sports entrepreneurs are receiving these days are often justified to the taxpayers in economic-development terms. Not only does a team contribute millions of dollars to the local economy along with hundreds of jobs, it is argued, but a new stadium can be a catalyst for economic growth. Indeed, a recent trend has been to take professional sports back downtown into facilities that become part of the entertainment complex of the center city, spurring, it is claimed, urban revitalization.

The weight of evidence suggests otherwise. Most analyses find the economic benefits of teams and stadiums questionable (see, e.g., Okner 1974; Baade 1987; Rosentraub 1988; Quirk and Fort 1992; Euchner 1993; Baade 1994; Baim 1994). Nevertheless, state and local policy makers are usually willing to accommodate the demands of franchise owners with the investment of significant public resources.

To understand why such decisions are made, we begin by examining how they are made. We examine sports as public policy. We are interested in how the business of professional sports franchises gets on the government agenda and why certain policies regarding sports stadiums are adopted and implemented. Although public officials have been asked to make policy choices with respect to franchises of every sport, we focus our attention on Major League Baseball. Its history is venerable. Its heroes are legendary. And it is with the game of baseball that the modern, high-stakes game of franchise politics began.

SPORTS AS PUBLIC POLICY

Baseball is a business. And for all of the romance and legend and unbridled affection the national pastime has engendered (see, e.g., Angell 1978; Kahn 1971; Ritter 1966; Thorn 1985, 1987), it has been so for a very long time. By the mid-1870s the club-based game grounded in local culture had become a national commercial enterprise dependent on business management, gate receipts, performance measured by statistics, and the paid labor of players (Goldstein 1989, 4, 101, 136–147). Harry Wright, one of the dominant figures of the baseball world during the late nineteenth century (p. 103) declared in 1871 to a friend, "Baseball is business now" (p. 138). Moreover, baseball has always had ties to politics. Almost every nineteenth-century professional team had a political connection (Vincent 1981, 98–99; see also Riess 1980, 49–77). Political clout helped to keep licensing fees at a manageable level, secured police protection at games, and, perhaps most important, facilitated the efforts of team owners to build a baseball park at a desirable location (Riess 1980, 49–77). Beginning in 1909, fireproof structures were built to increase seating capacities and replace wooden stands. The expense of such ventures prompted owners to either buy their own sites or obtain long-term leases for security. Political allies supplied inside information critical to selecting a site where land was cheap and accessible by mass transit, protected the team against community opposition, and obtained a variety of city services for the ball club (p. 110).

Given its historical underpinnings, there should be no surprise that the current state of affairs is one in which politics and the business of baseball (and, of course, other professional sports) are inextricably entwined. In the parlance of public policy, government decisions to build stadiums and accommodate team owners in other ways constitute distributive policies. As Anderson (1994, 11–12) states it, distributive policies involve the allocation of services or benefits to particular segments of the population. The benefits do not represent a direct cost to any specific group; rather, the costs are charged to the public treasury, that is, the taxpayers. As more and more cities and states respond to team owners' demands, the cumulative effect of these individualized decisions (see Lowi 1964, 690) is the creation of sports policy. Government policies that promote business activity include subsidies, favorable tax provisions, and the construction and maintenance of facilities (Anderson et al. 1984, 260–265). So it is with sports.

Though clearly it is the specter of an empty ballpark, broken-hearted fans, a tarnished public image, and obsolete T-shirts that prompts politicians to take seriously the escalating demands of team owners, the pattern in Major League Baseball has been one of teams staying rather than leaving. To be sure, modern baseball franchise relocation began in the early 1950s with the moves of the Boston Braves to Milwaukee, the St. Louis Browns to Baltimore, and the Philadelphia Athletics to Kansas City. These early moves did not stir much passion, since each of these franchises were weak counterparts to more successful major league teams—the Boston Red Sox, the St. Louis Cardinals, and the Philadelphia Phillies—which remained in those cities.

The threat of losing a team became more salient when the Dodgers and Giants, teams with loyal fans and more-recent successful seasons, left New York for the West Coast. Still, only ten franchise relocations have occurred in Major League Baseball in the modern era, and none since the Senators moved to Texas and became the Rangers in 1972. While the public perception may be that teams are on the move (and, indeed, there seems to be no end to the number of "team-less" cities that would love to become "big league"), the real story in baseball may be one of cities actively working to keep the teams they have. The game has become one of high-stakes policy making that has, in most instances, resulted in keeping the franchise from taking the ultimate road trip.

In order to identify the patterns that characterize public policy making aimed toward retaining Major League Baseball franchises, we examine the policy processes that resulted in the construction of new stadiums in Chicago, Baltimore, Cleveland, and Detroit. We chronicle the decisions made by "official policy makers," that is, legislatures, executives, administrative agencies, and courts. We also highlight the actions of the "unofficial participants," that is, interest groups, political parties, research organizations, the media, and individual citizens (see Anderson 1994, 54–79). We trace the development of the policy from problem identification and agenda setting, through policy-proposal formulation and adoption, to implementation (see pp. 84–148, 188–236). By treating political decisions regarding Major League Baseball franchises as part and parcel of public policy making, we will be able to determine how private and public interests converge—or collide—when the issue at hand is keeping the game in town.

COMISKEY PARK II

The construction of the new Comiskey Park, which was completed for the 1991 season, was the culmination of a process that evolved over several years. The Chicago White Sox had been sold to Jerry Reinsdorf and Eddie Einhorn in 1981, and while they pledged to keep the team in Chicago, by 1985 Reinsdorf and Einhorn began arguing that they needed a new stadium. A market analysis commissioned by the White Sox advised them to develop a suburban fan base, a goal that was not facilitated by the location of the old Comiskey Park in the predominantly black South Armour Square neighborhood on Chicago's South Side. Structural engineers hired by the owners also reported that Comiskey, the oldest facility in the major leagues, was crumbling (Euchner 1993, 135; Richmond 1993, 111). Almost immediately, the issue of a new stadium for the White Sox found a place on the government agenda.

Initially, the White Sox promoted a plan for stadium construction on land they had purchased in west suburban Addison.[1] The site was attractive because of predictions that attendance would increase, the team would garner more skybox and parking revenues, and maintenance costs would be lower under a long-term lease arrangement with a DuPage County Stadium Authority. The Republican governor, James Thompson, favored the Addison site, as did leaders of the Republican party in the General Assembly. House Speaker Michael Madigan, a Chicago Democrat and South Sider, was reluctant to support a highway and public-works improvement package that would help the White Sox leave Chicago and reward the heavily Republican DuPage County. Instead, he joined forces with Chicago's reform mayor, Harold Washington, supporting the mayor's efforts to keep the team in the city.

To counter the Addison plan, Mayor Harold Washington advanced a proposal in April 1986 for constructing a dual-purpose stadium for football and baseball as the linchpin of an economic-redevelopment package for the South Loop. The project would have been financed through $255 million of industrial revenue bonds, and would have enjoyed state and county financial support as well. Neither the White Sox nor the NFL Chicago Bears would agree to a shared space, however, and the proposal was dropped.

The potential move to Addison was also thwarted in 1986 when the U.S. Environmental Protection Agency took action in July to prevent the White Sox from developing the wetlands adjacent to their proposed site and when, in November, Addison voters approved an advisory referendum against building a stadium. Responding to community opposition, Thompson and other political leaders stopped pushing the suburban stadium plan.

In December 1986, at the urging of the Washington administration and the White Sox owners, the Illinois General Assembly created the Illinois Sports Facilities Authority (ISFA) to build and operate a new stadium across the street from the original Comiskey Park. The initial terms of the legislative package provided that the White Sox would rent the $120-million facility for $4 million annually. The team would receive all gate receipts and would be assessed higher rent only when attendance and skybox revenues were significantly greater than that yielded by current operations. A combination of the lease payments and a 2-per-cent tax on hotel rooms in the city was designated for construction-bond retirement. The city of Chicago also agreed to split operating losses of as much as $10 million per year with the state of Illinois.

Implementation of the plan was delayed for nearly a year, however, as Governor Thompson, a Republican, and Mayor Washington, a Democrat, battled over control of the ISFA board (McCarron 1987). The White Sox, meanwhile, publicly complained about certain parts of the legislative package, the delay in organizing the stadium author-ity, and neighborhood resistance to the proposed redevelopment. Reinsdorf also entertained proposals from Denver, New Orleans, Buf-falo, and Washington. He was most interested, however, in an offer from St. Petersburg, a small city that had built a $100-million domed stadium in the hopes of luring a team (Helyar 1994, 452). By 1988 the possibility that the White Sox might move to Florida had become a real threat, intensifying public interest and providing further leverage for the franchise in the negotiations with Chicago. In John Kingdon's (1995, 165–166) terms, the courting of St. Petersburg helped open the policy window and moved the stadium issue onto the decision agenda. An amended agreement provided for $150 million and additional rev-enue opportunities for the team. The ISFA agreed to a construction completion date of March 1, 1991; if the date was not met, $5 million in penalties would be paid to the team. The ISFA also agreed to as-sume the costs of continuing operations at Comiskey Park until its demolition. Furthermore, the agreement stipulated that the ISFA pay the White Sox a maintenance subsidy of $2 million a year (with an increase after the tenth year), and the ISFA must buy 300,000 tickets in those years in which attendance falls below 1.5 million in the second decade of the twenty-year lease. The franchise pays no rent on the stadium up to 1.2 million in yearly attendance. Above that, $2.50 per ticket is paid to the ISFA (Helyar 1994, 453).

This policy solution to the problem presented by the specter of the White Sox moving to Florida was adopted in a classic scene of hardball politicking. It was June 30, 1988, the last day of the Illinois legislative session. By law, no bills could be enacted after midnight. As Helyar (1994) replays it,

> It was 10:30 P.M. when Big Jim Thompson strode onto the floor of the Senate and started twisting arms. An hour later, the stadium was approved there, 30–26. Thompson raced across the capitol rotunda and into the House chamber. He threw off his coat, rolled up his sleeves, and began calling in every damned chit that was owed him.
>
> But at 12:00 A.M., Central Time, Thompson was still short of the sixty votes he needed. Cheers rang across Tampa Bay—but Florida didn't know Illinois politics. The clock on the House floor had been turned off, the deadline ignored. A few minutes after midnight, Thompson picked up his sixtieth vote. The stadium was approved, 60–55, and the House Majority Leader declared the time 11:59 P.M. (p. 453)

Implementation of the stadium deal required the acquisition of the necessary land, the first major task faced by the ISFA. As many as 100 families, dozens of businesses, a school, a church, and some industrial sites had to be relocated. Hit hardest by the stadium site redevelopment was South Armour Square, a neighborhood of mostly working-class black families who had lived in the area for generations. The legislation adopted by the state had given the ISFA "quick take" power of eminent domain; most of the land could be acquired within thirty days of notification of the property owner. Mayor Washington's stadium and economic-development advisors worked with the ISFA to overcome the community opposition that was voiced primarily through the South Armour Square Neighborhood Coalition. Following Washington's death, acting mayor Eugene Sawyer oversaw a program that gave homeowners market price for their houses, a $25,000 cash bonus, moving expenses, and legal fees. They could opt to have a new home built for free if their mortgage was paid off, or they could obtain mortgage payments identical to what they were currently paying. Renters received moving expenses, $4,500 bonuses, and a $250 monthly rental differential for one year. A significant number of contracts for minorities in the construction and operation of the ballpark were also negotiated.

The new Comiskey Park opened in 1991. After an eighty-year run, the original Comiskey Park, once called the Baseball Palace of the World (Gershman 1993, 92), became a parking lot for baseball fans on Chicago's South Side.

ORIOLE PARK AT CAMDEN YARDS

When Bill Veeck brought his St. Louis Browns to Baltimore in 1954, the franchise began its stint as the Orioles on a very favorable note. Baltimore's mayor, Thomas D'Alesandro Jr., gave the team generous terms for the lease of Memorial Stadium, revenues from parking and food concessions, free stadium maintenance, and office space. By 1957, however, both the NFL Colts and the Orioles began lobbying actively for stadium improvements. City residents supported a $1.2-million recreation loan in 1962 to upgrade the stadium to meet club needs, but strains in the city–team relationship grew during the 1960s as public funding became scarce (Miller 1990, 69–72).

By the late 1960s and early 1970s, however, the Orioles were baseball's dominant franchise, and their success, together with that of the championship Colts, helped foster a sense of local pride. Baltimore was also engaging in a major effort of urban renewal, including the redevelopment of its Inner Harbor into a complex of retail stores, offices, residences, and restaurants. In 1971 William Donald Schaefer, the city council president, was elected mayor. He was a pragmatic reformer who fully supported the development strategy and who was convinced of the important role professional sports could play in it. The Colts were campaigning for a publicly financed stadium in the rebuilt city center, and by 1972 Orioles owner Jerold Hoffberger was also convinced that a new stadium would help him secure his financial base (Miller 1990, 150–152, 179).

When Colts owner Carroll Rosenbloom announced in 1971 that he would leave Memorial Stadium and Baltimore when his lease expired the following year, Governor Marvin Mandel pushed the General Assembly into approving the establishment of a Maryland Sports Complex Authority; its final report of 1973 recommended the construction of a new stadium in the Camden Yards in downtown Baltimore. The Colts (now owned by Robert Irsay) and Orioles, however, refused to sign long-term leases until construction began, and the authority refused to request legislative permission to sell bonds to finance construction without signed leases. The following year Baltimore voters approved a referendum barring the use of public funds to build a stadium (Miller 1990, 200–205).

Edward Bennett Williams bought the Orioles in 1979; in the early 1980s the team was among the best in baseball and the city supported it with continued improvements to Memorial Stadium and with publicity and promotional activities (Miller 1990, 267–271). At the same time, Irsay was speaking to a number of other cities about relocating his franchise. State leaders attempted to appease him with major funding for stadium expansion, and ultimately the city, the state, and corporate leaders offered Irsay a multi-million-dollar package to counter the lure of Indianapolis, with its brand-new stadium and other incentives (Johnson 1986, 414; Harris 1986, 605–606). In the end there was probably nothing Baltimore could have done to save the Colts; Irsay's disagreeable personality had contributed to a city–team relationship that had become untenable. It was, however, the Colts' departure in the middle of a March night in 1984 that provided the window of opportunity to transform a new stadium for the Orioles from a frequently mentioned idea floating about in the policy primeval soup (Kingdon 1995, 116–144) to a prominently placed issue on the government's decision agenda. Mayor Schaefer emerged as the most ardent supporter of a new facility. He took the loss of the Colts personally, but also saw it as a chance to get Williams his stadium by appealing to the climate of panic in the city. Behind the scenes, he also started talking about bringing the Cleveland Browns to Baltimore (Richmond 1993, 65).

After a year of task-force and sports-commission reports, consultant recommendations, and political wrangling with state legislators, stadium site selection was one of the few issues of the 1986 Democratic gubernatorial primary (Johnson 1993, 98). Schaefer easily won both the primary and the November general election. In November 1986 Governor-elect Schaefer called for quick legislative action on stadium funding, and soon thereafter the newly created Maryland Sports Authority delivered its plan to build two separate facilities, for baseball and football, adjacent to the Harbor Place development at Camden Yards. In 1987 the Maryland legislature passed authorizing legislation for land acquisition and financing, including $235 million in revenue bonds, two to four sports lotteries annually to pay bond debt service, and $1 million each year from the city. Attempts by Marylanders for Sports Sanity (MASS) to put the legislation to a statewide referendum failed (Miller 1990, 300–302; Richmond 1993, 92, 127; Euchner 1993, 121).

Final negotiations resulted in a fifteen-year lease agreement under which the team pays no rent but splits stadium profits with the Sports Authority. The agreement detailed the number of seats and luxury boxes in the new stadium and gave the franchise a major voice in the stadium design. It also isolated the team from sharing the burden of cost overruns, thereby increasing its attractiveness to potential buyers. In December 1988 the Orioles were sold to a group headed by New York investor Eli Jacobs, who pledged to keep the team in Baltimore into the next century (Miller 1990, 311–312).

Implementation of the stadium plan finally took on a tangible quality in June 1989 at a demolition ceremony at the Camden Yards site (Richmond 1993, 178–179). On Opening Day 1992, in a stadium that went millions of dollars over budget, baseball was played in Oriole Park at Camden Yards.

JACOBS FIELD

When Cleveland Municipal Stadium opened for baseball in 1932 it was called by National League President John Heydler the "last word in baseball parks" (Torry 1995, 206). Built and paid for by the people of Cleveland (it was not, as frequently thought, a WPA project), the stadium was the creation of William Hopkins, an extraordinarily persuasive politician who became the city's first manager in 1924. By the late 1960s, however, Cleveland Stadium was no longer a showplace, but was a relic from another era (Torry 1995, 206–214).

New ballparks were being built all over the country while the Indians were playing in an aging behemoth of a stadium. Indians owner Bill Daley, tired of battling poor attendance, wanted a $4-million overhaul of Cleveland Stadium, threatening Mayor Ralph Locher with a move to Seattle if he didn't get what he wanted. In fact, financial offers had come from as many as twelve cities. There had been hints of relocation as early as 1957; in 1958 the team's lease with the city thwarted a move to Minneapolis.[2] But the lease had expired in 1964, and Daley could now make demands on a city eager to negotiate a new agreement. Mayor Locher ultimately approved a ten-year lease, the $4 million in improvements, and a reduction in the team's rent, and agreed to a clause that would allow the Indians to cancel the lease on ninety days' notice (Torry 1995, 72–103).

In 1966 the Indians were sold to Vernon Stouffer, who, after a failed attempt to split the team's games between Cleveland and New Orleans, sold the club in 1972 to a group headed by Nick Mileti. Mileti had brought an NBA franchise to Cleveland, though he soon moved the Cavaliers to Richfield, near Akron. By 1973 Mileti was too financially strapped to hold onto the Indians, and Ted Bonda took over as president. Steve O'Neill assumed control of the franchise in 1978, and he became increasingly convinced that the team's financial problems stemmed from the lousy lease the Indians had with Art Modell, the Browns owner who had taken control of Cleveland Stadium in 1974. When the lease with Modell expired in 1983, the Indians filed suit against Modell, contending that his Stadium Corporation owed the baseball club $1.25 million more in concession revenues from the past ten years. A settlement was eventually reached in 1985, but the Indians' dissatisfaction with their situation at Cleveland Stadium had been made clear (Torry 1995, 104–176).

An ambitious politician took up the stadium cause. In the spring of 1983 Vince Campanella, a Republican county commissioner, abruptly announced to his budget assistant, "We're going to do a stadium" (quoted in Torry 1995, 214). Republicans considered Campanella a potential challenger to Governor Richard Celeste in 1986, and Campanella hoped to improve his chances by taking the lead on an impressive downtown project for Cleveland. Campanella preferred a large dome that could house the Browns, the Indians, and the Cavaliers, and he favored the Central Market area at the southern edge of the city. Art Modell, an influential player in Republican politics, was willing to move into a dome, as long as it had at least 70,000 seats and his Stadium Corporation was repaid for the $12 million Modell had spent renovating Cleveland Stadium. Campanella proposed raising $150 million through an increase in the county's property tax for the next twenty-five years, and was successful in placing the issue on the 1984 primary ballot. Cleveland Mayor George Voinovich, also a Republican, was appalled by the notion of a tax increase, and gave his half-hearted support for a dome only after Campanella signed a nonbinding agreement that the county would try to raise $75 million from private sources. The voters defeated the property tax issue, and that fall Campanella lost his reelection bid to Mary Boyle, a close friend of Richard Celeste, the Democratic governor (pp. 214–216).

Although Voinovich had been lukewarm about a dome that was funded in large part by an increase in property taxes, he was worried that the loss of the Indians would jeopardize the major redevelopment of Cleveland's downtown that was in progress. Baseball Commissioner Bowie Kuhn and American League President Bobby Brown told Voinovich that the rest of the American League owners had lost patience with Cleveland; they were tired of playing before small crowds and losing money every time they played in Cleveland Stadium. The owners wanted to sell thousands more season tickets, something that would only be possible in a smaller park. Others were also talking about a new stadium, including Jeff Jacobs, an Ohio legislator who became intrigued with an architect's proposal for a six-sided domed facility. Jacobs suggested a "sin tax" on beer and cigarettes to construct the project just off Lake Erie by City Hall, but Voinovich rejected the plan in 1985.[3] Instead, he and Celeste joined forces to support business executives and politicians who had formed the Greater Cleveland Domed Stadium Corporation, an organization that included representatives from the Indians, the Browns, the county board of commissioners, and the business community (Torry 1995, 216–218).

Suburban officials offered sites on which to build, but the corporation wanted to build downtown. It considered two sites on the east side, but favored the Central Market area. By late 1986 the corporation had added to the six acres of city-owned land by borrowing $18 million from city banks and convincing Celeste to kick in money from the state treasury in order to purchase additional acres. Originally, the plan was to use a large infusion of private money to build a 70,000-seat, multipurpose domed facility with a retractable roof that could be reconfigured to 40,000 seats during the baseball season. When the Indians were sold in 1986 to Richard Jacobs (Jeff Jacobs's father) and his brother David, however, it became clear that the new owners, who intended to run the team like a business rather than a civic enterprise, would move to the Central Market, but only to a small park built for baseball, with real grass (Torry 1995, 183, 219–220).

In 1989 close advisors to Richard Celeste urged him to secure his power base during his last years as governor by getting behind one last effort to build a ballpark and keep the Indians in downtown Cleveland. Celeste, of course, had heard this before. In 1983 American League President Lee MacPhail had confided that the only way Cleveland was going to keep the team was to get a new stadium. Now, six years later, Celeste decided to pursue a new stadium project. He told one of his advisers, Tom Chema, to work quietly behind the scenes to forge a consensus among key public officials for putting public money into a new ballpark (Torry 1995, 202–204).

Chema began with Mayor-elect Mike White, who had denounced the proposed domed stadium as a "sports palace for the Republican privileged." (quoted in Torry 1995, 220). But White told Chema that if it could be shown that a stadium made sense from an economic-development standpoint, he would support it. Chema knew that very few permanent jobs would be created by moving the Indians from one site to another; the only way to satisfy White's demand for an economic boost was to build an indoor arena as well. He approached the Cavaliers about returning to Cleveland from their home in suburban Richfield, a possibility that also appealed to Tim Hagan, a contentious Democratic county commissioner (pp. 220–223).

After holding several rounds of talks with Cleveland's political and business elite, Chema proposed an indoor basketball arena and an open-air park for baseball in the Central Market. The Jacobs brothers committed the Indians to a twenty-year lease if the stadium was built. The agreement signed with both teams provided that half of the estimated cost of $344 million for the two facilities would come from the public; the teams would raise the remainder through the sale and rental of luxury loges and club seats. For the source of public funding, Chema turned to a fifteen-year levy on cigarettes and alcohol; Celeste pushed a bill through the Ohio legislature allowing county officials to tax beer and wine at the retail level, supplementing earlier legislation that had authorized Cuyahoga County to impose a sin tax (Markiewicz 1990; Torry 1995, 223–225).

The county commissioners agreed to put the tax on the May 1990 primary ballot. The corporate community raised $1 million to produce commercials and print ads for the campaign to win Gateway, the stadium project. When tracking polls showed that people were not eager to pay more taxes for a new stadium, the campaign organizers adopted the slogan, "More Than a Stadium." They emphasized the economic boost the project would give to downtown. Day after day, a series of county officials and organizations were choreographed to endorse the stadium plan, and, close to the election, Baseball Commissioner Fay Vincent appeared before a city council finance committee. He warned that if the voters rejected the sin tax he would probably give the Indians permission to move to another city (Torry 1995, 225–229).

Cuyahoga County voters narrowly approved the sin tax, though residents of Cleveland rejected it. As governor, George Voinovich steered $43 million ($12 million of which was a loan) in state dollars to the project for public landings, sidewalks, and street improvements. On Opening Day 1994, Dick Jacobs watched the game in county-owned Jacobs Field, having paid nearly $14 million for the privilege of having the park, which cost about $180 million, bear his family's name (Euchner 1993, 7; Green 1994; Torry 1995, 235–237; Verducci 1994, 43, 48).

COMERICA PARK

Tiger Stadium, Detroit's historic ballpark, was built in 1912, the same year that Boston's Fenway Park was built. Originally named Navin Field, and then Briggs Stadium, the park was christened Tiger Stadium in 1961. The stadium's location in Detroit at the intersection of Michigan and Trumbull became known simply as "The Corner."

The policy story that culminated in a new home for the Tigers began many years ago. Detroit opinion leaders began touting a new downtown stadium after the race riots of 1967 led many Detroit business leaders to believe that the city and their investments were in jeopardy. The Tigers' 1968 World Championship convinced them that baseball could save Detroit. William Clay Ford, owner of the NFL Lions, was dissatisfied with his team's secondary role at Tiger Stadium and wanted his own place to play. Tiger owner John Fetzer also wanted a modern ballpark. In 1970 a working group appointed by Detroit Mayor Jerome Cavanaugh and Governor William Milliken recommended a domed stadium on the riverfront. Key politicians and business leaders lined up behind the plan, and a Wayne County Stadium Authority was created. Financing options were explored, and Detroit Renaissance, a civic organization founded in the wake of the riots, came to see a stadium as integral to rebuilding the city (Betzold and Casey 1992, 85, 89–93).

In 1971 Ford became increasingly doubtful about the riverfront site, and turned his attention to suburban Pontiac's plans to build him a domed stadium. Fetzer wanted to stay in the city, and in 1972 he signed a forty-year lease to play in the stadium to be built downtown, agreeing to pay an annual rent of at least $450,000. The stadium plan unraveled, however, when two private citizens filed an eleventh-hour lawsuit to halt the sale of bonds to finance stadium construction and when the town of Belleville in Wayne County also filed suit against the stadium deal. The lawsuits were joined, and after a nine-day trial Wayne County Circuit Court Judge Blair Moody ruled that the stadium authority's agreement was too one-sided in favor of the Tigers. The case was immediately sent to the Michigan Supreme Court, which struck down the project. The court ruled that stadium proponents had misled the public into thinking the stadium would be financed by revenue bonds (in addition to a 5-percent county hotel/motel tax and other annual revenues), when in fact they were more akin to general obligation bonds, meaning that county taxpayers would have to foot the bill if the stadium failed to pay its own way. With the riverfront plan derailed, the state of Michigan spearheaded a new proposal to build a multipurpose dome in Pontiac, financed with $55.7 million in public revenue bonds and city millage taxes. Fetzer stuck to his decision to stay in Detroit, and the Lions moved to the Pontiac Silverdome in 1975 by themselves (Betzold and Casey 1992, 94–100, 103).

In 1976 Detroit's mayor, Coleman Young, told Mike Ilitch, owner of the National Hockey League Red Wings, that the city would build a $20-million arena on city-owned riverfront property to keep that team from moving near the Silverdome. Federal and city loans were used to finance public revenue bonds for the Joe Louis Arena, which opened in 1979 at a cost of $57.8 million. The NBA Pistons moved to Pontiac in 1978, and ten years later moved into a privately financed arena in nearby Auburn Hills. Fetzer, meanwhile, wanted Tiger Stadium repaired. In 1978 he sold the park to the city for a dollar and agreed to a thirty-year lease with three optional ten-year renewals. The city issued bonds for $8.5 million to be repaid with a surcharge of fifty cents per ticket, and the federal government granted $5 million. A second phase of renovations took place in the early 1980s, financed by additional bonds paid by a ninety-cents-per-ticket surcharge (Betzold and Casey 1992, 107–110). In 1983 Fetzer sold the team.

When Domino's Pizza magnate Tom Monaghan purchased the Tigers, he said that as long as he owned the team he would not build a new stadium. In the aftermath of the violent frenzy that accompanied the Tigers' World Series victory in 1984, however, club officials started talking about a new park. Publicly, Monaghan waffled. But Mayor Young did not even wait until the stadium renovations were completed before he started talking about a new domed stadium like Toronto's that would be part of a grand redevelopment strategy (Betzold and Casey 1992, 113, 118–125). A city councilman took a more jaundiced view: "I think what Coleman Young is looking for is a stadium named Coleman A. Young Stadium" (p. 125).

Sensing that Tiger Stadium was in real danger of being replaced, a small group of Detroiters formed the Tiger Stadium Fan Club in 1987.

The following year the stadium was put on the National Register of Historic Places, and in 1991 the National Trust for Historical Preservation included it on its fourth annual list of the nation's most important endangered historic sites. Public-opinion polls showed that area residents favored saving the stadium and were opposed to using public money for a new park. The Tigers organization, however, maintained that the stadium had become structurally unsound. Bo Schembechler, the legendary University of Michigan football coach who became Tigers president under Monaghan, told the Economic Club of Detroit in April 1991 that it was unfair to shackle the Tigers to a rusted girder in Tiger Stadium when the Pistons, the Lions, and the Red Wings all played in new arenas. Then he gave the city and Wayne County an August 1 deadline to arrange financing for a new county-owned stadium that the Tigers would rent (Betzold and Casey 1992, 131–145; Montemurri and Mitchell 1991; Montemurri 1991b).

As three areas near Tiger Stadium were being considered for a new ballpark and additional development, Wayne County Executive Ed McNamara announced that a public vote would be taken on the stadium project. Mayor Young called McNamara "crazy" to give voters a chance to decide the stadium issue. Meanwhile, state legislators were taking action to block plans for a new stadium (Montemurri and Mitchell 1991; Prater 1991; Christoff 1991a, 1991b; Montemurri 1991a). The acrimony between the county and the city intensified during the next few months. Mayor Young claimed Detroit could finance a stadium on its own; McNamara and Deputy Wayne County Executive Michael Duggan responded that the financing options available to the city were too costly. The county revealed its own plan for a $200-million stadium project, financed, in part, by a 5-percent hotel/motel room tax (Montemurri and Prater 1991a, 1991b; Montemurri, Gallagher, and Gavrilovich 1991).

Though the turf wars appeared to be over in July 1991, when Young and McNamara announced a deal to form a city–county stadium authority, plans began unraveling in the fall, when Schembechler rejected two Detroit stadium sites that had been proposed by public officials and said the Tigers would now start over and consider offers from all comers in the city as well as the suburbs (Betzold and Casey 1992, 252–260). Schembechler's arrogant campaign for a new stadium exacerbated public resentment about paying for it, and the unthinkable firing of Hall of Fame Tigers broadcaster and Detroit icon Ernie Harwell in 1990 soured even the most loyal fans. To Monaghan's statement that Detroit had all of a sudden become one of the worst baseball cities in the United States, a minister in the city replied, "If it's a bad baseball town, maybe we need to look and see if it could be a bad pizza town" (pp. 226–227; see also 160–163, 198, 256–257).

Relations between the Tigers and the city improved when Monaghan sold the team in 1992 to another pizza baron, Mike Ilitch, who owns the NHL Red Wings in addition to the Little Caesars pizza chain. Ilitch had already established a rapport with Detroit through his building of a very successful hockey team and his revitalization of the Fox Theater area. Those good feelings were strengthened when he brought Ernie Harwell back upon assuming ownership of the Tigers. A new mayor, Dennis Archer, worked to smooth over some of the animosity that had characterized relations between the city and the rest of the state during Young's tenure. The momentum of the Tiger Stadium Fan Club was also slowed by the coming of stadiums like Oriole Park at Camden Yards and The Ballpark in Arlington, which demonstrated that "new" was not synonymous with "sterile." In 1995 a deal was announced between the state, the city, and the Tigers for a $55-million grant from the Michigan Strategic Fund for a new stadium. The total represents $26 million from Indian casino profits, $19 million diverted from a fund to pay for high-tech research, and $10 million from other accounts. The city put up $40 million in Downtown Development Authority bonds, and the Tigers promised to contribute $145 million to a ballpark to be built near the Fox Theater in downtown Detroit. In 1996 the Tiger Stadium Fan Club was able to put the question of city funding for the stadium on the ballot, but 81 percent of Detroit residents voted against reversing the city ordinance which allowed the $40 million to be used for ballpark construction. The fan club also lost a suit against the state challenging the $55-million grant from the strategic fund (Johnson 1996; Basheda 1996; Haglund 1996b).

While the Tigers waited for the suit to be resolved, talks between the baseball franchise and the football Lions resulted in an August proposal to build adjacent stadiums across Woodward Avenue from the site originally chosen by the Tigers. The new stadium deal involves a buyout of the approved $240-million baseball facility by a newly created Detroit–Wayne County Stadium Authority, which will also own the new Lions stadium. The cost of the project will come from the Lions ($70 million), the Tigers ($145 million), corporate contributions ($50 million), county taxes on hotels and car rentals ($80 million), the state ($55 million), Detroit's Downtown Development Authority ($85 million), and the sale of land the county no longer needs ($20 million). The teams will sign thirty-five-year leases and get virtually all the revenues from their stadiums. The city's payback will come from expected development near the complex and a new image (Haglund 1996a; Lam and Fricker 1996). Despite opposition from TAP"S" (Taxpayers Against Proposition "S"), Wayne County voters overwhelmingly approved excise taxes of 1 percent on hotel and motel rooms and 2 percent on car rentals (Bradsher 1996; Guest 1996).

The naming rights to the new baseball stadium were sold in December 1998. A Detroit-based banking company took the opportunity to be associated, its chairman said, with the "hallowed traditions of baseball and the Detroit Tigers" for $66 million over thirty years (quoted in Associated Press 1998). Comerica Park is set to open for the 2000 season.

CONCLUSION

The recent flurry of stadium construction in major league cities around the country—Baltimore, Chicago, Cleveland, Detroit, Houston, Milwaukee, Seattle, and a host of others—has sparked a new round of journalistic agony about the greed of professional team owners. The charge is frequently made, both by casual spectators and more knowledgeable analysts, that cities are being held "hostage" by wealthy sports entrepreneurs who threaten to leave town if their demands for new facilities and other concessions are not met. Our examination of the policy processes that eventually resulted in new ballparks for the White Sox, the Orioles, the Indians, and the Tigers, however, suggests that it is too simplistic to view what's happening as "stadium stick-up." The decision to build a stadium with public funds is a public-policy decision. Like other policy decisions, it is often the culmination of years of demands by a variety of interested parties, numerous proposals floating about in the policy primeval soup, politicians worried about their political reputations and legacies, and events that create an opportunity for an idea to become a done deal.

Chicago's new Comiskey Park opened after seven years of extensive negotiation over the site, the funding, and land acquisition. Two forceful politicians, Mayor Harold Washington and Governor James Thompson, were not about to have their reputations sullied by the loss of the South Side team. Washington had no interest in being known as the mayor who lost the Sox; he took a personal interest in leading the drive to retain the franchise. There is evidence to suggest that former mayor Jane Byrne had prepared commercials for the 1987 campaign that charged Washington with losing the team, and he was committed to defusing that criticism (McCarron and Egler 1986; Euchner 1993, 139). Thompson was adamant about the issue: "I'll bleed and die before I let the Sox leave Chicago" (quoted in Shropshire 1995, 11). Indeed, Thompson may have been instrumental in foreshadowing the strategy the Sox would adopt to secure their policy goal: seriously threaten to move to St. Petersburg if demands for a new stadium were not met. It is reported that team owners Reinsdorf and Einhorn hosted Thompson (their fellow Northwestern University Law School alumnus) on Opening Day 1985, and brought up the subject of their

Comiskey problem. Thompson agreed they needed a new park, and also agreed to help. But, he told them, "You'll never get one built unless there's a crisis—unless people think you're going to leave if you don't get one" (quoted in Helyar 1994, 451). A politician's concern for his or her place in history can play an influential role in the policy decisions that are made (Anderson 1994, 126–129) and may create willing "accomplices" for sports franchise owners. The serious threat to move to St. Petersburg opened the policy window wide enough to move the stadium project onto the decision agenda, and ultimately to policy adoption.

The White Sox did not leave Chicago for the suburbs or another state, but keeping the team was not the result of simply caving in to owner demands. It is certainly true that the team got a sweet deal, but it is also the case that some social goals were included in the redevelopment of the stadium area and the construction of the stadium itself. Indeed, if Euchner is correct in his assessment that what the White Sox really wanted was to get out of South Armour Square (Euchner 1993, 141–142), it is somewhat ironic that the tortuous path of policy making landed them in a new Comiskey Park in the same old neighborhood.

A new ballpark for the Orioles was even longer in the making. Team owner Jerold Hoffberger began to talk about a stadium as early as 1972, two decades before the opening of Oriole Park at Camden Yards. Here, too, a dominant politician played a critical role in the process. Mayor-turned-Governor William Donald Schaefer epitomizes the political leader who, "whether motivated by thoughts of political advantage, the public interest, or their political reputations, may seize upon problems, publicize them, and propose solutions" (Anderson 1994, 92). As Jon Miller, the Orioles broadcaster, put it, "The new stadium was never about EBW [Edward Bennett Williams] and that regime making money. It was about William Donald Schaefer realizing that when he died they could have been the St. Pete Orioles" (quoted in Richmond 1993, 65). The Colts' departure provided the window of opportunity Schaefer needed to push through stadium development at Camden Yards.

The policy process that led to the construction of Jacobs Field was characterized not so much by public officials who staked their political careers on building a new ballpark to save a team or by a defining moment or event that produced optimal conditions for action. Rather, an almost seamless web of wealthy, well-connected sports entrepreneurs, politicians, and business executives were interested in continuing downtown revitalization and saw a new stadium complex as part of the strategy. But it didn't happen overnight; proposals to build a new ballpark started floating seriously in the policy soup a dozen years before Jacobs Field opened. Moreover, the Jacobs brothers had not said (at least not publicly) that they would move the team from Cleveland if a new park was not built. They had, however, cultivated both Democratic and Republican politicians in the city and spent hundreds of millions of dollars on downtown office buildings and a shopping complex (Markiewicz 1990; Torry 1995, 180). Consensus building in the political stream (Kingdon 1995, 159–163) facilitated a public–private partnership that brought a new ballpark to a classic American League franchise.

In Detroit, on the other hand, the feisty personalities of Mayor Coleman Young and Tigers president Bo Schembechler did little to smooth the way for the new stadium they both wanted. Though a new ballpark for the city of Detroit had been discussed by local politicians and franchise personnel since the 1960s, efforts intensified after the 1984 championship season. Nevertheless, a decade passed before proponents of a new stadium could claim success. It wasn't until there were changes in the political stream (Kingdon 1995, 145–164)—a new mayor, a new team owner with strong ties to the city, a weakened opposition interest group—that a deal was struck to replace one of the last remaining turn-of-the-century ballparks.

As noted, most analysts have concluded that building a new stadium for a team, or trying to lure a team by doing so, does not pay off economically. This isn't new. A 1957 article in *American City*, "Is Big League Baseball Good Municipal Business?" noted that all municipal stadiums were losing money, and questioned whether big cities, with their declining tax bases and growing social problems, could afford to invest public dollars in sports facilities (Miller 1990, 71). Indeed, even at the turn of the century the ballfields did not have much fiscal impact on a locality (Riess 1980, 111). But it is also not a new argument for those who seek to benefit from favorable distributive policies to advance. When sports franchise owners tout the positive economic impact their presence has on a city, or the increased flow of benefits new stadium construction will bring, they are using tactics common to the politics of business promotion. Similarly, when it is argued that every political effort should be made to ensure that the team stays in town because the image of the city and the public interest is at stake, sports entrepreneurs are echoing claims made by other businesses seeking government aid (Anderson et al. 1984, 261–262).

Sports, it is true, have a great deal of symbolism attached to them, and it may be some intangible value associated with having a common identification symbol which brings major league status to a city that is the driving force behind public investment in sports (see, e.g., Johnson 1985, 224; Quirk and Fort 1992, 176; Baim 1994, 218; Shropshire 1995, 62). But our examination of the processes that led to the decisions to build new baseball stadiums for several major league franchises has shown that policy making here, like that in other substantive areas, often evolves over long periods of time in a manner that can hardly be described as linear. As for the policies that are ultimately produced, perhaps things political are not always rational.

NOTES

1. The discussion which follows draws on our previous research on Chicago sports policy. See Pelissero, Henschen, and Sidlow (1991, 1992, 1993).

2. Cleveland Mayor Anthony Celebrezze had big plans for Cleveland, hoping to revitalize the lakefront area. He told Daley that the Indians were critical to downtown Cleveland, and noted that the team had guaranteed the city $360,000 for the final six years of their lease. Daley countered with the declining attendance figures and his increasing financial difficulties. Celebrezze responded to Daley, "I'll give you a bit of advice. Your attendance will go up when your club starts winning" (quoted in Torry 1995, 76–77).

3. In 1985 Jeff Jacobs had much to do with starting Cleveland's renaissance by buying an old Coast Guard station in the area known as the Flats, where the Cuyahoga River empties into Lake Erie, and turning it into a bar and restaurant. Other restaurants soon dotted the riverbanks (Torry 1995, 181–182).

REFERENCES

Anderson, James E. 1994. *Public Policymaking: An Introduction.* 2d ed. Boston: Houghton Mifflin.

Anderson, James E., David W. Brady, Charles S. Bullock III, and Joseph Stewart Jr. 1984. *Public Policy and Politics in America.* 2d ed. Monterey, Calif.: Brooks/Cole.

Angell, Roger. 1978. *The Summer Game.* New York: Popular Library.

Associated Press. 1998. Tigers' New Home Is Comerica Park. *Ann Arbor News,* 21 December, A1.

Baade, Robert A. 1994. Stadiums, Professional Sports, and Economic Development: Assessing the Reality. *Heartland Policy Study* 62 (28 March). Detroit: The Heartland Institute.

Baade, Robert A. 1987. Is There an Economic Rationale for Subsidizing Sports Stadiums? *Heartland Policy Study* 13 (23 February). Detroit: The Heartland Institute.

Baim, Dean V. 1994. *The Sports Stadium as a Municipal Investment.* Westport, Conn.: Greenwood Press.

Basheda, Valarie. 1996. Land Acquisition for Ballpark May Stir Up the Next Legal Fight. *Detroit News,* 7 July, 1B.

Betzold, Michael, and Ethan Casey. 1992. *Queen of Diamonds: The Tiger Stadium Story.* West Bloomfield, Mich.: A&M.

Brady, Erik, and Debbie Howlett. 1996. Ballpark Construction's Booming. *USA Today,* 6 September, 13C–14C.

Bradsher, Keith. 1996. Football Team Plans to Return to Detroit. *New York Times*, 21 August, A8.

Christoff, Chris. 1991a. Legislators Hope to Force Renovation. *Detroit Free Press*, 24 April, 10A.

Christoff, Chris. 1991b. Senate OKs Stadium Plan Limit. *Detroit Free Press*, 25 April, 1B.

Euchner, Charles C. 1993. *Playing the Field: Why Sports Teams Move and Cities Fight to Keep Them.* Baltimore: Johns Hopkins University Press.

Gershman, Michael. 1993. *Diamonds: The Evolution of the Ballpark.* Boston: Houghton Mifflin.

Goldstein, Warren. 1989. *Playing for Keeps: An Early History of Baseball.* Ithaca: Cornell University Press.

Green, Richard. 1994. A Field of Their Own. *Cincinnati Enquirer*, 15 May, A01.

Guest, Greta. 1996. Wayne County Voters Approve New Taxes to Help Build Stadium. *Ann Arbor News*, 6 November, A1.

Haglund, Rick. 1996a. Lions Will Move Back to Detroit. *Ann Arbor News*, 20 August, A1.

Haglund, Rick. 1996b. Tigers Get Supreme Blessing. *Ann Arbor News*, 15 August, B1.

Harris, David. 1986. *The League: The Rise and Decline of the NFL.* New York: Bantam Books.

Helyar, John. 1994. *Lords of the Realm: The Real History of Baseball.* New York: Villard Books.

Johnson, Arthur T. 1993. *Minor League Baseball and Local Economic Development.* Urbana: University of Illinois Press.

Johnson, Arthur T. 1986. Economic and Policy Implications of Hosting Sports Franchises: Lessons from Baltimore. *Urban Affairs Quarterly* 21: 411–433.

Johnson, Arthur T. 1985. The Sports Franchise Relocation Issue and Public Policy Responses. In *Government and Sport: The Public Policy Issues*, edited by Arthur T. Johnson and James H. Frey. Totowa, N.J.: Rowman and Allanheld.

Johnson, Malcolm. 1996. Court Upholds Stadium Funding. *Ann Arbor News*, 6 July, B3.

Kahn, Roger. 1971. *The Boys of Summer.* New York: Harper & Row.

Kingdon, John W. 1995. *Agendas, Alternatives, and Public Policies.* 2d ed. New York: HarperCollins.

Laing, Jonathan R. 1996. Foul Play? *Barron's*, 19 August, 23–27.

Lam, Tina, and Daniel G. Fricker. 1996. Team Effort. *Detroit Free Press*, 21 August, 1A.

Lever, Robert. 1995. Stadium Mania Puts Cities Over a Barrel. *Planning*, December, 22.

Lowi, Theodore J. 1964. American Business, Public Policy, Case Studies, and Political Theory. *World Politics* 16: 677–715.

Markiewicz, David A. 1990. Cleveland Voters Decide Tuesday on New Baseball Stadium. *Detroit News and Free Press*, 6 May, 10A.

McCarron, John. 1987. Politics Ties Up New Sox Park. *Chicago Tribune*, 15 July, sec. 1, p. 3.

McCarron, John, and Daniel Egler. 1986. Mayor Covered All Bases to Swing Sox Deal. *Chicago Tribune*, 7 December, sec. 1, p. 1.

Miller, James Edward. 1990. *The Baseball Business: Pursuing Pennants and Profits in Baltimore*. Chapel Hill: University of North Carolina Press.

Montemurri, Patricia. 1991a. County Cools to New Stadium. *Detroit Free Press*, 26 April, 1B.

Montemurri, Patricia. 1991b. Tigers Sold on County's Vision. *Detroit Free Press*, 23 April, 1A.

Montemurri, Patricia, John Gallagher, and Peter Gavrilovich. 1991. County Unveils Stadium Plan. *Detroit Free Press*, 6 June, 1A.

Montemurri, Patricia, and William J. Mitchell. 1991. Stadium Plan Will Be Voters' Call. *Detroit Free Press*, 24 April, 1A.

Montemurri, Patricia, and Constance C. Prater. 1991a. County Insists City Plan for New Stadium Is Costly. *Detroit Free Press*, 2 May, 1A.

Montemurri, Patricia, and Constance C. Prater. 1991b. Mayor Swings at Ballpark Proposal. *Detroit Free Press*, 1 May, 1A.

Okner, Benjamin A. 1974. Subsidies of Stadiums and Arenas. In *Government and the Sports Business*, edited by Roger G. Noll. Washington, D.C.: The Brookings Institution, 325–348.

Pelissero, John P., Beth M. Henschen, and Edward I. Sidlow. 1993. Community Development or Business Promotion? A Look at Sports-Led Economic Development. In *Community Economic Development: Policy Formation in the US and UK*, edited by David Fasenfest. Houndmills, England: Macmillan.

Pelissero, John P., Beth M. Henschen, and Edward I. Sidlow. 1992. The New Politics of Sports Policy Innovation in Chicago. In *Politics of Policy Innovation in Chicago*, edited by Kenneth K. Wong. Greenwich, Conn.: JAI Press.

Pelissero, John P., Beth M. Henschen, and Edward I. Sidlow. 1991. Urban Regimes, Sports Stadiums, and the Politics of Economic Development Agendas in Chicago. *Policy Studies Review* 10: 117–129.

Prater, Constance C. 1991. Mayor's Auditorium Setback Raises Fear of Defeat on Stadium. *Detroit Free Press*, 25 April, 1B.

Quirk, James, and Rodney D. Fort. 1992. *Pay Dirt: The Business of Professional Team Sports*. Princeton: Princeton University Press.

Richmond, Peter. 1993. *Ballpark: Camden Yards and the Building of an American Dream*. New York: Simon & Schuster.

Riess, Steven A. 1980. *Touching Base: Professional Baseball and American Culture in the Progressive Era*. Westport, Conn.: Greenwood Press.

Ritter, Lawrence S. 1966. *The Glory of Their Times*. New York: Macmillan.

Rosentraub, Mark S. 1988. Public Investment in Private Businesses: The Professional Sports Mania. In *Business Elites and Urban Development: Case Studies and Critical Perspectives*, edited by Scott Cummings. Albany: State University of New York Press.

Shropshire, Kenneth L. 1995. *The Sports Franchise Game: Cities in Pursuit of Sports Franchises, Events, Stadiums, and Arenas*. Philadelphia: University of Pennsylvania Press.

Thorn, John, ed. 1987. *The Armchair Book of Baseball II*. New York: Charles Scribner's Sons.

Thorn, John, ed. 1985. *The Armchair Book of Baseball*. New York: Charles Scribner's Sons.

Torry, Jack. 1995. *Endless Summers: The Fall and Rise of the Cleveland Indians*. South Bend, Ind.: Diamond Communications.

Verducci, Tom. 1994. Grand Opening. *Sports Illustrated*, 11 April, 42–48.

Vincent, Ted. 1981. *Mudville's Revenge: The Rise and Fall of American Sports*. New York: Seaview Books.

9

Major League Baseball and American Cities: A Strategy for Playing the Stadium Game

Neil J. Sullivan

We know that Senator Joe McCarthy was no bargain, but he was not the worst thing to come out of Wisconsin in the 1950s. Using a publicly financed stadium as bait, the otherwise sensible city of Milwaukee enticed the Braves to relocate from Boston in 1953, and the relationship between communities and sports franchises has suffered ever since.

Cities across America have been lavishing ornate stadiums and arenas on sports franchises despite the ability of these businesses to pay for the facilities themselves. Economic development is one of the explanations for these curious decisions, but economists are unpersuaded that the investments yield financial benefits to the public (see Baim 1994; Baade 1987; Baade and Dye 1988).

Civic pride can be another reason why cities pursue ball clubs. Some boosters insist that a community cannot be "major league" without one of these professional teams. The argument raises political questions about public choice that can be answered in various ways (see Sullivan 1987).

Whether the motives behind public stadiums can be justified or not, cities face keen competition from one another to attract or to hold sports franchises (see Eucher 1993; Whitford 1993). Taking Major League Baseball as a case study, the fundamental complication for citizens and public officials who play the stadium game is one simple but powerful economic fact: Far more cities want major league teams than the supply allows.

This chapter proposes that to play the stadium game in the public interest public officials need to appreciate that the market for ball clubs is distorted; that is, the scarcity of teams is contrived. With that awareness in mind, these officials need a strategy for negotiating with club owners over new stadiums. The chapter first establishes an empirical basis for concluding that the number of baseball teams is artificially low, and then proposes a method for reviewing the decisions about a new stadium with suggestions about the allocation of public and private responsibilities.

THE ARTIFICIAL SCARCITY OF FRANCHISES

The number of teams in the American and National Leagues is a decision reserved to the owners of the existing teams. Since scarcity enhances the value of each franchise, the owners have been reluctant to add clubs despite the demand of cities, the Players Association, and prospective owners. The limitation on creating more teams is an obvious restraint of trade, but one that is allowed by baseball's antitrust exemption that the Supreme Court conferred in 1922.[1] If the number of major league teams is being held artificially below what a market would generate, the implications for cities is significant. The pressure to spend hundreds of millions of dollars on new stadiums would ease considerably if cities were not faced with being without a major league club. But what is the evidence that the current number of major league franchises is a contrived scarcity?[2]

Major league baseball is played by a cohort of the population that is fairly easily defined: males between the ages of approximately twenty and forty. Assuming that major league players represent a fixed percentage of that labor pool, we can get an idea of how many men at any particular time are blessed with the skills to play baseball at the highest professional level. Establishing a ratio of major league players to the larger male population in the applicable age group demonstrates an extraordinary point about the number of major league teams (Table 9.1).

From 1900 to 1960 the number of major league players remained at 400 despite a doubling of the labor pool during those six decades. In 1998, with the addition of two more teams, the number of major league jobs will have increased to 800, but the labor pool has effectively doubled again since 1960.

The scarcity of franchises is clear if we use the ratio from 1900–1910, and apply it to today's labor market. If 1 of every 27,670 young men could play major league baseball, the country would field sixty major

Table 9.1
Percentage of Male Population in the Major Leagues

Census	Males, Ages 20–39[a]	Major Leaguers	Ratio
1900	11,068,157	400	1:27,670
1910	14,184,350	400	1:35,460
1920	15,174,484	400	1:37,936
1930	17,413,164	400	1:45,533
1940	18,833,339	400	1;47,083
1950	22,855,322	400	1:57,183
1960	22,531,151[b]	500	1:45,062
1970	25,547,049	650	1:39,303
1980	35,906,643	650	1:55,241
1990[c]	41,577,000	700	1:59,396

Source: U.S. Bureau of the Census, *Historical Statistics of the United States: Colonial Times to 1970* (Washington, D.C.: U.S. Government Printing Office, 1975), 15–16.

Note: The ratio for the 1960s is calculated by taking the census of 1960 as a pool for the sixteen original major league teams plus the four expansion teams of 1961 and 1962. The 1970s ratio compares the population figures with the first twenty major league clubs plus the four teams added in 1969 and the two that joined in 1977.

[a]White males only, 1900–1940; all races, 1950–present.

[b]The decline in the pool from 1950 to 1960 is likely a result of marriages deferred by the Great Depression and World War II.

[c]Estimated.

league teams. This figure, of course, represents a statistical conclusion; it does not necessarily indicate that sixty teams should be playing today. But in response to the hoary claim that the quality of baseball is not what it used to be, the answer seems quite clear: If 400 young men were good enough to play major league baseball in 1900, it is not statistically unreasonable to conclude that 1,500 are equally qualified now.

Several factors complicate a purely statistical analysis. One is the drain on these athletes from other sports. Some current members of the National Football League and the National Basketball Association might have gone into baseball when that was clearly the preeminent professional sport. These alternatives to baseball might convert some second basemen into point guards, but the other sports require physical qualities to play some of their positions that would limit their impact on baseball. Seven-footers and three-hundred pounders would have a difficult time finding a suitable place on the baseball diamond.

The enhanced social status of professional athletes is another factor that suggests that the ratio of major league players to the labor pool underestimates how many more potential ball players are in the population. Wealthy college graduates can now pursue a career in sports without a stigma. Playing ball was a rather scandalous decision in the days of Bucknell graduate Christy Matthewson and Columbia University's Lou Gehrig.

Finally, baseball has recently extended its international labor pool to Asia and Europe, areas that will join with Latin America to provide millions of additional candidates for the major leagues. The quality of major league baseball earlier in this century may well have been quite poor compared to what is available today, but if we are content to watch the caliber of play that our grandparents watched, then far more teams could be added to the major league roster.

The critical public-policy implication of this statistical analysis is that the existing clubs enjoy far greater political leverage than the economics of baseball can justify. A greater supply of teams would diminish the pressure on cities to attract or to hold one of the existing clubs. Public officials could more vigorously defend the public purse in the knowledge that if a club left for a more generous community it could be more easily replaced.

A STRATEGY FOR NEGOTIATING

Since major league franchises began moving in the 1950s, many cities have tried to attract or to hold them by providing stadiums. Of the twenty-three ballparks now in use and built in the United States since 1954, only Dodger Stadium in Los Angeles and Joe Robbie Stadium in Miami were privately financed.[3]

During the 1960s and 1970s, multipurpose stadiums became the norm as cities across America sought to make the most efficient use of their investment. The record has been very disappointing. In his study of privatization, E. S. Savas (1987) has pointed out that the public financing of stadiums has been unsuccessful in controlling their costs, and it has also contributed to franchise instability. Savas concludes, "In retrospect, perhaps the stadium should not have been built at public expense" (p. 222).

In these budget-balancing times, public spending is scrutinized with great care. Stadiums are increasingly financed through public–private partnerships, a fashionable label but one that can be vague concerning the distribution of costs, risks, and benefits. Public officials need to be clear about what role governments should play in these partnerships and what obligations they should avoid.

A negotiating strategy can be developed in nine stages, or innings, if the metaphor is tolerable, from the location for the new stadium through its opening. At each point, the ball club or the government has a possible role to play, and determining who does what should be developed with great precision.

This strategy makes the normative assumption that the public purse should be reserved for two general categories: (1) public goods that a market would ignore and which will return benefits to the community, and (2) the care of people at a decent standard of living when those people are unable to care for themselves. When negotiating with baseball owners, public officials should keep these primary obligations in mind.

The First Inning: Find the Site

This function can be performed by the state, the ball club, or some other private party. The productive use of public assets gives the state an interest in being active in the land market. As part of its privatization strategy, a government may want to unload land that was acquired for a purpose that is no longer feasible or even desirable. The site might be an undeveloped private parcel, the area encompassing an existing stadium, part of a little-used public park, an antiquated public facility like a rail car storage site, or a public housing project set for demolition.

An economic-development office may also help to bring private parties together. News that a ball club is interested in a new stadium may trigger an official's recollection that a large parcel of land near transit sources remains available. Perhaps a shopping center never materialized, or one went bankrupt. Government could serve as a link among private parties.

Public and private sectors routinely become familiar with land that is potentially useful for a baseball stadium. The cost of that knowledge is marginal, so public participation in finding a new stadium site is a reasonable role for the state.

Second Inning: The Environmental Impact Statement (EIS)

Once the location for the stadium has been determined, the developer faces the state-imposed burden of showing that the project is not going to impose unacceptable costs on the environment. The EIS reflects strong public support for the protection of natural resources, but the method of making that assessment can be crucial to the outcome of the development.

The state needs to work to avoid an administrative filibuster in developing the EIS. Hearing upon hearing can drive up the cost of a project to unacceptable levels. To be sure, if the stadium were to cause unacceptable damage to the environment the state should be able to block the project; but the stadium should not be prevented simply because the process of making the EIS is prohibitively expensive.

A reasonable time limit on environmental objections is the kind of reform that the state should consider. A stadium, unlike a nuclear power plant, poses no inherent threat to the public's safety or health. Complex analysis of emissions or effluents is unnecessary, so one of the reasons for lengthy environmental studies is unwarranted.

Both the environmental impact statement and the consideration of political opposition give the state an opportunity to experiment with new methods of determining public choice. The experiment should try to develop a model that avoids making decisions in the expectation of a lawsuit, an exercise that has frustrated many interests who compete in the arenas of government. The significant financial dimensions of stadium decisions combined with the relatively straightforward health and safety factors make this subject well suited for some fresh ideas about decision making.

The Third Inning: Political Opposition

Aside from environmental considerations, other interests can be expected to oppose the stadium for reasons unrelated to safety, health, or endangered species. Traffic, noise, potentially unruly crowds, and stadium lights are all reasons why neighbors of the facility may prefer a less-intrusive project.

As with the EIS, the state can expedite the consideration of these objections. The benefits of the new stadium will be spread over the entire community, but the costs may well fall disproportionately on those who live in the immediate area of the ballpark. The determination of whether the costs are justified against the benefits is the essence of political calculus, and it should be made on the merits rather than the duration and expense of the process.

Just as the administrative process needs to avoid a filibuster, so too the judicial review of administrative action needs to respect a streamlined method of decision making. Unless a constitutional claim can be credibly proposed, the courts need to defer to the judgment of the community that it prefers to resolve its political disputes in an expeditious manner.

The Fourth Inning: Paying for the Site

This is strictly a responsibility of the ball club. Once the site has been determined, the purchase of the property should be left to the private sector.

A public acquisition sticks the state with an asset that is of limitd value. What can the state do with land on which a stadium is located, other than pursue another ball club? If the land is in private hands, then the incentives to maintain the site and the risks of an economic downturn stay focused on the ball club. They need to keep the location attractive and accessible if their profits are to continue. By contrast, government might be forced to curb the maintenance of the site during hard fiscal times.

The Fifth Inning: Infrastructure

Linking the stadium to highways, water and sewer lines, utility wires, and other public resources is the principal expense that the public should bear. The state normally makes these investments for projects that promise a significant return to the public treasury. The millions of dollars spent on roads and pipes are recovered through the taxes that the new venture generates.

Ancillary projects for the stadium should be privately financed. Parking is one such example. Private companies routinely build and maintain the structures where we park, and there is no reason to have the state assume this responsibility for baseball stadiums. Other economic development can be expected, with restaurants, souvenir shops, and other retail stores relying on the fans to stop by and spend a little more cash to round out the day. Private development thus promotes itself.

The Sixth Inning: Stadium Design

The public sector does not necessarily make a mess of the aesthetics of stadium design, but generally that is so. In the 1960s and 1970s the pursuit of efficiency led many states to replace aging city neighborhood ballparks with multipurpose suburban stadiums that required low maintenance.

The doughnut design, sometimes with a plastic roof, became a fashion in stadium architecture. Plastic grass permitted the use of the facility by both baseball and football teams without undue wear on the field. The circular shape of these stadiums proved to be a poor setting for the arc of the baseball field and the rectangle of football.

Oriole Park at Camden Yards in Baltimore demonstrates that a public facility can be elegant. This baseball-only ballpark recaptures the charm of the old neighborhood fields. Along with Royals Stadium in Kansas City, this park shows that utility need not overwhelm grace in the design of the stadium. But there remains no reason why the public should recruit the architect for stadium construction.

The major firms are well known, and the tremendous success of Camden Yards has confirmed the wisdom of retaining the heritage of the game in the design of its parks. New stadiums in Cleveland and Texas have been built along similar lines, in public–private partnerships. In stadium design, the ball club has the clearest interest in making sure its home is a gracious one.

The Seventh Inning: Paying for the Stadium

With the exception of the racial ban that kept blacks from the game until 1947, the publicly financed stadium is the most regretable feature of the business of baseball. By assuming the cost for the major fixed capital asset, the state weakens the bond between the ball club and its community. The franchise becomes essentially the highly portable aggregate of players that the owner can move to any city that offers even more largesse.

A baseball stadium inherently has exceptionally few potential users. If a city is abandoned by its team, the stadium is not so much an asset for the community as the whitest of elephants. Whatever rock concerts, papal masses, tractor pulls, or motocross events the stadium might have housed, the facility's primary function is baseball, and without a team the stadium has no serious purpose.

Boosters of public stadiums promote the economic-development angle and stress the rents that the city will collect. But a private stadium stimulates the economy in the same way, and the state can collect property taxes as easily as rents, without assuming the burdens of ownership.

The Eighth Inning: The Private–Private Partnership

The primary reason why stadiums are not privately financed is that they do not have to be. Public officials are sufficiently eager to keep or attract a ball club that they will assume the obligation that should fall to the club owner. The argument that the stadiums cost too much to finance privately begs several crucial points.

The first is that grandiosity need not guide the design of the stadium. If private funds cannot support a $200-million stadium, then a more modest complex should be built. If a grander stadium makes more commercial sense, then the club owners can bring in partners. The need for additional capital to finance a new facility is one of the most common reasons why business owners take in partnerships.

In the case of a baseball stadium, the opportunities for private–private partnerships are abundant. Parking, the scoreboard, concessions, billboards, and broadcast rights all give other private parties access to

the fans of the ball club. The public-relations benefits of being affiliated with a ball club are attractive to many firms. The contention that
stadiums will not be built if the state does not finance them ignores
the financial realities that businesses face in every other industry. The
prosperity of this particular industry makes that contention particularly problematic.

The Ninth Inning: If All Else Fails

Public officials may make a responsible offer to the local club owner,
including a proposed site, a streamlined process to answer statutory
and political challenges, and an adequate infrastructure, and they may
find that the club owner wants more. If another community is willing
to go beyond reason, the first city faces a hard choice: Do they let the
ball club leave without crossing the line beyond the limits of reason?
In a word, yes, but that does not doom the community to life without
professional baseball.

The threat to remove the antitrust exemption has already proven to
be a formidable tool. In almost every case, cities that have lost baseball franchises have either retained a club in the other major league or
have received a replacement expansion franchise in rather short order
(see Table 9.2).

The nation's capital is the only city that once enjoyed major league
baseball but now has no team. Other cities threatened to press for federal review of the antitrust exemption and, to quiet the waters, the
major league owners expanded back into markets that were once de-
rided as "bad baseball towns." This record suggests that a far more
aggressive strategy by public officials would be beneficial even while
the market for teams remains artificially scarce.

This chapter has established that major league owners have taken advantage of their antitrust exemption to keep the supply of franchises far
below what a free market suggests is possible. The exaggerated dispro-

Table 9.2
Cities Losing a Franchise and Acquiring Another

City	Abandoned by	Replaced with
New York	Dodgers and Giants, 1958	Mets, 1962
Washington, D.C.	Senators I, 1958	Senators II, 1961
Washington, D.C.	Senators II, 1972	No Replacement
Milwaukee	Braves, 1966	Brewers, 1970
Kansas City	A's, 1968	Royals, 1969
Seattle	Pilots (Brewers), 1969	Mariners, 1977

portion between cities that want teams and the number of clubs available gives team owners a great advantage in negotiating over stadiums.

While this imbalance persists, public officials need to have a careful and thorough plan for bargaining with the clubs over stadium issues. Part of that plan should include the awareness that, even under current law, cities have successfully pressured MLB to replace ball clubs that abandon their communities.

The current stadium game is tilted in favor of some of the wealthiest and most privileged members of our society. The cost to buy their attachment comes at the expense of some of our weakest neighbors and the ever-beleaguered middle class. Such a game is not particularly engaging, and the means are at hand for a more sensible and proper contest.

NOTES

1. *Federal Baseball Club of Baltimore, Inc. v. National League of Professional Baseball Clubs et al.*, 259 U.S. 200, 1922.

2. In 1997, thirty teams will play in the American and National leagues with two more franchises joining in 1998.

3. Fenway Park in Boston, Wrigley Field in Chicago, and Tiger Stadium in Detroit date to the World War I era, and Busch Stadium in St. Louis was publicly financed, but later purchased by the Cardinals.

REFERENCES

Baade, Robert A. 1987. Is There an Economic Rationale for Subsidizing Sports Stadiums? *Heartland Policy Study* (23 February) Detroit: Heartland Institute.

Baade, Robert A., and Richard F. Dye. 1988. Sports Stadiums and Area Development: A Critical Review. *Economic Development Quarterly* 2: 265–275.

Baim, Dean V. 1994. *The Sports Stadium as a Municipal Investment.* Westport, Conn.: Greenwood Press.

Euchner, Charles, C. 1993. *Playing the Field: Why Sports Teams Move and Cities Fight to Keep Them.* Baltimore: Johns Hopkins University Press.

Savas, E. S. 1987. *Privatization: The Key to Better Government.* Chatham, N.J.: Chatham House.

Sullivan, Neil J. 1987. *The Dodgers Move West.* New York: Oxford University Press.

Whitford, David. 1993. *Playing Hardball: The High-Stakes Battle for Baseball's New Franchises.* New York: Doubleday.

IV

MEDIA, THEATRICS, AND POLITICAL ACTORS

One way that sports, players, and owners hold our attention is through the "drama" surrounding their actions. Much of our information about sports comes from the media. In Chapter 10, Robyne S. Turner and Jose F. Marichal explore the role of local media in stadium development. Ferdinand Mount's The Theatre of Politics *(1973) examines how politicians use theatrics to sell policies. Owners and politicians also use theatrical techniques in building sports arenas and stadiums. Mount identifies two types of theater, the theater of embarrassment and the theater of sentiment. The theater of embarrassment entails scandals and human errors. One gets some of this type of theater when an athlete becomes involved in domestic violence or in a gambling scandal. The theater of sentiment involves politicians and owners personalizing political decisions. In Wilbur C. Rich's review in Chapter 11 of the* New England Patriots *fiasco, an enormous amount of time was spent focusing on two actors to give the impression it was a personal feud. The rivalry between Robert Kraft and Speaker Tom Finnenan proved to be highly dramatic, with each issuing official statements and making appearances before different audiences.*

One can think of the politics involved in building a new stadium as a play in which the politicians and the owners are the actors while the media serves as the supporting cast. The public is the audience. The purpose of the play is to widen the constituency for a new stadium beyond the loyal fan base. The owners pitch their appeals to the various groups they believe will be crucial in the decision-making process. The owners often come up with a catchword or slogan to drive or frame the campaign. By using facts, threats, and policy statements, politicians and owners are trying to sell the stadium to the public. The audience will applaud or jeer at the performance of the two group of actors.

Finally, there is the melodrama of sports. Fans often invest a lot of emotion in supporting "their team." Indeed, teams encourage the idea that they are a part of the community (see Danielson 1997). A true sports fan follows his or her team, feels depressed if his or her team loses, and buys sports memorabilia and season tickets. In addition to being a psychological investment for its fans, a team is also a financial investment. Although television revenues dwarf ticket revenues, the fan is still a major player in the history of a franchise. The lack of fan support can undermine the owners' attempt to build new facilities or attract quality players. This is why sports reporting is critical to the process of nurturing fan supports. Murray Edelman's (1964) observations about the impact of news stories applies to sports stories.

Politicians, officials, journalists whose careers depend on news stories, advocates of causes, and a fair number of people who are continually concerned, shocked, entertained, or titillated by the news, constitute an avid audience for the political spectacle. For them, there are weekly, daily, sometimes hourly triumphs and defeats, grounds for hope and for fears, a potpourri of happenings that mark trends and aberrations, some of them historic. Political life is hyperreal: typically more portentous than personal affairs. (p. 6)

And so it is with sports fans. This explains why the sports pages provide a steady diet of tidbits about players' personal lives in the off-season, report threats of owners, seriously examine comments by coaches, and deconstruct stadium deals. The construction of this discourse is analogous to that of a political spectacle. As the fan searches for certainty in an era of mobile franchises, ownership changes, and intercity competition, the building of stadiums, ballparks, or arenas represents a relatively sensible investment in an industry that provides tremendous psychological rewards.

This discourse is also closely related to the famous Cox and Mair (1988) observation about the redemptive ideology of locality. Briefly, the argument holds that the pro-growth business elite needs to legitimate projects that are planned for the community. Residents are encouraged to believe that their collective identity is somehow connected to the success of project like a stadium. Accordingly, they must rally behind what Cox and Mair call Urban Propaganda Projects (UPP) to save the city and themselves from further decay. In the case of the New England Patriots, the ideal was promoted that Boston's reputation as the hub city of New England would be injured if the team moved to Hartford. Hence, they should pay for a new stadium to keep the team. When the team owner decided to stay in the Boston area, residents were encouraged to believe they had been redeemed. This might seem somewhat abstract, but Rich's review of the stadium politics in Boston helps to explain this phenomenon.

REFERENCES

Cox, Kevin, and Andrew Mair. 1988. Locality and Community in the Politics of Local Economic Development. *Annals of the Association of American Geographers* 78: 318–319.

Danielson, Michael. 1997. *Home Team*. Princeton: Princeton University Press.

Edelman, Murray. 1964. *The Symbolic Use of Politics*. Urbana: University of Illinois Press.

Mount, Ferdinand. 1973. *The Theatre of Politics*. New York: Schocken Books.

10

Exploring Politics on the Sports Page

Robyne S. Turner and Jose F. Marichal

The images evoked by some of the more hallowed American football and baseball stadiums across the country have been so firmly ensconced in the American psyche that it is difficult to view these venues in anything but a positive light. Sports teams have traditionally carried great symbolic meaning to the cities that house them. The acquisition of a franchise is regarded as an emblem of world-class-city status. More important, stadiums are widely perceived as economic magnets that create jobs by attracting capital from outside the central city (Baade and Dye 1990). Yet the effectiveness of a stadium strategy as an economic-development policy approach has been successfully challenged in many cities.

The purpose of this chapter is to examine the publicly reported positions taken by policy actors on the issue of stadium development and to understand those positions within the context of local policy systems. Different sets of actors within the city will propose different responses to economic-development approaches. Pro-growth advocates in many communities will present a new stadium as a solution to the economic-development needs of a region. Challenges come from a variety of local actors who see the opportunity to gain politically from opposing the project. These responses, for and against, illustrate how different communities of policy actors treat different solution sets as these actors try to optimize sports as a policy response.

THE LURE OF SPORTS POLICY

Because of the highly coveted nature of sports franchises, cities compete with each other to put together the most attractive package to either lure or maintain sports teams in given localities. A sports team may be sold to local taxpayers as a profit-making venture, as teams bargain for a city's desire to have a sports franchise. Teams leverage an offer from a competing city in order to force the team's home city to renegotiate more-favorable lease terms, make renovations to existing facilities, or build new facilities. Charles Euchner (1993) points out that "at some point in the past decade, virtually all professional franchises publicly threatened to move to a different city in order to extract the benefits they desired from local governments" (p. 5).

This has been a profitable strategy for sports franchises. The Seattle Mariners received free rent, a 40-percent share of skybox revenue, and a right to break their lease if the franchise did not draw 1.4 million fans in a given year when they intimated they might move to Indianapolis (Euchner 1993, 54). When the Chicago White Sox threatened to move to St. Petersburg, the Illinois legislature intervened and guaranteed minimum ticket sales and a statewide television package (p. 54). This leverage position can also manifest itself in the construction of new state-of-the-art facilities with retractable roofs and luxury skyboxes. The taxpayers of New Orleans had to pay an $11-million annual debt service for the construction of the Superdome (Johnson 1986, 421). Newspaper sports pages chronicle celebrated franchise moves, such as when the NFL Brown's moved from Cleveland to Baltimore, where the city and the state of Maryland teamed to build a new stadium in order to lure the team.

Many local leaders justify public assumption of a large debt service to finance a stadium by arguing that there will be long-term economic benefits for the city. Yet several studies have shown both minor and major stadium projects often have a negligible or incalculable effect on the overall economic health of a city (Rosentraub and Swindell 1991; Johnson 1986). Baade and Dye (1990) found that "the presence of a new or renovated stadium has an uncertain effect upon development in a region" (p. 13). These studies asks the question: Why do cities implement a stadium-development strategy as an economic-development policy if it is presumably such a financially risky proposition?

Stadium Projects as Economic-Development Solution Sets

Stadium-development projects may be locally justified by the short-term symbolic impact they have on the local business economy with the expectation of long-term spinoff benefits to the region. Yates (1977) contends that it is impossible for public officials to develop cut-and-dried policy approaches because problems are unpredictable and in continual flux. Given this to be true, it is more practical for a policy maker to work backward. Instead of attempting to apply approaches to existing problems, it is more practical to plug problems into well-tailored policy approaches. Bachelor (1994, 605) outlines this phenomenon as "solutions looking for problems." This suggests that specific development projects can be solution sets to be used by public-policy actors as needed to address larger economic-development problems. Their effectiveness is ultimately measured in terms of political mileage.

In this case, the stadium strategy allows elected officials to cater to business interests and still maintain legitimacy among the electorate. Though the economic benefits of building a facility are debatable, there are symbolic benefits which compel public officials to act. The end result of the policy becomes a secondary consideration (Bachelor 1994).

Conversely, if a franchise leaves a city, there are significant symbolic costs to be paid by not offering incentives. The political liabilities are magnified in the case of a sports franchise because of the strong psychological attachments that exist between a team and its fans. No politician would want to be in the unenviable position of losing the home team, which may be viewed by the public as the first indicator of a decelerating economic environment.

Though losing a franchise is considered a political liability, the team's demand for the construction of a new stadium might be turned into a positive if the construction can be justified as urban redevelopment. In this way, the team demand is packaged into an existing economic-development strategy the city is undertaking (see also Rosentraub et al. 1994). Examples of this approach are the new baseball parks in Baltimore, Denver, and Chicago. While retention or acquisition of the team in these cities was a primary goal, the new ballparks were attached to other projects and sold as gateways to future development. The effectiveness of this strategy will be known only after the team and stadium are firmly in place.

Policy Communities and Urban Political Economy

The effectiveness of this symbolic strategy depends on the makeup of the policy community, which is defined as "the existence of a community of policy actors pursuing common interests in a restricted political space" (Goetz and Sidney 1994, 1). Those who dominate a policy community serve as gatekeepers for the types of solution sets that are proposed. Yet most policy communities can only capture temporary monopolies in any arena, because the policy system is in constant flux. Through the mobilization of "latent or potential members, whose indifference can be overcome either by disturbances external to the sub-system, or by strategies employed by coalitions within the subsystem," those opposed to a policy subsystem can change the composition of the system (Sabatier and Jenkins-Smith 1993).

There are characteristics unique to each group of actors within policy-making communities that influence policy outcomes. These groups can be broken down into relatively simple classifications: territorial groups, elected officials, and administrative officials (Clarke 1987). Territorial groups, such as business groups, team representatives, and community interests, place short-term distributional demands on the system and seek to maximize benefits while minimizing costs. Elected officials must balance the needs of all interests but are usually biased toward the business community. Administrative officials are gener-ally out of the public eye, but may have their own identifiable con-stituencies as well as the goal to acquire institutional power and control.

The composition of policy systems is largely determined not only by their monetary resources, but also by the effectiveness of the sym-bols they employ (Baumgartner and Jones 1994). At the local level the sports stadium issue imbues the strong emotional bond between a community and its franchise. Euchner (1993) points out that "if a sport-ing event is considered an essential part of the community, a contrary politician or activist group can be seen as anti-community" (p. 170). Yet opposition groups attempt to dislodge the policy support for sports by suggesting that a sports strategy is an inefficient use of resources that carry opportunity costs. The difficulty these opponents confront is that it is difficult to convert these arguments into effective symbols.

UNCOVERING SPORTS POLITICS

We expect to see an alliance of growth/business actors and local government, which together act as a booster of growth interests, to push for large-scale, publicly funded infrastructure projects that cre-ate capital (Molotch 1976; Mollenkopf 1983). Yet we are uncertain who in the alliance acts as the public advocate and who stays behind the scenes. Nor are we sure who publicly challenges these efforts. In this chapter the development issue of sports stadiums is assessed through news quo-tations from different public- and private-sector actors. This approach allows us to penetrate the issue in order to reveal the positions of the actors who are, by definition, central to urban growth politics.

One potential problem is that the local print media is also a political actor in growth politics (Logan and Molotch 1987). The newspapers are expected to be sympathetic to the demands of other growth actors because the paper stands to profit from growth through circulation and advertising sales. Beyond that association, some news organiza-tions own sports teams and have a significant interest in their profitability, which is affected by the team's stadium agreement. It is beyond the scope of this chapter to assess whether there is any bias in the coverage of sports-stadium issues by newspapers. However, if such a bias exists, it may affect the selection of quotations used in stories about stadium deals.

Public-Sector Actors

Politics is as important a determinant of policy selection and process as economic analyses (Stone 1989). Local government actors can be parceled by subgroups of actors with different motivations, constituencies, and, therefore, preferences. Local government actors may not have enough independent autonomy to select or determine policy outcomes, yet they can set minimum standards for a specific project as well as leverage the specific costs and benefits of a stadium proposal. Identifying their positions on stadium-development projects should provide indicators to understand more fully the parameters of sports-development politics.

For the purposes of this chapter, we have divided the public sector into three subgroups: elected officials and staff in their offices, other administrative officials such as planners, and officials in quasi-governmental units such as economic development authorities. Policy solutions may compete for the attention of different public actors based on individual actor needs. Elected officials may be boosters if the project is defined as economic development. Their position, however, may be tempered by administrative planners and service departments that work with interest groups and neighborhoods. These are groups that are likely to define the issue in terms of the equitable distribution of development costs and benefits. On the other hand, administrative actors may be information providers, providing expert analysis and a rationally detached policy perspective. Quasi-government officials are most likely to be supportive of stadium projects in which they can be development partners. Because they are housed in separate agencies with separate budgets, it benefits them economically to approve development projects.

Who Says What about Sports Stadiums

Our study tries to identify which actors take opposing and favoring positions toward a proposal to develop a sports stadium, and the nature of those positions. We examined articles from local daily newspapers around the country for five years during the period from 1982 to 1990 that dealt specifically with the topic of stadium-development proposals.[1] In each article we coded the quotations of each actor according to the type of position they took on the stadium project in their community or the nature of the information they gave about the project. We also classified the actors as elected, administrative, or territorial interests. This effort produced a database that allows us to analyze policy actors according to the statements they make on this issue in different locations over a multiyear period as relayed by the print media. The analysis presented here treats the data cumulatively and does not employ any variable of time.[2] The database was created by subjective coding of the contents of each article. The reported quotation by an actor is the unit of analysis. Analysis of this database must be tempered by the understanding that the newspaper may selectively include quoted statements in each article, limiting the scope of our ability to accurately portray the position of each actor. Therefore, the analysis is limited to a cumulative treatment of the coded statements by categories of actors and categories of statements.

Over half of the 1,443 total quotations in the newspaper article database come from government actors.[3] Community-based actors such as neighborhood groups represent no more than 10 percent of the quotations. Project-related actors include the representatives of the sports teams, developers, and business interests, and are the source of more than 30 percent of the quotations. There is a preponderance of government and project-related sources quoted, leading us to expect a very positive treatment of this policy issue overall. However, more than 70 percent of the subset of 1,227 quotations classified for the analysis are either neutral (information providing) or challenging some element of the proposal, rather than an overt statement of support for a stadium project. These data suggest that there is no overt evidence of a unanimous consent for stadium-development projects as a local policy issue.

Table 10.1 shows the type of actor by type of statement, providing evidence that policy communities view these proposals distinctly. Not surprising, community-based and project-related actors exhibit opposite positions by their statements. This is particularly revealing as it relates to the position taken by government actors. Approximately 28 percent of the government-actor quotations are classified as challenging some aspect of the stadium-development project. There is no unanimous support for stadium-development proposals even in the public sector, generally considered a booster of sports teams. It is necessary, therefore, to further break down public-sector actors into subgroups in order to more clearly assess their policy positions. This subgroup analysis should provide some insight into understanding how the stadium issue is considered in the policy process, and perhaps the attractiveness of stadium-development proposals as solution sets. Elected officials included in this part of the analysis include the mayor and staff of the mayor's office (representing the mayor's point of view), city commissioners, and county government; appointed or staff officials represent local governments involved in the decision process;

Table 10.1
Types of Actors Quoted by Categories of Statements (n = 1,227)

Quoted postion on proposal	Quotes by government actors	Quotes by project related actors	Quotes by community-based actors
Challenging	188 (28%)	66 (15%)	67 (54%)
Neutral/info	236 (35%)	147 (34%)	24 (20%)
Supporting	249 (37%)	218 (51%)	32 (26%)
Totals	673	431	122

appointed actors include city government staff, city manager, and quasi-governmental agencies or authorities (such as an economic-development authority).

In a further refinement in the analysis of only government actors, the types of quotations are collapsed into the three categories: challenging, neutral/informational, and supporting/advocacy. Several types of statements are not sufficiently definitive and were deleted from the collapsed categories (see types marked with an * in the appendix). Therefore, in this analysis six types of statements comprise the challenging category, three types of statements make up the neutral category, and six types of statements comprise the supporting category.

Table 10.2 shows a breakdown of types of statements made by type of local government actors.[4] All cross-tab results are statistically significant. This breakdown clearly shows that elected officials are likely to take different positions, hedging their support or opposition to a stadium project. Appointed officials are more likely to be boosters of the project, while, surprisingly, quasi-governmental actors are more likely to be information providers. One explanation may be that quasi-governmental actors restrict their public role to that of information providers and supporters of the decision process in order to avoid the criticism that they are seeking their own interests. As the examination of the groups of statements reveals, appointed officials may issue statements that are both supporting and challenging, perhaps depending on the nature of their department's constituent group.

The data in Table 10.3 suggest that appointed officials (city manager and city government staff) are more likely to support the projects in their statements than are elected officials (mayor, city commissioner, county government). This divergence of appointed and elected actors

Table 10.2
Local Government Actors by Categories of Statements (n = 531)

Quotation type	Elected official	Appointed officials	Quasi-governmental Officials
Challenging	36.8%	27.7%	7.7%
Neutral/info	29.0%	30.9%	52.4%
Supporting	34.2%	41.5%	40.0%
Totals	307	94	130

Note: All are at p = <0.001

Table 10.3
Specific Local Government Actor Quotations by Categories of Statements (n = 531)

Actors	Challenging statement	Neutral statement	Supporting statement	Totals
Mayor	39 (30.0%)	53 (40.7%)	38 (29.0%)	130
City Commission	31 (46.0%)	10 (15.0%)	26 (39.0%)	67
County Government	43 (39.0%)	26 (23.6%)	41 (37.2%)	110
City Manager	5 (29.4%)	5 (29.4%)	7 (41.0%)	17
City Staff	21 (27.0%)	24 (31.0%)	32 (41.5%)	77
Quasi Governmental Authority Staff	10 (7.5 %)	68 (53.0%)	52 (40.0%)	130
Totals by category of statement	149 (28.0%)	186 (3 5.0%)	196 (37.0%)	531

Note: All are at p = <0.001

may be due in part to a defensive posture taken by administrative staff who feel they must defend their expertise. Such defensive statements may appear to be supportive in the quotations. This may be particularly true when administrators are defending an economic analysis or facility-development plan. As expected, quasi-governmental actors are by far the least likely to challenge the proposal. Elected officials, particularly city commissioners, are more likely to be polarized in their support and opposition, with more negative statements than positive. Commissioners often represent specific place-based constituencies and stadium proposals often have significant impacts on specific locations. This need to accommodate NIMBY (not in my backyard) challenges may explain why the majority of the commissioners' statements are classified as challenging stadium proposals.

Similar results are found when mean responses are examined. Elected officials have a lower mean response (1.97) than either appointed officials (2.13) or quasi-governmental officials (2.32) (where challenging = 1, neutral/info = 2, and supporting = 3). Elected and appointed officials have a standard deviation of more than 0.8, suggesting some volatility in their responses (as Table 10.3 indicates). Quasi-governmental officials have a standard deviation of 0.6, indicating they have a greater concentration of responses. All differences in the means are statistically significant at the $p = <0.05$ level.

Discussion

Though this is a limited overview analysis of the data, there are some indications that we can extract about the quoted statements of public officials and the implications for policy development as far as it concerns stadium proposals as a means for urban economic development. Public officials do not exhibit uniform sentiments about this type of development project. Different types of officials have different constituencies, and perhaps different roles to play. It is clear, though, that for the most part the public sector takes a positive, although tempered, position on such development proposals. It is not accurate, however, to state that the public sector uniformly supports stadium developments. There are distinctions as to the type of support or information and advocacy roles those different actor groups take. Though this analysis does not provide statistical evidence, there are instances where individual public-sector actors make contradictory statements, such as supporting a proposal in principle but questioning the costs or location. Overall, however, these data seem to support the notion that public-sector officials may support stadium-development proposals as part of a larger economic-development strategy but question the specifics according to the needs of their different constituencies.

The data also indicate that government actors do not widely challenge stadium proposals. On balance, their quoted statements primarily are not challenging the development of stadiums, but instead reflect sentiments ranging from oblique support of the process, and thus the project itself, to outright support for the project (boosterism). It seems, then, that the primary public question is not whether to build, but where and how to build. Few government officials are quoted as challenging the presence of a sports team. The dissention is in the project details. This assessment suggests that sports teams may find the public sector a willing listener, if not a deal maker. Conversely, the variety of opinions taken by public-sector actors suggests that they are not blind boosters for sports team interests and potentially can act as an effective gatekeeper in the policy community. Their role seems to be pivotal, not only in terms of the nuts and bolts of regulatory approval and sentiment, but in the policy process where approval and consensus are necessary.

CONCLUSION

Policy actors play varying roles in the midst of decision making concerning stadium-development projects. Even when collapsing those roles into broad categories of public, project-related, and community-based actors, the subtext suggests that there are important distinctions that may alter the course of the decision-making process. Public-sector officials are not autonomous in their positions toward stadium-development proposals, but neither are they in lockstep with the proposal supporters, even though public officials may support the development as a long-term economic-development strategy. Their ties to constituency groups may temper their statements, increasing their likelihood to be deal-makers as well as boosters. Elected officials and administrative officials differ in their positions, suggesting that there are subgroups of the public sector in the policy community and that they are likely to attach themselves to different elements of a stadium development as an economic-development solution set.

By and large, though, we can depend on public-sector actors to be generally responsive to these types of development projects. Unfortunately, these data must treat all actors equally in terms of their weight in the decision-making process. In different locations, different public-sector actors may have essential or actual veto power over a development project. Certainly, if the quasi-governmental-actor group does not favor a stadium proposal, it may never get discussed. If a powerful elected official is opposed to the project, it may die a thousand deaths of review and analysis. The bottom line for local governments may be to determine if they are asking the right questions about a stadium-development project: to build or not to build, and when to evaluate the benefits and costs of the project—the obvious short-term benefits as well as the eventual long-term gains and losses.

APPENDIX: TYPES OF STATEMENTS QUOTED
IN NEWSPAPERS

Types indicated by an * were not used in Table 10.2 and Table 10.3 analysis.

Category 1: Challenging Types of Statements

Questioning the costs; economic consequences of the project

Questioning the benefits; need for the project, who is actually benefiting

Challenging the proposal; merits and specific items of the deal

Challenging the proposed location of the stadium; intergovernmental concerns

Challenging the decision-making process; its fairness, openness, use of discretion

Challenging the positions taken by individuals; finger pointing to undermine the proposal

Category 2: Information Types of Statements

Information about the decision-making process; poll results, time frame and sequencing, process rules, status of various elements of the project proposal

Descriptive information about the proposal; design, costs, terms of the deal

Neutral reply to questions about the proposal; noncommittal replies, further study, caution, and deliberation

*Requesting or demanding information and action; ultimatums, call for specified action, threats, conditions for action

*Predicting and analyzing the project; explaining victory or defeat of the proposal, status of the plan, postponement, assumptions

Category 3: Supporting Types of Statements

Consensus building; empathy, flexibility of expectations, peacemaking

Explaining and rationalizing the project and specific aspects

Defending the decision-making process and methodology to evaluate and support project

Reassuring the public on project proposal issues

Boosterism; rewards, profit, spin-offs, growth potential, city exposure, limits, and losses if not completed

Outright support of the project; state-of-the-art facility, praise of project, innovative and visionary, evaluations are positive

*Commitments; if plan A fails, implement plan B

NOTES

1. The Newsbank data source was used to extract 159 articles from thirty-six cities nationwide. The articles were found under the heading "planning and proposals" and the subheading "sports facilities: stadiums." Articles on sports arenas were not considered, as they are often used as venues for concerts and other revenue-producing functions. The authors devised their own coding scheme to capture twenty-two types of positions taken by actors on stadium proposals in their locality; these were collapsed for analysis. There are eighteen actor categories that were collapsed into three types of actors; public sector, project related, and community based. The public-sector group was later distilled to three categories; elected officials (and their office staffs), appointed officials, and quasi-governmental officials.

2. We collected the quotation data over a multiyear period in order to avoid any single year that may have been skewed due to abnormally high or low stadium-construction activity. It also allows coverage of different economic conditions that may have occurred at different times in different regions of the country.

3. Government actors include mayor and mayoral staff, city commission, city manager, city staff, quasi-governmental officials, county elected officials, state government, and federal government.

4. Elected officials include mayor and mayoral staff, city commission, and county officials. Appointed officials include city manager and city government staff. Quasi-governmental officials is a separately coded category.

REFERENCES

Baade, Robert A., and Richard F. Dye. 1990. The Impact of Stadiums and Professional Sports on Metropolitan Area Development. *Growth and Change* 21: 1–14.

Bachelor, Lynn. 1994. Regime Maintenance, Solution Sets, and Urban Economic Development. *Urban Affairs Quarterly* 4: 596–616.

Baumgartner, Frank, and Bryan Jones. 1994. Agenda Dynamics and Policy Subsystems. *Journal of Politics* 53: 1045–1073.

Clarke, Susan. 1987. More Autonomous Policy Orientations: An Analytic Framework. In *The Politics of Urban Development*, edited by C. Stone and H. T. Sanders. Lawrence: University of Kansas Press, 105–124.

Euchner, Charles. 1993. *Playing the Field: Why Sports Teams Move and Cities Fight to Keep Them*. Baltimore: Johns Hopkins University Press.

Goetz, Edward G., and Mara Sidney. 1994. *Policy Subsystems in Local Community Development*. Paper presented at the annual meeting of the American Political Science Association, New York.

Johnson, Arthur T. 1986. Economic and Policy Implications of Hosting Sports Franchises: Lessons from Baltimore. *Urban Affairs Quarterly* 21: 411–433.

Logan, John, and Harvey Molotch. 1987. *Urban Fortunes*. Berkeley and Los Angeles: University of California Press.

Mollenkopf, John. 1983. *The Contested City*. Princeton: Princeton University Press.

Molotch, Harvey. 1976. The City as a Growth Machine. *American Journal of Sociology* 82: 309–331.

Rosentraub, Mark S., David Swindell, Michael Przybylski, and Daniel R. Mullins. 1994. Sport and Downtown Development Strategy: If You Build It, Will Jobs Come? *Journal of Urban Affairs* 16: 221–239.

Rosentraub, Mark S., and David Swindell. 1991. Just Say No? The Economic and Political Realities of a Small City's Investment in Minor League Baseball. *Economic Development Quarterly* 5: 152–167.

Sabatier, Paul, and Hank Jenkins-Smith. 1993. *Policy Change and Learning*. Boulder, Colo.: Westview Press.

Stone, Clarence. 1989. *Regime Politics: Governing Atlanta, 1946–1988*. Lawrence: University of Kansas Press.

Yates, Douglas. 1977. *The Ungovernable City*. Cambridge: MIT Press.

11

Who Lost the Boston Megaplex and Almost the New England Patriots?

Wilbur C. Rich

In the 1950s a famous rhetorical question within foreign-policy circles was, "Who lost China?" The assumption was that America once owned China and that now it belonged to the Communists. Of course, the United States never owned China, but in the minds of some it was a virtual ownership. For the last four years the "Who lost the Megaplex?" question filled the sport bars of Boston. The Megaplex, a planned multipurpose facility that would combine a football stadium, a baseball park, and a convention center, was heavily discussed in the media and became a part of the virtual reality of Boston's sports scene. The proposal was intensely promoted by the ownership of the New England Patriots as a way to solve its football stadium problem. A new convention center had been on the city agenda for a long time. Despite the commonalty of interest, the idea was abandoned after the Megaplex coalition could not agree on location and financing. What happened? Why are the city politicians now thinking about three separate facilities instead of one? Who fumbled the ball? The failure of the Megaplex proposal poses several issues about the efficacy of sports facilities and economic development. Was the proposal an example of poor marketing on the part of the governing regime?

This chapter will discuss the failure of the Megaplex proposal and its meta-meaning for Boston's pro-growth coalition. Although plans for the Megaplex have been dropped, there is still no resolution of the need for a stadium and a convention center. Sports-stadium controversies offer a fascinating opportunity to examine the conflicts between a mayor-centered coalition and the downtown development interest. An examination of the Megaplex planning supports Pressman and Wildavsky's (1973) admonition about "complexity of joint action." There were so many decision points, veto groups, and delays that the final resolution increased the cost and proved to be unsatisfactory.

SPORTS POLICY AND CITY LEADERSHIP

Professional sports and urban politics meet when cities are asked to subsidize the renovation, expansion, and rebuilding of any professional sports facility. In this post-industrial age, a professional sports team can become an important part of a city's political and economic identity. A mayor's reputation as job developer can become caught up in a fight to build a facility or keep a franchise in the city. Generally speaking, mayors do not preside over the loss of professional sports franchises. Fans are also voters. Besides, sports facilities can be revenue providers rather than revenue spenders. Boston was inclined to support a stadium facility because of the possibility of creating 10,000 to 15,000 new jobs and $100 million in the hotel business.

A sports facility is not a one-time subsidy or investment. Cities bear the cost of increased traffic, wear and tear on infrastructure, pollution, and safety for the life of the facility. In order for a team to raise the money (usually in the form of state revenue bonds) to build a new stadium, they need the support of the governing regime as well as of the general public. Accordingly, the team owners form a coalition with politicians to mobilize support for the funding. This coalition can form an entangling relationship, as this review of the Megaplex suggests. In other states, officials have had to bend their constitutions to keep their team (see Bardson 1998).

The sports franchise issue engages politicians and their business counterparts because it gives them a chance to demonstrate civic leadership. This melding of political and economic interest has been called regime politics (Elkins 1987; Stone 1989). Pelissero, Henschen, and Sidlow (1991) identified three types of regimes. A corporate regime promotes the corporate agenda, which usually includes downtown development and amenities. In other words, whatever the corporate community wants in terms of amenities, it gets. Corporate regimes have traditionally supported stadiums and other concessions for professional sports teams. In an interview, Joseph Corcoran (1997), the developer and a leader of the Megaplex coalition, asserted that Boston doesn't fit this model:

[In] Atlanta they form committees and come out together. In Boston everybody works separately and works at cross-purposes. Everybody has a separate agenda. People don't come together. Too many turf wars. If it is one person's interest, then it is the best interest of the other to be against it. The Governor is in one place. The mayor is in another. The Speaker in a different place. President of the Senate is in a different place.

At least for the Megaplex proposal, Boston's governing coalition did not behave like a corporate regime. Although Corcoran's comments were mostly directed toward elected officials, there were also considerable disagreements within the downtown community. Without unity, the downtown coalition could not use singleness of purpose in negotiation with the city.

Pelissero, Henschen, and Sidlow's (1991) second type of regime is called a progressive regime, as it promotes neighborhood-group agendas. These regimes are less likely to support "growth machine projects" or downtown development in general. The South Boston neighborhood, a predominately working-class white ethnic community (i.e., Irish-American) fought the idea of a stadium in their community. Their representatives in the city council and in the state legislature led the fight against the stadium and the convention center. The mayor has also consistently opposed a stadium in the South Boston area. Does Boston fit this model? Mayor Menino has followed his predecessor Ray Flynn's mantra of being a neighborhood mayor, but it is not clear that neighborhood opposition will prevail in this case.

The final type of regime, the caretaker, describes a governing group that is not able to promote any agenda because of the weak relationship between the business community and home owners. I have argued elsewhere that Mayor Tom Menino's leadership is a caretaker regime (Rich 1995). This does not mean that he can safely ignore the electoral backlash from losing the Patriots over a location fight. Hence there is great incentive for the mayor to stay engaged and not let his career get mangled in the stadium.

MAYOR MENINO AND THE CROWDED PLAYING FIELD

Who are the other members of the Megaplex coalition? They include Governor William Weld, leaders of the state legislature, Robert Kraft (owner of the Patriots), construction companies, the Massachusetts Convention Center Authority, the Boston Redevelopment Authority

(BRA), and downtown business leaders such as real estate developer Joe Corcoran of Corcoran and Jennison Companies. Kraft has attempted to assume the leadership of this coalition, but so far has not been able to move the coalition forward. Governor Weld supported the notion that a stadium in Boston will stimulate the economy. The stakes are high for Governor Weld and Mayor Menino, but they can't do it alone. Because the project was bigger than Boston and its suburbs, other state political actors were allowed to play a role in planning. Therefore they needed to market the proposal statewide.

In 1993 a *Boston Globe* poll (Sit 1993, 53) found that the majority of state residents wanted a combined convention center and sport stadium. They surveyed 402 people statewide and found that 73 percent supported the project if it was linked to economic improvement of the entire state. The level of support fell when respondents were asked if they supported public spending for the facilities. On the question of public funding, 47 percent supported the idea and 41 percent did not. A larger percentage of respondents (66 percent) opposed the project if it would raise the debt level for the state. A more telling response was related to whether they supported using taxpayer money to support the stadium if that was the only way to keep the Patriots. Of the total respondents, 63 percent of them would rather lose the team. Among football fans, 55 percent agreed to spend the money to keep the team.

In 1994 the mayor instructed the Boston Redevelopment Authority to conduct a study of the proposals. The BRA recommended building a freestanding convention center. The mayor then took a stand against a doomed stadium for football. He thought that a larger convention center would best serve the city's interests. Menino's plans for a stand-alone convention center would be financed by a $1 hotel fee. The center would be financed with over $400 million of public funds. After the mayor made his preference public, the governor, a Republican, supported an alternative site for the Megaplex in Roxbury, a predominately minority neighborhood. A city–state agreement on cost and location is essential if the state is to be the senior partner in this development. This disagreement is significant because of the comingling of state and local politics in facility financing. The state legislature is controlled by Democrats, and it sought to create its own proposals.

The state legislature called a Megaplex summit and established a thirteen-member Megaplex commission under Chapter 6 of the Acts of 1995, *An Act Relative to Development of Convention Facilities in the Commonwealth* (Commonwealth of Massachusetts 1995). The commission toured six cities (Atlanta, Baltimore, Chicago, Indianapolis, New Orleans, and St. Louis) and examined their financing, impact, and physical construction. The state commission decided that the stadium should accommodate both a football stadium and convention center. They also supported a stand-alone open-air stadium for the Boston Red Sox. They predicted that the cost of the Megaplex facility would come close to $1 billion. The big question was where to locate the facility.

BOSTON, A SPORTS TOWN?

Boston often revels in its reputation as a great sports town. The love affairs with the Boston Red Sox, Celtics, and Bruins is as strong as with any sports fans in America. But despite Boston fans' love of sports, the Red Sox and the Patriots need new playing facilities.

Although the New England Patriots are a relatively new professional football franchise, they have attracted a loyal following in the city and region. However, the Patriots' fans live with the continuing threat of seeing moving vans each time there is a change of ownership. A city without a professional football team does not have cachet to compete for industries that employ a young middle-class professional workforce. Because the NFL has packaged itself as a status symbol, attending an NFL game has become a part of the male success ritual. The NFL has become so prestigious that cities will lure even an established franchise with outstanding fan support (i.e., the Cleveland Browns in 1996). The competition has gotten so fierce that few city franchises are safe.

As is the case for several NFL teams, residents of Boston have to travel to the suburbs to see the team play. The Patriots play their games in Foxboro, ten miles from Boston. The town is only accessible by car or a special commuter train. Although the Patriots are considered Boston's team, the team has changed its name to New England Patriots to a create regional identity. Indeed, 33 percent of the Patriots fans base lives outside the state.

Some people believe that having the Patriots inside Boston's city limits would consolidate fan support and loyalty. Mr. Kraft, the new owner, wants a new stadium that is close to the planned convention center to benefit from the new traffic. With these two attractions, the Central Business District's local hotels, restaurants, and bar businesses would also benefit. The strategy of the proponents of the economic-development argument is to repeat it frequently in the media (see Euchner 1993). The noneconomic proponents play on the emotional needs of the fans and the status needs of the city.

Aside from the economic and noneconomic arguments, why should there be a linkage between the stadium and the convention center? First, the 1986 federal tax law changed the tax exemptions for building stadiums. According to Marisa Lago (1996), BRA director, the decision to link the stadium to the convention center "was a reaction to public attitude against public financing of a sports stadium. One could indirectly subside the football stadium with a convention center. There was a demonstrated need for a convention center. The football propo-nents saw an opportunity to latch on to it. The stadium was artificially appended to it." Apparently, the governing regime thought a stadium facility combined with a larger convention center would also convince investors to create more hotel rooms in the city. This would make Bos-ton a competitive location for conventions with over 10,000 attendees. In order to make this plan work, the linkage had to be maintained.

Robert Kraft was aware of the need for a new stadium when he brought the team. While other NFL franchises were shopping for new stadiums in new cities, Kraft was busy trying to make a deal to stay in Boston. Kraft made it clear that he did not want to be remembered as the man who took the Patriots out of Boston. Kraft's responsible-owner persona won him praise from fans and state and local politicians. He wants a first-class NFL stadium, and leaders in the Boston area want to keep the team. Yet the dynamics of new ownership are working against the Kraft pledge. Euchner (1993) observed,

Franchise turnover produces a steady influx of new ownership groups, which usually want to negotiate new arrangements with their stadium landlords, in turn producing more intercity bidding for franchises. Team sales are encour-aged by the unique prerogative of franchises to depreciate player salaries for five years. As new owners negotiate more lucrative deals with local authori-ties, other teams in the league seek similar advantages just to keep pace. The cycle of some teams gaining business advantages over other teams, and those other teams playing catch-up, begins anew. (p. 25)

The economics of franchise ownership can be so capricious and daunting that even a community-minded owner like Kraft would be forced to entertain outside offers to increase his leverage with city and state politicians. Because other cities had been so generous with NFL owners, building them luxury boxes, making lease concessions, or paying with other features, some Boston politicians felt that their bar-gaining position was relatively weak.

At first glance it appeared that there was a mutuality of interest between city leaders and Robert Kraft. There was land to build a 70,000-seat fixed-seating stadium, and fans supported the idea; several sites were considered to be ideal locations. Consensus for a joint conven-tion center–stadium facility was building, and the public thought the construction cranes were on their way.

A closer look, however, reveals significant disagreements about the mode of financing for the new facility, the location, and the efficacy of a multipurpose facility. Location emerged as the most difficult part of the proposal.

LOCATION AND FINANCING POLITICS

At first the location game was played by neighborhoods and local politicians. Several sites had been suggested for a possible stadium and convention center. These included Beacon Yard, Kenmore/Mass Pike, Back Bay, North Station, Neponset Drive-In, Boston State Hospital, Boston Sand and Gravel and Suffolk Downs, C Street and Northern Avenue, and Commonwealth Flats. There seemed to be many suitable locations, but there was no agreement on any one of them. The mayor wanted to locate the convention center in South Boston. The governor wanted to locate the facilities in Roxbury. The minority community in Roxbuxy supported the idea, but when the Megaplex plan was abandoned, Kraft insisted on locating a stadium in South Boston.

The location game was also played by rival cities. As Charles Euchner (1993) has pointed out, owners increase their profits by creating competition among cities. Franchise owners are not above playing one city, neighborhood, or suburb against another in order to get a better deal. Cities in New England have had the welcome mat out for the Patriots for several years. As early as 1993 the state of Connecticut tried to make a preemptive strike for the Patriots. Governor Lowell Weicker of Connecticut signed a bill authorizing $252 million in bonds to build a professional football stadium in Hartford if the New England Patriots would move there. Apparently the legislature sensed a lack of resolve on the part of the Bay State legislature.

The potential backlash of losing the Patriots has never been lost on Massachusetts Governor William Weld. He has been fighting to control the location and financing of a facility since as early as 1993. When a few people began singing "St. Louis, here we come," the governor announced publicly that the Patriots would leave the state "over his dead body."

To keep the Patriots, there were renewed efforts at solving the financial problem. Several questions had to be addressed. Should the stadium and convention center be connected? Should the convention center be built first? What type of taxes would pay the debt services for the stadium bonds? What was the best location for the facilities? What would be the probable impact of the facilities on the economy? How many permanent jobs would the new facilities create? As a result of these questions, a series of studies was launched to provide answers. Three different impact studies disagreed on all these questions. A 1993 Cooper & Lybrand study sponsored by the state Office of Economic Affairs gave optimistic answers for these questions. Coopers & Lybrand estimated the impact to be $1.01 billion and the creation of 13,300 jobs. Under this proposal the state share would be $63 million. The state commission estimated $500 million, with 7,500 jobs created. The state share would be $22.9 million. The Coopers & Lybrand study does not take into account the competition from the Hynes Convention Center. Seven months later, the Price Waterhouse study, sponsored by the Massachusetts Center Authority, gave equally optimistic recommendations for the proposal. The Price Waterhouse study included the convention center and the stadium. It estimated that the total impact would be $860 million, and 11,900 jobs would be created. The state revenue share would be $46.9 million.

However, the 1994 BRA study was less supportive of the idea of a combined convention center with fixed-seat stadium. The interim report stated, "After an extensive analysis, the BRA concluded that the exposition center and football stadium should be built separately in different locations. It estimated that the total impact of the project would be $419 million and would generate 6,560 new jobs. It would require $18.9 million of state revenues." In an interview, Marisa Lago (1996), BRA director, stated that the "two structures idea could not sustain itself. For football, you need 70,000 seats and for the convention you need 5,000 seats. There were programmatic differences. The two structures could not work together." Yet the BRA study and its differences with the other studies did not quiet the critics. Each study reflected the different assumptions of the various proposals. It became harder to estimate cost and impact as the project configurations continued to change.

Accordingly, these studies did not help the credibility problem or the promotional need of state and local politicians. Kenneth Shropshire (1995) has argued that all impact studies "are crafted to support an advocacy role" (p. 61). Should urban regimes take seriously the predictions that are based on an exaggerated multiplier that overstates the economic benefits of the project? Sports facilities did change the reputation of Indianapolis, but will they do the same for Boston?

BOSTON AND THE INDIANAPOLIS MODEL

The analogy between Boston and Indianapolis, with its downtown domed stadium, is perhaps overdrawn. Boston is no Indianapolis and Tom Menino is no Bill Hudnut (see Hudnut 1995). Granted, locating the stadium in Boston will change the dynamics of business and traffic, but it will not transform Boston into a sports city. The political culture of Boston, with its prestigious academic institutions, high-tech industry, and historical traditions, works against a Indianapolis-type transformation.

Nevertheless, Boston wants to stay competitive as a major convention town. To remain competitive, it needs a larger convention center with 600,000 square feet of exhibition space and more hotel rooms.

Would such a facility make Boston competitive with Chicago and Atlanta for the big conventions? Would it be competitive for the Super Bowl, political conventions, and a future Olympics? Maybe. Boston and Indianapolis are only marginally similar, and differ greatly in their political cultures. An attempt to import a solution set from a Midwestern city to an Eastern one is problematic (see Bachelor 1994). Rosentraub et al. (1994) warns against using sports as a downtown development strategy or adopting an Indianapolis model:

Given how small sports is as an industry and the low pay associated with the numerous service sector jobs created by sports activities, sports is not a prudent vehicle around which a development or redevelopment effort should be organized. A sports strategy will not be an economic stimulus for a community or region. (pp. 237–238)

Domed facilities are multi-million-dollar enterprises that are increasingly complex and expensive to build and maintain. A state-of-the-art domed stadium built in the year 2000 could become obsolete within ten years. The city of Boston could find itself the owner of a new facility and a team with a new owner, and could be back in the cycle of cities on the verge of losing their teams.

No decision the city makes is risk free. Therefore, the mayor had no choice but to state publicly what he had said in private: "Everyone agrees we need a convention center. . . . What's holding it up is the how to finance the stadium piece. We don't need a new football stadium right away, but we do need a convention center for business and jobs. So let's do what's doable and what's needed today" (Vaillancourt and Walker 1995, 1). Without the mayor's support, the Megaplex was comatose. Don Lowery (1996), the Patriots' public-relations director, stated publicly and categorically that the "Megaplex is dead. We will never see the Megaplex in our lifetime." This was yet another indicator that his boss, Mr. Kraft, had given up on the Megaplex idea. Earlier, Joe Corcoran, one of the leaders of the Megaplex coalition, had conceded defeat in a private discussion with the mayor. However, the mayor was not off the hook, as Kraft continued the fight for a stadium.

According to Marisa Lago (1996), "The politics on Beacon Hill [the state house] favored a Megaplex. Every technical expert saw no synergism between the two facilities. The state legislature accomplished two key things, location and convention only. We are getting clarity on those two points. It will be a convention center only at Four Points." The clarity to which Ms. Lago refers came eleven months later, when the state legislature voted to build a $700-million convention center at a sixty-acre South Boston site. Meanwhile, Mr. Kraft continued his efforts to build a new stadium.

REVIVING THE STADIUM IDEA

When it became clear that a joint stadium and convention idea was dead, Mr. Kraft began lobbying for a stand-alone open-air stadium in South Boston. He proposed a privately financed $200-million open-air stadium and entertainment complex that would require less public money. This plan received the support of Governor Weld. This plan, which calls for the Massachusetts Port Authority to make land available, received mixed reactions from the press and the South Boston community. More important, Thomas Finneran, Chair of the House Ways and Means Committee, reported responded with "a yawn and a sigh" (Halbfinger 1995b, 1).

This time Kraft proposed the Carolina Plan for financing the stadium: a one-time extra fee on season-ticket-holding fans. The fans would pay from $250 to $1,500 to retain a permanent designated seat. This fee, called a personal seat license, would give the fan the rights to transfer or sell the seat privilege, and would also include an option on the seat for nonfootball events, such as concerts (Halbfinger 1995a, 49). Kraft introduced his new plan to the city council; it was promptly rejected.

In December 1996 another attempt was made to build a stadium on the South Boston Waterfront. Kraft was determined to build his privately funded stadium near the Waterfront in South Boston called Commonwealth Flats. The new Kraft plan would include an NFL entertainment pavilion and a year-round restaurant. He reportedly spent $4 million on designing the facility. The plan envisioned restaurant traffic from the nearby convention center. This time the Massport-owned land near Summer Street became a talking point between Mayor Menino, banks, and Mr. Kraft. The political leaders of South Boston, State Senator Stephen Lynch, City Council President James Kelly, and Rep. John Hart were still opposed to a stadium in South Boston. Lynch asserted, "It doesn't do anything for me, or the neighborhood" (Halbfinger 1996, 1A). Most of the residents of South Boston were opposed to increased traffic and crowds caused by NFL games. Nevertheless, Kraft met with the South Boston Waterfront Advisory Board, the South Boston Chamber of Commerce and Building Trade Council, and residents of South Boston. When Kraft tried to sell the idea to the South Boston Waterfront Advisory Board, they rejected it.

The more people Kraft tried to mobilize or win over, the more problems he encountered. One can understand why Pressman and Wildavsky (1973) concluded their book with the admonition that the "fewer the steps involved in carrying out the program, the fewer the opportunities for a disaster to overtake it" (p. 147). Unfortunately, Boston's sports leaders and politicians kept creating new steps and allowing the stadium to sink deeper into the policy quagmire.

The whole stadium controversy became more complicated because of the success of the 1996 Patriots season. During an AFC Championship game in Foxboro, the power went out for eleven minutes. This faux pas on national television became a symbol of the Patriots' poor facility. This incident only served to make Kraft's case that a new stadium was imperative. Opponents of the new stadium were now accused of mistreating a winning franchise. The pressure was on the elected officials to keep the team at all costs. Time for a compromise was running out as Mayor Menino approached a reelection campaign.

The attack on the mayor became more strident. He was called a "small-time mayor." He was accused of losing his temper and acting like a "child." Menino responded, "I don't want to lose the Patriots, but that's not going to make the decision on whether it's a first-class or second-class city. I hate to see them go, and I'll do everything I can to keep them here, but it is not the be-all and end-all of everything" (Aucoin and Lehigh 1997, 1A). Menino kept to his priority of getting a new convention center for Boston. The mayor had the support of South Boston residents, and they were getting more visible and vocal. At a meeting at the Gavin School, 1,300 of them voiced their opposition. The solidarity of the South Boston Community against the stadium reminded reporters of the infamous fight against busing (Aucoin 1997).

The Patriots' trip to the Super Bowl was almost overshadowed by the continuing political controversy. In addition to the hoopla over the team, there were two subtexts to this drama. Would Mr. Kraft dismiss Coach Bill Parcells after the game? The second subtext was the added pressure on Mayor Menino to support a stadium in Boston. Emotions among fans were intense and the mayor was booed at the pep rally for the team. The national sports media sided with Mr. Kraft and the new stadium. Although most out-of-towners did not understand the nature of the disagreement between the mayor and Mr. Kraft, they supported Kraft (see Cassidy 1997b, 1E). Although the Patriots lost the game, the team's future looked bright. Fans still wanted to keep their winning team.

In 1997 the actors changed. Governor Weld resigned to run against John Kerry for a U.S. Senate seat. William "Billy" Bulger resigned the Speaker position to become the president of the University of Massachusetts. Paul Cellucci became acting governor and Thomas Finneran became Speaker. The new Speaker let it be known early that he was opposed to any stadium plans with public financing. A war of words ensued between Finneran and Kraft. Several financing schemes were floated. The sports-radio talk shows and sport writers joined in, taking sides in the debate.

Mr. Kraft made a last ditch effort to win over Acting Governor Paul Cellucci and Speaker Finneran with a proposal to build a new stadium in Foxboro with state support for infrastructure improvement along highways (Route 1). Kraft wanted the state to pay $30 million for the infrastructure and $20 million for a land deal surrounding the stadium. This idea was initially rejected, and the search for a new home for the Patriots began anew.

CAN'T WIN FOR LOSING

Prospects for a stadium in Boston or Foxboro grew dimmer. Yet Kraft and his ally, Acting Governor Cellucci, continued their quest for a new stadium plan. A political stalemate developed at the state house (Beacon Hill), and there seemed to be little movement in either direction. Kraft met with the governor of Rhode Island regarding moving the team to Providence. Negotiations looked promising for awhile, but disagreements developed. Governor Lincoln Almond was quite anxious to have the Patriots, but wanted an 8-percent tax on each ticket to pay for the proposed $250-million stadium in downtown Providence. The governor refused to lower the tax proposal and the negotiations broke off (see Cassidy 1997c, 1B). The ball was back on Boston's side of the field.

Speaker Finneran was delighted that the Rhode Island deal fell through, but still insisted that no public money should be spent on rehabilitating the Foxboro stadium. Meanwhile, the tension between Kraft and Finneran intensified. Name calling such as "whining multimillionaire" became a part of the discourse over the stadium (Phillip 1997, 1A). Behind the scenes a new compromise was being forged. It was reported that the Speaker was amenable to a $50-million proposal to improve the infrastructure around the Foxboro site. A poll taken by the *Boston Globe* found that 57 percent of the public supported using public money to improve the infrastructure. In a 1995 poll the same percentage had approved public money for improvements. However, when respondents were asked if they would use state funds to keep the Patriots, support dropped to 51 percent. Emboldened by the poll results, Finneran finally came up with a proposal which called for over $50 million for infrastructure improvement in return for $2 million in annual parking fees. He asserted, "He [Kraft] can take it or leave it" (Cassidy 1997a, 1A). Finneran had cast his lot. The town of Foxboro was ready to deal. The ball was now in Senate President Thomas Birmingham's court.

Four months passed and the stadium deal left the front pages of newspapers. The air was full of rumors of new sites for the Patriots. Scenarios included the Patriots going to Providence, Hartford, and even Storrs, Connecticut. Birmingham, a consistent supporter of a stadium and emboldened by the recent $17.6-billion TV deal signed by the NFL, took up the stadium deal in the next session of the legislature. In February 1998 Birmingham began to push for a new $200-million stadium at Foxboro instead of the $50-million renovated one. Under the Birmingham plan the state would pay $20 million for 380 acres of the land that Kraft owns and then lease it back to Kraft. Kraft would build a privately funded $200-million stadium and return $2.4 million per year in parking and ticket fees. In effect, the state would have to pay $7 million in debt service on the $72 million of state bonds. With the income of $2.4 million, the annual cost to the state would be $4.6 million. On twenty-year bonds, the state would spend $92 million.

At a press conference with Mr. Kraft, Birmingham proclaimed that the deal would assure that the Patriots stay in the area for twenty-five years. Acting Governor Cellucci and the *Boston Globe* editorial page endorsed the plan, but the Speaker didn't. He stood foursquare on the principle that taxpayers should not subsidize a lucrative franchise. A day after the plan was unveiled the Speaker refused to accept the deal. He wanted more income to cover the debt. Kraft refused to change the deal. The Speaker was adamantly opposed to the land-purchase part of the deal. He called it a $20-million gift. On March 18 the Speaker formally rejected the Birmingham/Kraft deal.

Through the spring of 1998 a stalemate incurred. In July Finneran admitted to the press that if the Patriots were lured away "it will not be for absence of legislative effort. . . . We've done about the best we can do" (Cassidy 1998b, 1D). Kraft did not agree and rejected the plan. Time ran out on the Birmingham plan as the Senate adjourned on July 31.

On that day Mr. Kraft took the unusual step of writing an op-ed piece outlining his disappointment over not reaching a deal with city and state officials. He accused Speaker Finneran of making a "number of false or misleading arguments" and stated that the Speaker's opposition to the sale and lease provision was "misleading and obstructionist." He concluded,

The reality of today's world of professional sports, and the NFL in particular, makes it imperative that franchises have stadiums and arenas that can generate revenues and allow teams to compete for the best players. The bottom line is that Foxboro Stadium on its own does not allow the Patriots to compete with the rest of the league. This is what this entire stadium effort is about. I feel that our team has brought a sense of pride and excitement to the region that has enhanced our quality of life. I believe the Senate bill would have provided the opportunity to create a public–private partnership that would have allowed the Patriots to continue to make these contributions. Unfortunately, the speaker does not agree. (Kraft 1998, 19A)

Following the Kraft editorial, there were halcyon days in the Patriots' nation. Again rumors began circulating that Mr. Kraft would move the team. Some believed that these new rumors of a move were just a ploy to move Finneran from his position. On November 17 the Speaker brushed off remarks attributed to Kraft regarding selling or moving the team. He stated, "It doesn't really mean anything. I don't know if the NFL wants to act in such a disrespectful fashion" (Cassidy 1998a, 2B).

NEXT STOP, CONNECTICUT?

Two days later the Patriots announced that the football organization had reached an agreement with the state of Connecticut to move the team to Hartford. In 1993 the state passed an anticipatory stadium bill to lure the Patriots. In the new proposed deal, Connecticut would build a $280-million, 68,000-seat open-air stadium. The new stadium would have up to 150 luxury boxes and 6,000 premium seats. Construction would be financed by the sale of state bonds. The team agreed to pay 10 percent of ticket prices to pay off the bonds. Mr. Kraft agreed to move the Patriots offices and facilities to Hartford and spend $50 million on a hotel for the Adriaen's Landing Development and an additional $20 million on an NFL entertainment center. The team would use the stadium rent free in exchange for a 30 year commitment and keeping all the revenues from concessions. There was even an agreement that if Kraft could not sell all of the luxury seats, the state would make up the difference. This guarantee could cost the state $17.5 million over 10 years. A KPMG Peat Marwick report concluded that the state would lose money for the first 14 years after the stadium. However, the Stadium would earn enough over 30 years to pay for itself (Cassidy 1998, 1A).

Kraft did not get tax-exempt status for his NFL entertainment center, and a $13-million cap was placed on the state liability for unsold luxury seats. The team would start to play in Hartford in 2001 and would share the stadium with the University of Connecticut football team. The new stadium would enable UConn to move up to NCAA Division I status.

This announcement created a new theater for the Patriots. The new players were Connecticut Governor John Rowland, House Speaker Thomas Ritter, and Hartford Mayor Michael Peters. They had high hopes for the deal and saw it as the salvation of their much-maligned city. Kraft was heralded by the state legislature. It was so overwhelming that he actually cried during his testimony before the legislature (Garber 1998, 1C). They voted overwhelmingly to accept the Kraft plan.

Politicians, the public, and fans in the mythical Patriots' nation couldn't believe or accept the loss. The new deal prompted Chad Gifford (1998), CEO of BankBoston, one of the city's largest banks and a major player in the various private-funding proposals, to write an editorial on the op-ed page. He asserted, "Make no mistake about it:

Boston is a tough town in which to get things done. Rivalries run deep and convictions are firmly held. Some say our three favorite pastimes are politics, sports and revenge. The decision on a new stadium for the Patriots provided all of that, and more." He asked rhetorically, "Can we change our civic culture and make this an easier place to do business, a city where consensus replaces confrontation as the primary orientation of our public and private sector leaders?" (p. 7D). The fact that Chad Gifford went public with his disappointment is quite unusual. Aiming his comments at schism, he cited Atlanta and Seattle as examples of cooperation. After visiting these cities, he saw how the elites worked together. He stated,

We learned in both cities, that civic leadership is reasonably united in terms of vision and that a consensus around priorities leads almost everyone to sing from the same song sheet. We learned that civic leadership is positive about the progress and enthusiastic about the future. And we learned that there is a deep level of trust, based on personal as well as institutional relationships, between elected officials, private sector, and community leaders. . . . Let's stop pointing fingers and start to learn the real lesson, by demonstrating civic leadership and a positive attitude around a focused agenda. Trust and respect must replace arrogance, cynicism, and turfism. (p. 7D)

To be outmaneuvered by Atlanta and Seattle would be one thing, but Hartford—most politicians were embarrassed and the fans were angry at the thought of traveling ninety miles to see a Patriots game. Fans vented their anger on sport-radio talk shows.

Although the Hartford deal had been signed, Boston politicians refused to accept the loss. They openly wished something would go wrong with the deal. State officials were busy preparing for the possibility that the Hartford deal would collapse. In December 1998 Mayor Menino stated that he would consider a site other than South Boston for a stadium. He suggested that Mr. Kraft take another look at the so-called incinerator site. There were no signs of a shift in Finneran's position.

On February 12, 1999, Mr. Kraft signed the final 300-page agreement to bring the team to Connecticut. It was a complicated agreement that reportedly tied the team to the state for thirty years. It had another deadline, April 2, for all barriers to the agreed-upon site to be removed before the move. This provision was a reference to a steam plant that supplied heat and air conditioning to downtown businesses. The clean-up of this contaminated site could cost millions. CTG Resources, which owned the plant, wanted $48.8 million to move their headquarters and additional money for a clean-up. The cost created a problem for Connecticut officials, and provided hope for Massachusetts politicians. At the end of March Finneran began offering plans and schemes to the Patriots if the Hartford deal failed. At first glance the Hartford deal seemed ironclad. A closer look revealed several loopholes for Mr. Kraft.

There were several preconstruction dates built into the deal. Before the final one of May 2, a series of league maneuverings took place and what looked like a sure thing unravelled. Mr. Kraft hired a consultant who reported the state could meet the construction deadlines.

On April 23, 1999, NFL Commissioner Paul Tagliabue entered the controversy when he met with Governor Cellucci, Speaker Finneran, Senate President Birmingham, and a new actor, Paul Kirk, who won fame as the former chairman of the Democratic Party, in a last ditch effort to keep the team in Boston. Four days later the Tagliabue/Kirk group decided that keeping the Patriots in Boston was in the interest of the NFL, CBS, Kraft, and the Massachusetts political leadership. The main argument was that Boston is a larger television market, with 2.2 million viewers (the sixth-largest national market), as opposed to the 909,930 (the twenty-seventh-largest market) in Hartford.

On April 27 the Tagliabue/Kirk group reached an agreement. Massachusetts political leaders agreed to spend $70 million on access infrastructure (e.g., roads and sewers) for a new Foxboro stadium. Kraft agreed to build a privately financed $250-million stadium, with the help of the NFL. The NFL got an agreement from business leaders to buy $15 million worth of luxury boxes for the new stadium. Kraft would be required to pay the state $1 million for the infrastructure. The state will also collect about $400,000 in parking revenues on land not owned by Kraft.

Kraft met again with Governor Rowland for reassurance that the state could meet the 2002 construction schedule they had agreed on. Armed with a consultant report that found Connecticut would not be able to meet the construction deadline, Mr. Kraft decided to terminate the deal on April 30. The Patriots would stay in Massachusetts. There would be no stadium in Boston proper. The team would continue to play in the old stadium until a new one could be constructed in Foxboro.

We had come full circle. With the exception of the luxury boxes, the new agreement was essentially the same deal Kraft had rejected earlier. The difference was a commitment by the NFL to help Mr. Kraft with financing a new stadium to be built next to the old one. Finneran held his ground. Mr. Kraft, Tagliabue, and Kirk were hailed as heroes (see Lehigh 1999). Rowland was reviled as a loser and the theater goes on.

CONCLUSION

This chapter is a summary of events up to this writing. It is impossible to make conclusions in sports politics or write the final word on stadium politics. What started out as Megaplex ended up as mega-drama, with Mr. Kraft and Mr. Finneran becoming larger-than-life figures. Their conflict alternated between the sports page and the front page. Bostonians liked the theater, but not with this ending. *Boston*

Globe reporter Charles Sennott (1997) tried to summarize the struggle for a Boston stadium in two sentences:

The stadium fight has become a tribal clash between the tough and tightknit neighborhood of South Boston and a brash industrialist who wants to put a 70,000-seat amphitheater in their backyard. Also in the mix are a pro-business, Republican governor who supports the stadium, a mayor conscious of his traditional political base in the city's neighborhoods, and a Democratic-controlled Legislature that seems to have dug in its heels against the proposal. (p. 1)

Our review of events suggest that stadium politics in Boston was a little more complicated than the Sennott (1997) characterization. It is true that neighborhood groups in South Boston were successful in resisting the stadium, but they were helped by some very powerful local politicians. Their struggle was helped by the minirivalries between the Speaker, the governor, the Senate president, and Mr. Kraft. State politicians were skillful in reconstructing the stadium controversy into a state issue. This undercut the mayor's ability to take the initiative.

Sennott's (1997) reference to "tribal clash" was an attempt to make something of the fact that Kraft is Jewish and most of the residents of South Boston are Irish. Kraft didn't help the situation much by saying to the press, "I spent nearly $1 million on Irish consultants" (Sennot and Cassidy 1997, 1A). Boston politics has always been tribal, but the fight over the stadium was not particularly anti-Semitic. It was more of who was going to pay for what.

The glaring omission in Sennott's (1997) characterization was the lack of coordination between the economic elite and the political elite. Chad Gifford's (1998) editorial was a telling statement about the internal dynamics of the governing regime. The public might have read the statement as a plea for civic leadership, but it must have sent shock waves among those who considered themselves a part of that leadership. The failure of the pro-growth coalition to achieve consensus and provide a united front is a barometer of the current state of the economic elites. Part of the difficulty can be traced to younger corporate leaders who are not interested in assuming leadership in the city's future. They seem to be more interested in global economic trends than in state and local politics (see Rich 1995). However, changing the civic culture will be difficult for Boston because, unlike Indianapolis, Atlanta, or Seattle, Boston is a made city, not a city on the make.

This is why the mayor was able to say that the loss of the Patriots would not hurt the city. Even Mr. Gifford, chairman of BankBoston, admitted that Boston can be a "world-class city without an NFL franchise." This is true, but enough people were worried about the reputation of the city to take another look at keeping the team in the state. If it was just a matter of $70 million and selling more luxury seats, then the deal was possible. After the deal was made, Paul Kirk stated that the $15-million commitment in luxury boxes "will be exceeded" (Krupa 1999, 12A). Buying luxury boxes could be a way to forge closer relationships within the business elite and show good faith to the NFL. A lot of time, money, and energy were spent to prevent a divorce between Boston and the Patriots; only time will tell whether the reconciliation works.

REFERENCES

Aucoin, Don, and Scot Lehigh. 1997. Stadium Dispute Puts Menino in the Hot Seat. *Boston Globe*, 14 January, 1A.

Aucoin, Don. 1997. South Boston Holds Its Ground. *Boston Globe*, 7 January, 1B.

Bachelor, Lynn W. 1994. Regime Maintenance, Solution Sets, and Urban Economic Development. *Urban Affairs Quarterly* 29: 596–616.

Bardson, Brent. 1998. Public Sports Stadium Funding: Being Held Hostage by Professional Sports Team Owners. *Hamline Law Review* 21: 505–535.

Boston Redevelopment Authority. 1994. *Site and Market Analysis for Boston's New Exposition Center and Stadium*. Boston: Boston Redevelopment Authority.

Cassidy, Tina. 1998a. Finneran Dismisses Kraft Remark on Patriots Sale. *Boston Globe*, 17 November, 2B.

Cassidy, Tina. 1998b. Patriots Reject Plan by Finneran: Speaker's Controversial Proposal Would Have Kraft Build a $200 M Stadium. *Boston Globe*, 28 July, 1D.

Cassidy, Tina. 1998c. Patriots Reported Close to an Accord with Connecticut. *Boston Globe*, 19 November, 1.

Cassidy, Tina. 1998d. Report Sees Slow Profits for Stadium: Connecticut Could Lose Money for Years Before Patriots Deal Earns Return. *Boston Globe*, 2 December, 1A.

Cassidy, Tina. 1997a. Finneran Offers New Foxboro Stadium Plan; $50 M in Improvements, but No Land Buy. *Boston Globe*, 15 November, 1A.

Cassidy, Tina. 1997b. Most Would Spend to Keep Patriots: Poll Shows Support for Improvement Near Stadium. *Boston Globe*, 31 October, 1A.

Cassidy, Tina. 1997c. Tax Proposal Threatern Stadium Deal; R.I. Asking for Surcharge of 8 Percent on Pats Tickets. *Boston Globe*, 28 September, 1B.

Commonwealth of Massachusetts. 1995. *Acts of the 1995 Commission*. Chapter 6, p. 12.

Corcoran, Joseph. 1997. Telephone interview with author, 12 February.

Elkins, Stephen. 1987. *City and Regime in American Republic*. Chicago: University of Chicago Press.

Euchner, Charles C. 1993. *Playing the Field: Why Sports Teams Move and Cities Fight to Keep Them*. Baltimore: Johns Hopkins University Press.

Garber, Greg. 1998. Brought to You by Kraft: All He Wanted Was a Home. *Hartford Courant*, 20 November, 1C.

Gifford, Chad. 1998. Local Leadership Failed Kraft and the Patriots. *Boston Globe*, 29 November, 7D.

Hudnut, William. 1995. *The Hudnut Years in Indianapolis, 1976–1991*. Bloomington: Indiana University Press.

Halbfinger, David. 1996. Kraft Has Rocky Day in South Boston. *Boston Globe*, 11 December, 1A.

Halbfinger, David. 1995a. The Bottom Line: Fans Mixed on Cost/Benefits Ratio of the Patriot Owner's Proposal: Sport Marketing, Seat Licenses. *Boston Globe*, 14 December, 49.

Halbfinger, David. 1995b. Weld Backs a Stadium for Patriots. *Boston Globe*, 17 November, 1.

Kraft, Robert. 1998. Blame the Speaker for Stadium Stalemate. *Boston Globe*, 31 July, 19A.

Krupa, Gregg. 1999. NFL Commissioner Put Luxury Box Blitz. *Boston Globe*, 8 May, 1A, 12A.

Lago, Marisa, Director, Boston Redevelopment Authority. 1996. Interview with author, 20 December.

Lehigh, Scot. 1999. Whining Millionaire Becomes "Public Hero." *Boston Globe*, 1 May, 1A.

Lowery, Don. 1996. Remarks at the annual meeting of the New England Political Science Association, Springfield, Massachusetts, 4 May.

Pelissero, John P., Beth M. Henschen, and Edward I. Sidlow. 1991. Urban Regimes, Sports Stadiums, and the Politics of Economic Development Agendas in Chicago. *Policy Studies Review* 10: 117–129.

Pressman, Jeffrey L., and Aaron B. Wildavsky. 1973. *Implementation*. Berkeley and Los Angeles: University of California Press.

Phillips, Frank. 1997. Finneran Stands His Ground. *Boston Globe*, 2 October, 1A.

Rich, Wilbur. 1995. Tom Menino and Boston Politics. Paper presented at the Northeastern Political Science Association, Newark.

Rosentraub, Mark S., David Swindell, Michael Przybylski, and Daniel R. Mullins. 1994. Sport and Downtown Development Strategy: If You Build It, Will Jobs Come? *Journal of Urban Affairs* 16: 221–239.

Sandomir, Richard. 1999. Tagliabue Fakes Out the Patriots. *New York Times*, 17 April, 27A.

Sennott, Charles. 1997. A Fortune Build: Bob Kraft Aims for Larger Goals; Friends and Foes Talk of Ambition, Ego Smarts. *Boston Globe*, 2 February, 1A.

Sennott, Charles, and Tina Cassidy. 1997. How Kraft's Grand Plan Unraveled Stadium Is a Lesson in Boston Politics. *Boston Globe*, 23 February, 1A.

Shropshire, Kenneth L. 1995. *The Sport Franchise Game: Cities in Pursuit of Sports Franchises, Events, Stadiums, and Arenas*. Philadelphia: University of Pennsylvania Press.

Sit, Mary. 1993. No-Taxes Megaplex Is Favored. *Boston Globe*, 6 January, 53.

Stone, Clarence. 1989. *Regime Politics: Governing Atlanta 1946–1988*. Lawrence: University of Kansas Press.

Vaillancourt, Meg. 1999. Patriots Sack Hartford Stadium Deal. *Boston Globe*, 1 May, 1A.

Vaillancourt, Meg, and Adrian Walker. 1995. Menino Urges Stadium Be Axed from Megaplex. *Boston Globe*, 13 August, 1A.

Conclusion:
The Future of Sports Stadiums

The chapters in this volume raise several important questions about sports stadium financing and its risks. Researchers found few stadiums that generated the type of muliplier effects that were expected. It is not clear if sports determine whether families and businesses locate in a city. The jobs created by a new stadium are not high-paying ones and they do not increase the city income. Besides, research suggests no differences in personal income of residents before in comparison to after the construction of a stadium or the arrival of a new team in their city. Baade and Dye (1988) suggest that stadiums may simply realign existing economic-development projects rather than stimulate new ones. If the city invests so heavily in one area, it may not be able to do so in other areas.

Having a stadium downtown does not automatically mean people will spend more money downtown. The stadiums themselves are becoming shopping centers and fast-food restaurants. There is little spillover to other businesses. Fans rarely rent hotel rooms or browse through shops after a game.

The real problem with stadiums is that they are now subject to changes in fashion. Whereas stadiums of the past could be expected to last for several decades, today stadiums quickly become obsolete within the decade they are built. Domed stadiums and articifial turfs were once in fashion, but now open-air stadiums have made a comeback. Today, Camden Yards in Baltimore is the model for all new multisports stadiums.

Despite the rush to put sports franchises in all sections of the country, there are the problems of size and distribution of wealth. Some wealthy cities have more resources and more entrepreneurs than their smaller counterparts. They will enjoy a permanent advantage over emerging cities. They will be able to spend more money on facilities and players. "Wannabe" cities will not able to compete with teams in the big-television-market cities. There is also the problem of the local economy. Some cities have a more diverse economy. They can withstand years of losing teams. Other cities cannot sustain losing teams. Some cities will struggle to meet their bond obligations and will have to reallocate scarce resources to meet the avaricious needs of owners. The truth is that medium-size cities simply do not have the population needed to sustain a major league franchise. Hartford tried to build a fan base with the National Hockey League Whalers and failed. Yet this did not dissuade state and city leaders from trying to entice the New England Patriots to move to their city. The Connecticut governor and the state legislators were willing to spend the money to build a publicly financed stadium in the middle of downtown Hartford. They were willing to spend the taxpayer's money, but they could not invent a large enough television market. Although the proposed Hartford stadium was linked to a larger project, it was never fully explained as to how the two projects would improve the plight of its increasingly poor inner-city community.

ECONOMICS AND SOCIAL ISSUES

Can a city build bigger and more modern stadiums and simultaneously stop the economic dislocation of inner-city residents? Would Oakland be a better place to live for the poor if the Raiders did not return? The short-term answer to both questions is no. The long-term answer is that it depends on whether politicians believe they had more than a Hobson's choice. As monopolies, the National Football League and Major League Baseball can detemine the number of teams in their leagues and can control where they will play. Cities have no alternative source of teams; they must deal with these established entities. Stadiums are relatively easy for politicians to support because they are one of the few things that the economic elite desire. While members of the economic elite will compete to secure a sports franchise, they often exhibit less enthusiasm about solving other needs of a city. A quote by Art Modell is quite revealing: "I feel for the schools. I feel for welfare. But look at the positive effect of pro football on a community, the emotional investment of people at large. You can't equate that with fixing up the schools" (cited in Leone 1997, 477).

The new stadiums in Detroit will have state-of-the-art facilities and will allow suburbanites to come to the stadium, park their cars, watch the game, and never go outside the stadium area. The pro-stadium coalition has the full support of elected officials. Mike Illich, the owner of the Detroit Tigers baseball team, and William Ford, the owner of the Detroit Lions, are considered heroes trying to rescue the city and restore the downtown area. Despite all the new infrastructure, the problems of Detroit will remain the same. William Neil (1995) concludes, "The city of Detroit now boasts a collection of image-conscious physical capital projects surreally floating free amidst a human capital wasteland" (p. 648). There are simply not enough semiskilled manufacturing jobs to sustain its predominately minority population. Most of these people cannot afford to buy tickets to see the Lions and the Tigers.

Economic rivalry between cities continues to be a reality. Peterson's (1981) market theory is correct in this regard. Nevertheless, there are distinct differences between Sun-Belt and Rust-Belt cities. The Sun-Belt cities, the southern tier of the United States, have enjoyed unparalleled growth. They are benefiting from the retirement boom, changes in lifestyles, and the invention of central air conditioning. On the other hand, old Rust-Belt cities, such as Detroit, Cleveland, Chicago, and St Louis, have suffered losses in population. Part of the reason these cities invest in stadiums and other entertainment amenities is to stem the population tide. Whereas they once only had Sun-Belt cities to fear, they now have to watch their own suburbs and satellite cities in competition. Providence, Rhode Island, wanted the New England Patriots to relocate to a downtown stadium. Boston barely escaped a similar raid from Hartford. If Kraft needed the money and the NFL did not need a franchise in that television market, the outcome might have been different. Football teams, which only play twenty games, twenty-three at the most, can force a city to make a commitment just by visiting a rival city. When the city of St. Louis lost the NFL Cardinals, they built a stadium and paid a heavy price for the Los Angeles Rams to move there.

THE MYTH OF THE QUICK-FIX RENAISSANCE

Most older cities believe that they are in a new renaissance period. The new facades and infrastructures are supposed to attract the middle class and create more economic opportunities for the poor. However, building a multi-billion-dollar stadium will do little to upgrade the quality of life for those living in inner-city neighborhoods. Allocating city resources in this way displaces the living space of the poor in order to build a playground for the rich. Yet the opponents of stadium building have no "uplifting" alternative projects. Many just want to stop the building of a new stadium or public funding for renovations. Often there are divisions between historic preservationtist and environmentalists. Rarely are such groups able to mount a serious challenge to pro-stadium coalitions. And as the chapters in this volume suggest, pro-stadium coalitions are formidable interest groups. Once they launch the idea for a new stadium, they coopt the politicians and the media into making the new stadium a reality. As Chapter 11 suggested, sports writers find themselves advocates for the owners. When there is a franchise crisis, they find themselves in the center of the newsroom. They are quoted by their colleagues and become the gurus to the main-line news reporters. The owner reaps publicity and sympathy from the public, who are led to believe that they are losing something dear to their city. The whole process works because the theater is so successful.

Are sports stadiums a big image-building item for cities? Can a city make claims to being a cosmopolitan or a national city without a professional team, preferably a football or baseball team? Unfortunately, many city leaders believe that they must have a professional team and so the idea has gained some currency. Chasing professional teams is an expensive and problematic proposition, since owners have little loyalty to a city that bears their team's name. The late Robert Isray, Art Modell, and Al Davis of the NFL come to mind as owners with teams who were willing to move them. What does a city do with a domed stadium after the team is gone? Houston is trying to answer that question. There are all sorts of data that question the multiplier effect and the job-creating ability of new stadiums (Baim 1994; Baade and Dye 1988).

WHAT CAN BE DONE?

There are several lessons to be drawn from reviewing the history of sports franchises and stadium construction, but few leaders are prepared to listen and learn. The city of Houston should have learned its lesson with the NFL Oilers, but they are now back in the hunt for a new franchise. Where is the citizen oppositon? Some cheered when the Oilers left, and most will cheer if the NFL installs a new expansion team. This suggests that educated citizens will be able to build opposition to a new stadium. However, the image of sports is such that it will be difficult to gain support from the community.

If not a citizen's committee, then what about a full disclosure of financial obligations in terms the layman can understand? They need to know what their elected leaders are agreeing to on their behalf. Leaders should openly state if a stadium is not likely to return enough money to pay for itself. The citizenry should be informed that if a stadium does not cover its expenses the taxpayers will be expected to pay more in taxes. This revelation may not mobilize citizens against a stadium proposal, but it would go a long way toward accountability.

THE ROLE OF GOVERNMENTS

Only Congress can force the owners to stay put or honor their commitment to a city and state (Beisner 1988). There have been several reform bills introduced in Congress. Chapter 2 examines the purpose of the Hoke bill (Fan Freedom and Community Protection Act of 1995). It is clear that Congress is not inclined to regulate professional sports. Owners of all sports have testified before Congress about the special nature of their business and have been granted special treatment (e.g., Professional Sports Community Act of 1985).

Some scholars have advocated a partial antitrust exemption for the National Football League so they can discipline owners and prevent them from relocating. They have also suggested that the NFL retain the team's name, colors, and logo on behalf of the city for a fixed number of years (see Leone 1997). A law could be written which restricts the ability of a franchise to move until all the city's debt from its investment is paid. Some have even advocated eliminating the tax-free status of bonds used to finance stadiums. Other scholars call for an end to the federal subsidy of sports stadiums (Lathrope 1997).

Congress has entertained many proposals, but it is still reluctant to regulate the sports business. John Biesner (1988) has suggested a sports arbitration board. This body would determine the criteria for team relocation. None of these changes will happen soon. Critics argues that such laws would infringe upon the property rights of owners and unnecessarily get Congress involved in the sports-regulating business. Yet this may be the price to pay because of the lack of accountability of sports-franchise owners to their cities. Fans are stakeholders in a sports franchise. They deserve a say in what happens. Hartel (1998) asserts that it is time to stop watching the "play-by-play pageants of opportunism and greed."

State and local governments should ask more questions about the overheated finanical world of sports. One writer suggested having a referendum when a stadium's cost exceeds $50 million, and requiring every stadium-financing plan to be consistent with the state's constitution (Bordson 1998). This may sound reasonable to some, but $50 million is too low because there are no stadiums available at that price. Perhaps $200 million would be more appropriate. In any case, there is a compelling public interest at any cost because owners are using public resources. If owners want cities to remain good hosts, they must become more accountable to them. We hope this volume stimulates a debate about the economics and politics of stadiums and the people who build them.

REFERENCES

Baade, Robert A., and Richard F. Dye. 1988. Sports Stadiums and Area Development: A Critical Review. *Economic Development Quarterly* 2: 265–275.

Baim, Dean. 1994. *The Sports Stadium as a Municipal Investment*. Westport, Conn.: Greenwood Press.

Beisner, John. 1988. Sports Franchise Relocation: Competitive Market and Taxpayer Protection. *Yale Law and Policy Review* 6: 429–448.

Bordson, Brent. 1998. Public Sports Stadium Funding: Communities Being Held Hostage by Professional Sports Owners. *Hamiline Law Review* 21: 505–535.

Hartel, Lynn Reynolds. 1998. Community-Based Ownership of a National Football League Franchise: The Answer to Relocation and Taxpayer Financing of NFL Teams. *Loyala of Los Angeles Entertainment Law Journal* 18: 589–628.

Lathrope, Daniel J. 1997. Federal Tax Policy, Tax Subsidies, and the Financing of Professional Sports Facilities. *South Texas Law Review* 38: 1147–1165.

Leone, Katherine. 1997. No Team, No Peace: Franchise Free Agency in the National Football League. *Columbia Law Review* 97: 473–523.

Neill, William. 1995. Lipstick on the Gorilla: The Failure of Image-Led Planning in Coleman Young's Detroit. *International Journal of Urban and Regional Research* 19: 639–653.

Peterson, Paul E. 1981. *City Limits*. Chicago: University of Chicago Press.

Index

About the Editor and Contributors

Robert A. Baade has been the James D. Vail Professor of Economics at Lake Forest College since 1986. He has published more than twenty articles, book chapters, and monographs about the economic impact professional sports exert on their host communities. In addition to his scholarly efforts, Baade has had considerable practical experience in assessing the economic impact of various projects, including some in the Chicago area where he resides. Most notably, he chaired the cost–benefits committee of Chicago's Metropolitan Planning Council's Stadium Task Force.

Lynn W. Bachelor is associate professor of political science and public administration at the University of Toledo. She has published articles about urban economic development in *Urban Affairs Review* and *Economic Development Quarterly*, and is the coauthor of *The Sustaining Hand*, a study of corporate influence in Michigan cities.

Beth M. Henschen has taught at Purdue University and Loyola University in Chicago. She now teaches political science at Eastern Michigan University and is a policy consultant. She has written extensively on American politics, including several articles on the relationship between politics and sports.

Arthur T. Johnson is provost and vice president for academic affairs at the University of Maryland Baltimore County (UMBC). His primary research field is public sports policy. He is the author of nearly two dozen articles and a book and coeditor of two books, all of which deal with the relationship of government to sports organizations. Dr. Johnson also conducts research within the field of public-personnel management. Most recently, he examined federal government recruitment on college and university campuses and patterns of entry-level hiring by the U.S. government. In connection with this research he served as Faculty Associate in the Office of Policy Evaluation—U.S. Merit Systems Protection Board during the 1998 academic year.

Jose F. Marichal is a Ph.D. political science student at the University of Colorado in Boulder. His interests include urban politics, community development, and public policy. He is currently looking at factors affecting creation and implementation of higher-education diversity plans.

Richard Temple Middleton IV is a Ph.D. political science student at the University of Missouri at Columbia. His interests include urban politics, race and ethnic issues, and environmental policy, as well as constitutional law. He has written extensively on American politics, including an article on cities and economic development.

Wilbur C. Rich is professor of political science at Wellesley College. He holds a doctorate degree from the University of Illinois and has taught at Columbia University and Wayne State University. Author of several articles and reports on the problems of local government administration, Dr. Rich's books include *The Politics of Urban Personnel Policy, Coleman Young and Detroit Politics,* and *Black Mayors and School Politics.* A fourth book, *The Politics of Minority Coalitions,* was published by Praeger in 1996.

Steven A. Riess is professor of American history at Northeastern Illinois University in Chicago. The former editor of the *Journal of Sport History,* he is the author of several books on sport, most notably *Coty Games: The Evolution of American Urban Society and Rise of Sports* (1989) and *Touching Base: Professional Baseball and American Culture in the Progressive Era* (2d ed., 1999), both published by the University of Illinois Press. He is also editor of the series *Sport and Entertainment* for the Syracuse University Press.

Edward I. Sidlow is professor and head of the department of political science at Eastern Michigan University. He has held positions at Miami University (Ohio), Northwestern University, and Loyola University in Chicago. He has written extensively on American politics, including several articles on the relationship between politics and sports.

Neil J. Sullivan is a professor in the School of Public Affairs at Baruch College, City University of New York. He is author of *The Dodgers Move West* (1987) and has written a history of Yankees Stadium. He has also written an article entitled "Baseball and Race: The Limits of Competition" for the *Journal of Negro History* (Summer 1998).

Robyne S. Turner is associate professor of political science at Florida Atlantic University. Her most recent publications focus on the politics of urban development and can be found in *Economic Development Quarterly* and *Urban Affairs Review*. She is the coeditor with Judith A. Garber of *Gender in Urban Research* (1995).

Robert K. Whelan studies urban revitalization, development, and public management in the United States, Canada, and France. He belongs to the American Society for Public Administration and the Urban Afairs Association and serves as the chairperson of the Slidell Planning and Zoning Commission. He was honored with the Donato J. Pugliese award for service to SECOPA. Dr. Whelan has published in the *International Journal of Public Administration, Public Administration Quarterly, Public Administration Review,* and *Journal of Urban and Public Affairs.* He coauthored *Urban Policy and Politics in a Bureaucratic Age,* with Clarence N. Stone and William J. Murin, and is finishing a manuscript on the response of Canadian local governments to fiscal crisis. His latest project focuses on economic development in Quebec City.

Alma H. Young, the Coleman A. Young Professor of Urban Affairs, is serving as interim dean of the College of Urban, Labor, and Metropolitan Affairs at Wayne State University. She has maintained an active agenda in both research and community outreach. Her research interests include the politics of urban redevelopment, the development of social policy (especially as it affects women and children), and the relationship between citizen groups and the state.

Andrew Zimbalist is a Robert A. Woods Professor of Economics at Smith College. He works in the areas of comparative economic systems and sports economics. He has published twelve books and dozens of articles in these fields, the most recent of which is *Unpaid Professionals: Commercialism and Conflict in Big-Time College Sports* (1999).

ISBN 1-56720-317-5

EAN

9 781567 203172

90000>

HARDCOVER BAR CODE